Conversations with John Updike

Literary Conversations Series

Peggy Whitman Prenshaw
General Editor

© Elena Seibert, courtesy of John Updike

Conversations
with John Updike

Edited by
James Plath

University Press of Mississippi
Jackson

97   96   95   94   4   3   2   1

The paper in this book meets the guidelines for permanence and durability
of the Committee on Production Guidelines for Book Longevity of the Council
on Library Resources.

Library of Congress Cataloging-in-Publication Data

Updike, John.
    Conversations with John Updike / edited by James Plath.
        p.   cm. — (Literary conversations series)
    Includes bibliographical references (p.) and index.
    ISBN 0-87805-699-8 (cloth : alk. paper). — ISBN 0-87805-700-5
(paper : alk. paper)
    1. Updike, John—Interviews.   2. Authors, American—20th
century—Interviews.   I. Plath, James.   II. Title.   III. Series.
PS3571.P4Z474   1994
813'.52—dc20   93-44741
                                                            CIP

British Library Cataloging-in-Publication data available

Books by John Updike

The Carpentered Hen and Other Tame Creatures: Poems. New York: Harper and Brothers, 1958.

The Poorhouse Fair. New York: Alfred A. Knopf, 1959.

The Same Door: Short Stories. New York: Alfred A. Knopf, 1959.

Rabbit, Run. New York: Alfred A. Knopf, 1960.

Pigeon Feathers and Other Stories. New York: Alfred A. Knopf, 1962.

The Magic Flute. Adapted for children from the opera by Mozart. New York: Alfred A. Knopf, 1962.

The Centaur. New York: Alfred A. Knopf, 1963.

Telephone Poles and Other Poems. New York: Alfred A. Knopf, 1963.

Olinger Stories, A Selection. New York: Vintage Books, 1964.

The Ring. Adapted for children from the opera cycle by Wagner. New York: Alfred A. Knopf, 1964.

Assorted Prose. New York: Alfred A. Knopf, 1965.

Of the Farm. New York: Alfred A. Knopf, 1965.

A Child's Calendar. New York: Alfred A. Knopf, 1965.

Verse: The Carpentered Hen and Other Tame Creatures (and) *Telephone Poles and Other Poems.* Greenwich, Conn.: Fawcett Publications, 1965.

The Music School: Short Stories. New York: Alfred A. Knopf, 1966.

Bottom's Dream. Adapted from William Shakespeare's *A Midsummer Night's Dream.* New York: Alfred A. Knopf, 1966.

Couples. New York: Alfred A. Knopf, 1968.

Bath After Sailing. Monroe, Conn.: Pendulum Press, 1968.

The Angels. Pensacola, Florida: King & Queen Press, 1968.

Three Texts from Early Ipswich. Ipswich, Mass.: 17th Century Day Committee of the Town of Ipswich, 1968.

On Meeting Authors. Newburyport, Mass.: Wickford Press, 1968.

Midpoint and Other Poems. New York: Alfred A. Knopf, 1969.

Bech: A Book. New York: Alfred A. Knopf, 1970.

Rabbit Redux. New York: Alfred A. Knopf, 1971.

Museums and Women and Other Stories. New York: Alfred A. Knopf, 1972.

Seventy Poems. Harmondsworth (UK): Penguin Books, 1972.

Warm Wine, An Idyll. New York: Albondocani Press, 1973.

Six Poems. New York: Aloe Editions, 1973.

A Good Place. New York: Aloe Editions, 1973.

Buchanan Dying, A Play. New York: Alfred A. Knopf, 1974.

Cunts. New York: Frank Hallman, 1974.

A Month of Sundays. New York: Alfred A. Knopf, 1975.

Picked-Up Pieces. New York: Alfred A. Knopf, 1975.

Marry Me: A Romance. Franklin Center, Pa.: Franklin Library, 1976; New York: Alfred A. Knopf, 1976.

Couples: A Short Story. Cambridge, Mass.: Halty Ferguson, 1976.

Tossing and Turning: Poems. New York: Alfred A. Knopf, 1977.

Hub Fans Bid Kid Adieu. Northridge, Calif.: Lord John Press, 1977.

The Coup. New York: Alfred A. Knopf, 1978.

From the Journal of a Leper. Northridge, Calif.: Lord John Press, 1978.

Too Far to Go: The Maples Stories. New York: Fawcett Crest, 1979.

Problems and Other Short Stories. New York: Alfred A. Knopf, 1979.

Three Illuminations in the Life of an American Author. New York: Targ, 1979.

Sixteen Sonnets. Cambridge, Mass.: Halty Ferguson, 1979.

Talk from the Fifties. Northridge, Calif.: Lord John Press, 1979.

The Chaste Planet. Worcester, Mass.: Metacom Press, 1980.

Ego and Art in Walt Whitman. New York: Targ, 1980.

Five Poems. Cleveland: Bits Press, 1980.

People One Knows. Northridge, Calif.: Lord John Press, 1980.

Rabbit Is Rich. New York: Alfred A. Knopf, 1981.

Hawthorne's Creed. New York: Targ, 1981.

Invasion of the Book Envelopes. Concord, N.H.: Ewert, 1981.

Bech Is Back. New York: Alfred A. Knopf, 1982.

The Carpentered Hen. New York: Alfred A. Knopf, 1982.

The Beloved. Northridge, Calif.: Lord John Press, 1982.

Spring Trio. Winston-Salem, N.Ç.: Palaemon, 1982.

Hugging the Shore: Essays and Criticism. New York: Alfred A. Knopf, 1983.

The Witches of Eastwick. Franklin Center, Pa.: Franklin Library, 1984; New York: Alfred A. Knopf, 1984.

Emersonianism. Cleveland: Bits Press, 1984.

Confessions of a Wild Bore. Newton, Iowa: Tamazunchale, 1984.

Jester's Dozen. Northridge, Calif.: Lord John Press, 1984.

The Best American Short Stories 1984, ed., with Shannon Ravenel. Boston: Houghton Mifflin, 1984.

Facing Nature: Poems. New York: Alfred A. Knopf, 1985.

Impressions. Los Angeles, Calif.: Sylvester & Orphanos, 1985.

Getting Older. Helsinki, Finland: Eurographica, 1985.

Roger's Version. Franklin Center, Pa.: Franklin Library, 1986; New York: Alfred A. Knopf, 1986.

A&P: Lust in the Aisles. Minneapolis: Redpath Press, 1986.

A Soft Spring Night in Shillington. Northridge, Calif.: Lord John Press, 1986.

Trust Me. New York: Alfred A. Knopf, 1987.

Forty Stories. Harmondsworth (UK): Penguin Books, 1987.

The Afterlife. Leamington Spa, England: Sixth Chamber, 1987.

More Stately Mansions. Jackson, Miss.: Nouveau Press, 1987.

S. New York: Alfred A. Knopf, 1988.

Going Abroad. Helsinki, Finland: Eurographica, 1988.

On the Move. Cleveland: Bits Press, 1988.

Getting the Words Out. Northridge, Calif.: Lord John Press, 1988.

Self-Consciousness: Memoirs. Pasadena, Calif.: Easton Press, 1989; New York: Alfred
    A. Knopf, 1989.

Just Looking: Essays on Art. New York: Alfred A. Knopf, 1989.

In Memoriam Felis Felis. Leamington Spa, England: Sixth Chamber, 1989.

Rabbit at Rest. Franklin Center, Pa.: Franklin Library, 1990; New York: Alfred A.
    Knopf, 1990.

Brother Grasshopper. Worcester, Mass.: Metacom Press, 1990.

Recent Poems. Helsinki, Finland: Eurographica, 1990.

Mites and Other Poems in Miniature. Northridge, Calif.: Lord John Press, 1990.

Odd Jobs: Essays and Criticism. New York: Alfred A. Knopf, 1991.

Thanatopses. Cleveland: Bits Press, 1991.

Memories of the Ford Administration. New York: Alfred A. Knopf, 1992.

Collected Poems 1953–1993. New York: Alfred A. Knopf, 1993.

Brazil. New York: Alfred A. Knopf, 1993.

Concerts at Castle Hill. Northridge, Calif.: Lord John Press, 1993.

Baby's First Step. Huntington Beach, Calif.: Cahill, 1993.

Contents

Introduction

My first contact with John Updike came in 1985, when I wrote to ask if he would grant an interview for *Clockwatch Review,* a nonprofit journal of the arts I still edit. His response was gracious—many writers, after all, ignore such requests—but Mr. Updike nonetheless made it clear that he couldn't oblige: "I really think being interviewed a great waste of time and energy, with results that generally leave you feeling embarrassed, or at least that you should clean your fingernails."[1]

In public, his feelings have been more bluntly declaimed. "Writers *can* get overinterviewed," Updike told fellow novelist Martin Amis. "It rots a writer's brain, it cretinizes you. You say the same thing again and again, and when you do that happily you're well on your way to being a cretin. Or a politician."[2]

As Updike explained to a National Public Radio audience, he once called interviews "a half-form, like maggots, and a form to be loathed," because "it's a little disconcerting . . . to realize that these remarks which you toss off, once they're in print, have an equal weight with all the words that you've labored to polish and make come out exactly right. So I do resist and resent the tendency of our age to milk people through interviews to get them to betray the 'real' whoever—John Updike, let's say—when John Updike has been trying to show the real John Updike in his writing all these years" (Gross, 1988).

While Updike certainly hasn't withdrawn from the media as fellow writer Thomas Pynchon has, his own feelings about the interview-as-genre are so well known that later questioners have approached him with some trepidation. "Fresh Air"'s Terry Gross, for example, confessed, "For years I'd hoped that I'd someday have the opportunity to do an interview with you, but I was very scared. . . . I think of all the people I've met, you have the strongest anti-interview feelings."

Jane Howard, in recalling her three-day interview visit with Updike at his home, at the beach, and on the links in 1966, likewise observed that "Of all the people I interviewed in my years at *Life,* only [Vladimir] Nabokov was more wary of how he would appear in print." That ex-

plains Updike's frequent insistence that he be allowed to proofread
interview transcripts and make not only corrections, but stylistic and
substantive changes as well. In the case of Lewis Nichols, one of the
earliest visitors to Updike's writing office, it also helps to explain why
the author responded immediately to oral questioning via typewriter:
"typing rapidly, beating time with a half-off loafer clinging to his toes"
and explaining to his interviewer that "as an old 'Talk of the Town' man
for the *New Yorker* he knew interviews"—meaning, one supposes, that
Updike learned firsthand the way words can bend and twist in the hands
of another on their way to the printed page. Yet, like those who would
follow, the interviewer found that Updike, once committed, was a
charming, gracious, candid, and generous subject, prone to offer such
unasked-for insights as the revelation that "For every novel I have
published, by the way, there exists one, or a fraction of one, that I have
scrapped,"[3] or that he chose the name "Eccles" for the first Rabbit book
because he wanted to have an Anglo-sounding name in order to set him
apart from Pennsylvania Germans—and because he played poker with a
fellow named Eccles. "It wasn't until I read a review that I learned I had
made that awful pun [with Ecclesiastes]," Updike said.[4]

His earliest apparent interview request, from *Library Journal*'s Judith
Serebnick, elicited a cornucopian response. While other emerging
writers replied to her questionnaire with a few scant paragraphs, Updike
sent three single-spaced, typed pages of answers that were "incredibly
well-written, thoughtful, and interesting," according to Serebnick. More
fascinating is that they included off-the-record remarks Updike asked
her not to publish. "And I didn't," Serebnick said. Updike later sent a
postcard thanking her for not violating his trust, and in that card one
senses the discomfort that must have occurred in the interim, of having
been possibly *too* forthcoming. "My father was a great do-gooder,"
Updike told an interviewer in 1981, "and I'm afraid I have a do-gooding
streak which unless severely curbed will run away with me."[5] That,
too, explains a great deal.

While Updike's aversion to interviews has become almost as legendary as his alter-ego Henry Bech's—who warded off would-be interro-
gators with an airy-but-erudite apology that "Henry Bech is too old and
ill and doubtful to submit to questionnaires and interviews"[6]—he has
given his time and energy to more than two hundred of them.

To a one, Updike's interviewers were struck by his great height and distinctive facial features, which Howard described as "oddly good-looking, with an arresting hooked nose and sea-captainish crinkled eyes." Almost all noted that his "cheerful, relaxed, friendly and modest" demeanor (Reston, 1968) and his tendency toward self-effacement was wholly unexpected, given his status as a genuine celebrity and "Great American Novelist"—a label Updike said brings pressure from two sides: "the media pressure and the academic pressure. And then there's that constant feeling that if you're not writing *Moby-Dick,* you're just clowning around."[7]

The body of interviews does, in fact, affirm Updike's status as a major American writer, one whose Rabbit tetralogy may indeed loom as large over time as Melville's whale. Though early detractors complained that Updike's fiction doesn't deal enough with important social issues, the introductions to these individual interviews—especially those from international publications—indicate otherwise. As *The Scotsman* reported in 1983, "At a time when novelists have been retreating into marginal fields or their own ethnic groups within that wider America" or writing "self-indulgent" and "academic" novels, "Updike had always kept his eye fixed on an older conception of the novel that it is making a statement about society. . . . His concern has been the point 'where culture changes.'"[8]

The interviews selected for this volume show Updike to be fully concerned with life as it is lived in America, which he said was "founded as a utopia, and that's always on our minds—that we're falling short of being a utopia" (Bragg, 1990). Having devoted his writing life to exploring small-town and suburban comings and goings—"the same old middle-class muddle that continues to charm me and that I continue to investigate as if it was going to reveal the secret of life" (Thomas, 1980)—Updike has never been reticent to explain his choice of subject matter. As he told a Boston radio audience in 1975, "I can perceive that this country has never been really at home with urban or urbane ideals. Its notions of virtue are all kind of countryside notions" (Stout).

Yet, according to Updike, the "chief glory" of post-WWII American literature has been the urban Jewish writers. And while he told *Hayden's Ferry Review* (1987) that "I really never set out to be a Christian writer or theological writer. I'm just trying to announce with a sense of wonder and surprise that I'm here at all," what becomes enormously clear from reading these interviews is how *much* of Updike's social fabric is spun from Protestant threads. Though he tells Jeff Campbell that "My art is Christian only in that my faith urges me to tell the truth, however painful and inconvenient, and holds out the hope that the truth—reality—is good," it becomes evident that Updike is writing as much out of the Christian experience as Bellow, Roth, and the Jewish writers he so admires are writing out of theirs.

Reading these interviews, one begins to understand the complicated way in which Updike perceives the world of the "real," and the spiritual ideals which have given shape to the objects he describes with such loving extravagance: "Any act of description is, to some extent, an act of praise, so that even when the event is unpleasant or horrifying or spiritually stunning, the very attempt to describe it is, in some way, part of the Old Testament injunction to give praise," Updike told Jan Nunley in 1993. "The Old Testament God repeatedly says he wants praise, and I translate that to mean that the world wants describing, the world wants to be observed and 'hymned.' So there's a kind of hymning under-current that I feel in my work. Even though my books strike people as immoral or morally useless," he told Nunley, "to me they are real moral investigations of how we live, and harsh, perhaps, because the standards are otherworldly." And his characters are ordinary because, as he explained early in his career, "the idea of a hero is aristocratic. As aristocracies have faded, so have heroes. . . . Now either nobody is a hero or everyone is. I vote for everyone" (Howard, 1966).

However unintentionally, these collected interviews also address the complaint that Updike is a prose stylist who doesn't deal enough with ideas. From his first interview—where he wrote Serebnick that he was attempting to do "any number of things" in "trying to write a first novel which would serve, in its breadth, as a base for further novels"—Updike has engaged questioners in often heady discussions of religion, philosophy, literary theory, ethics, and science, articulating the interplay of ideas that rests beneath the surface of his elaborate descriptions. What becomes clear as well is Updike's seriousness in trying to attempt visual to verbal transformations. He told Christopher Lydon that painting is this century's "heroic art," and that "I, myself, in my attempts to be an artist in words, have looked to museums—especially modern museums—as some sort of example of what art might do now. The little *frisson* or the big *frisson* I get in the museum is something I hope to translate into my own writing" (1989).

Reading these interviews, one comes to realize that Updike's luxuriant style, his drive to produce work (to stay "just ahead of total silence. That's why I have to produce a book a year"[9]), his interest in "'middleness' or the quality of things at rest"[10] and his fascination with what he termed the "Three Great Secret Things" (sex, religion, and art)[11]—even his sense of writing as "paying homage to the world" (Winkler, 1985)— have been formed by a number of things. With interviewers he openly discusses the shaping influences of a nurturing family and small-town upbringing, the Great Depression, the Cold War, his early exposure to Vermeer and modern art, early stinging dismissals of his work, and family failures for which he seems driven to atone.

"In the course of a life, a dozen people really matter," Updike told then-high school student Lorrie Dispenza in 1977. "We're born into a family of some kind, and a lot of what we know about how life is lived comes from that family" (Christian, 1985). "There's something about the impressions gathered in the first 18 or 20 years of life that I think have shaped almost all writers," Updike explained to Alvin P. Sanoff (1986). In Updike's case, Shillington, Pennsylvania, has shaped his work to the extent that more than a few interviewers have prefaced their remarks by comparing Updike's strong sense of place to Faulkner's.

Updike's life, as revealed in these interviews, lends itself less to vivisection than most, because the factors of his life have changed very little over the years. For one thing, he is, as he's often admitted, "a domestic creature" who has lived in a family situation all but two of the years since his first book was published in 1958. Then too, fame came early and stayed throughout his career, as did notice of his considerable talents and the resultant high expectations which followed—which is to say that from the very beginning, Updike has had to field questions about critics. As he told Howard, "There's a 'yes-but' quality about my writing that evades entirely pleasing anybody. It seems to me that critics get increasingly querulous and impatient for madder music and stronger wine, when what we need is a greater respect for reality, its secret, its music."

If there is a progression, it's that his early annoyance with "the people who have been really out to puncture me"[12] which occasionally surfaces in interviews, yields, eventually, to apparent resignation and to a reaffirmation of the regenerative aspects of writing. Updike explained it best in 1987: "Robert Lowell, in one of the poems in *The Dolphin*,

talks about a critic who was sent by God to chastize him, but he and I
go on typing for the same reason: to go on living" (McNally & Stover).
One other progression of sorts: Those familiar with the charge that
Updike's work is sexist will also find it interesting to read the pro-
women remarks he made before the accusations began, or to read, in a
1975 interview, his apparent surprise at the backlash, as well as the responses that follow in later interviews.

Although no distinctive "periods" emerge, what does, in fact, surface
is Updike's ever-evolving willingness to share biographical details.
Guarded and even defensive at first about the autobiographical nature of
his work, age as well as critical success and a succession of awards has
generated increasingly specific responses—as when he named, for a
roomful of booksellers and reviewers in 1990, two actual Shillington
athletes who inspired his choosing "Rabbit" as a nickname: "I admired
Bob Arndt, and there was something very pale and rabbity about him.
And there also was a boy in Shillington High called Rabbit Easter. I
think the two things merged in my mind."[13]

Often, a remark lightly touched upon in one interview will be fully
developed in another conducted shortly thereafter—which suggests that
the interviews have engaged Updike perhaps more than he might care to
admit. In one such case, when William Findlay gets Updike talking
briefly about influences—"I think that Marquez's *One Hundred Years
of Solitude* did help give me the courage to try *The Coup*. . . . And
[Carlos] Fuentes did write a book, *The Death of Artemio Cruz,* which
was one of the books in my mind when I was trying to write my own
book about a dying man [*Buchanan Dying*]"[14]—a year later Jean-Pierre
Salgas is the beneficiary. Updike reveals, in that interview, an extensive
list of influences on specific novels, adding that "I have almost always
begun a book with another book in mind." And as the interview with his
Japanese translator shows, Updike's *Rabbit, Run* also provided the inspiration for at least one book. Through such intertextuality, Updike
feels, "writers give each other the courage to carry on" (Salgas).

While surprisingly few interviews appear to have been conducted
prior to his winning the National Book Award in 1964 for *The Centaur,*
or even during the next few years—one can only speculate that the
mixed critical reaction was in part responsible—requests began to pour
in after *Couples* made Updike an international celebrity in 1968. In
addition to the Rabbit books, which were eagerly anticipated by readers

and reviewers, the periods which generated the most interviews were those which followed publication of *Marry Me: A Romance* and *The Coup,* as well as both Bech collections and *Roger's Version.* Updike granted the fewest interviews during 1974–75, the two years he was separated from his first wife and living in Boston. Now, his publisher reports that he receives four to five requests per month, many of them from foreign magazines so anxious to publish *anything* from him that they say he can talk about whatever he wants, or answer in brief by mail. Despite his willingness to grant roughly one out of ten interview requests, Updike told Sanoff that "Too much talk can make you fatheaded. You get the idea that everything you say is worth being recorded and that you are in some sense a wise man and an interesting person."

The bottom line, of course, is that Updike *is* a wise and interesting person, who has emerged as—if not *the* pre-eminent American novelist—certainly one of America's most celebrated writers and literary ambassadors. What he says is of great interest, and his place in American literary history is, as even his detractors must concede, well assured. After Updike received his first Pulitzer Prize in 1982, *Time* wrote that "No one else using the English language over the past 2½ decades has written so well in so many ways as he." [15]

In conversation, however spontaneous, Updike's love of language shines through—a love he told an interviewer that arose, in part, from his grandfather, who was "a lovely talker. He really had that old-fashioned way of talking as a kind of performance" (Christian, 1985). These 32 interviews were chosen not only because they span the full range of Updike's writing career, but because they also cover the full range of voices and levels of response that Updike has given, each prompted by different interviewers and concerns. Updike told one of his questioners that *Of the Farm* was meant to be a "sort of musical" novella, where "The four people are like the four instruments of a string quartet: they talk to each other in their duets and trios within the quartet" (Dispenza, 1977). Included in this collection are interviews given to scholars, graduate students, talk-show hosts, large and small-town newspaper reporters, international publications, a religious journal, a fellow Harvard alum—even a high-school girl who Updike said "brought out the garrulous father" in him, [16] and the coach of the NBA Champion Chicago Bulls. Because of the sheer volume of interviews available, many excellent interviews obviously had to be omitted—left for Updike fans and scholars to discover on their own. But within the range of voices and interviews included here, Updike's own voice and remarks resonate in fascinating ways and reverberate with the texts that prompt each discussion.

As is customary with the Literary Conversations series, the interviews are reprinted largely uncut and as they first appeared, because the publisher recognizes the importance to scholars of unedited interviews. While this leads to a certain amount of repetition, it also provides interesting variations (or apparent contradictions) for scholars to consider. For stylistic consistency, American spellings have been used and book titles have been regularized into italics. Factual and typographical errors have been silently corrected. Four of the interviews appear in English for the first time, while three—Iwamoto (1978), Winkler (1985), and Nunley (1993)—contain additional material from the interviewer's original notes or audiotapes that never appeared in the published articles.

Like Blanche DuBois, a researcher is always dependent upon "the kindness of strangers," many of whom I've talked with so often that they can no longer be considered as such. First, I must thank Sue Ponsford, my research assistant, for helping me track down a good many of these interviews, working on transcriptions, and doing a thousand time-consuming things, both large and small. Special thanks goes to the Joyce Foundation and Illinois Wesleyan University for the grant support which allowed me to complete work on this book. Thanks also to Seetha Srinivasan, my editor at the University Press of Mississippi for her patience and guidance, and to all those who cheerfully provided me with interviews, technology, and information, especially Jane Beal (WGBH-Boston Film & Video Resource Center); Gordon Boltz and Ed Shultz (*Reading Times-Eagle*); Richard Burgin (*Boulevard*); Ed Byers (Reading Public Library); Sophie Cottrell and Kathy Zuckerman (Alfred A. Knopf); Tom Flynn (Rochester *Democrat and Chronicle*); Ron Fried and Judy Englander ("The Dick Cavett Show"); Professor Donald J. Greiner (Univ. of South Carolina); Terry Gross and Dorothy Ferebee ("Fresh Air," WHYY-Philadelphia); Jane Howard; Professor Iwao Iwamoto (Kyoritsu Women's University); Bob Mowery and the staff at Sheean Library (IWU); Salima Keegan (*Hayden's Ferry Review*); Jan Nunley and Nan Cobbey (*Episcopal Life*); Adelaide J. Pearson (Ipswich

Public Library); Eulalie Regan (*Vineyard Gazette*); Professor Charlie
Reilly (Montgomery County Community College); Judith Serebnick;
Diane Windham Shaw (Skillman Library, Lafayette College); Michael
Sragow; Edney Silvestre (*O Globo*); Professor Campbell Tatham (Univ.
of Wisconsin-Milwaukee); Michael Whalton (Hemingway Days Fes-
tival); Willi Winkler; and Herb Yellin (*The John Updike Newsletter,*
Lord John Press).

But of course, my greatest thanks goes to John Updike himself, who
has provided me with interviews I never knew existed, who has meticu-
lously gone over the chronology and bibliography and offered to help in
additional ways, and who once wrote, when I first proposed the project,
that he wasn't quite sure if he was emotionally up to it. I know, now,
exactly what he meant.

JP
September 1993

NOTES

1. From a letter to the author, 19 October 1985. Subsequent quotations from interviews included in this volume are cited in-text by interviewer, publication, and/or year.
Quotations from other interviews, articles, and books are footnoted.

2. Martin Amis, "Updike's Version," *The Observer* (30 August 1987): 15–16.

3. Lewis Nichols, "Talk with John Updike," *The New York Times Book Review* (7
April 1968): 34–35.

4. From "John Updike Offers Peek behind Curtain of Writer's Window," *Bethlehem*
(Pa.) *Globe Times* (13 March 1982): B-2.

5. Curt Suplee, "Women, God, Sorrow & John Updike: Rabbit Runs Again for the
Cool Master of Life's Small Punches," *The Washington Post* (27 September 1981): F-1,
F-2.

6. John Updike, *Bech: A Book* (New York: Alfred A. Knopf, 1970): 148.

7. Louise Lague, "A Novelist's Reflection: 'I Don't Like to Be Watched': And That
Is Just One of the Ironies of Updike," *The Washington Star* (9 December 1976): D-1,
D-2.

8. Allan Massie, "Updike: Rabbit-hunting in Middle America; Allan Massie talks to
John Updike after his Edinburgh Festival appearance," *The Scotsman* (3 September
1983): Weekend Scotsman sec., 2.

9. Craig MacDonald, "A Chat with John Updike," *Writers Digest* (Sept. 1977): 5.

10. Frank Gado, *First Person: Conversations on Writers and Writing* (Schenectedy, New York: Union College Press, 1973): 80–109.

11. John Updike, "The Dogwood Tree: A Boyhood," (*Assorted Prose,* New York: Alfred A. Knopf, 1965): 151–187.

12. Richard Burgin, "A Conversation with John Updike," *New York Arts Journal* 9 (April/May 1978): 21–23 and 11 (September/October 1978): 20–21.

13. Roger Miller, "Updike Says This Year's will be the Last Rabbit Tale—But No Promises," *The Milwaukee Journal* (1 July 1990): E-6.

14. William Findlay, "Interview with John Updike," *Cencrastus: Scottish and international literature, arts and affairs* 15 (New Year 1984): 30–36.

15. Paul Gray and Peter Stoler, "Perennial Promises Kept," *Time* (18 October 1982): 72–74, 79–81.

16. From a letter to the author, 26 July 1993.

Chronology

1932   John Hoyer Updike is born on 18 March in Reading, Pa. (model for the fictional Brewer), the only child of Linda Grace Hoyer, an aspiring writer, and Wesley Russell Updike, a junior high-school mathematics teacher. From ages "Zero to 13" he lives at 117 Philadelphia Ave. in Shillington (model for the fictional Olinger).

1936   Raised in a Lutheran/Democratic household, he enters the Shillington public schools and aspires, by age 12, to become a contributor to *The New Yorker*.

1943   Updike enters Shillington High School, where, as a seventh grader and with the publication of "A Handshake with the Congressman," he contributes the first of some 285 drawings, articles, and light verse to the school newspaper, the *Chatterbox*. In his sophomore year, he tries to write a mystery novel and as a senior serves as class president. His yearbook bio notes that "the sage of Plowville hopes to write for a living."

1945   Updike's family moves on Halloween day to his mother's birthplace on a 93-acre farm in nearby Plowville, Pa., and takes up residence in the six-room stone farmhouse—a move that makes him feel isolated.

1950   His first summer out of high school and for two successive summers Updike works as a copy boy for the *Reading Eagle* and writes a few feature stories. In the fall he enters Harvard College on a tuition scholarship. He is first a cartoonist, then a poet and prose writer, and eventually President at the *Lampoon*.

1951   He works at *Willow,* an unfinished novel.

1953   On 26 June, he marries Radcliffe fine-arts major Mary
            Pennington, daughter of Rev. and Mrs. Leslie T. Penning-
            ton of Chicago, where Rev. Pennington is minister of the
            First Unitarian Church.

1954   Updike graduates *summa cum laude* as an English major
            from Harvard. That same June, *The New Yorker* buys one
            story and one poem—his "literary breakthrough." The first
            poem to appear is the light verse "Duet, with Muffled Brake
            Drums" (14 August); his first *New Yorker* story, "Friends
            from Philadelphia" (30 October), concerns a small-town
            adolescent. He attends the Ruskin School of Drawing and
            Fine Art in Oxford, England, on a Knox Fellowship for the
            1954–55 school year, while continuing to write. In
            England, he meets Katherine White and is offered a staff
            job at *The New Yorker.*

1955   Oldest daughter Elizabeth is born on 1 April. In August, the
            Updikes move to Manhattan, where he works as a reporter,
            writing "Talk of the Town" columns for *The New Yorker.*
            He is declared 4-F because of psoriasis.

1957   In January, son David is born. Early in the year, Updike
            completes *Home,* a 600-page novel he had been working
            on, but decides not to rewrite it. In March, to concentrate
            on his fiction and poetry, he quits his staff job at *The New
            Yorker* and relocates his family to Ipswich, Mass. (site of
            his honeymoon and model for the fictional Tarbox). They
            move into the house called "Little Violet" on Essex Rd.,
            where he writes *The Poorhouse Fair.*

1958   His first book, *The Carpentered Hen and Other Tame
            Creatures,* is published by Harper and Brothers. Rather than
            change the ending of *The Poorhouse Fair,* Updike changes
            publishers. In spring, the Updikes buy and move into a

seventeenth-century clapboard house at 26 East St., Ipswich.

1959   Alfred A. Knopf publishes both his first novel and his first short story collection, *The Same Door*. In England, *The Carpentered Hen* is published as *Hoping for a Hoopoe*. Son Michael is born in May, and a grant from the John Simon Guggenheim Foundation helps enable Updike to work on a longer novel, *Rabbit, Run*.

1960   *Rabbit, Run* is published, and *The Poorhouse Fair* receives the Rosenthal Award of the National Institute of Arts and Letters. In December, daughter Miranda is born.

1961   After writing his first books at home, Updike rents a one-room office above a restaurant in the Caldwell Building on South Main St., where he will work every morning, six days a week.

1962   During the summer, Updike teaches creative writing at Harvard—his only try at his father's occupation.

1963   *The Centaur* is published.

1964   Updike is elected a member of the National Institute of Arts and Letters and receives the National Book Award for Fiction for *The Centaur*. *The Olinger Stories, A Selection* is published. Travels in Russia, Bulgaria, Romania, and Czechoslovakia for the U.S. State Department.

1965   Updike is elected to the American Academy of Arts and Sciences.

1966   He receives the First O. Henry Prize for "The Bulgarian Poetess."

1967   Updike and other writers sign a letter drafted by Robert

Penn Warren urging Soviet writers to use the pen to help restore Jewish cultural institutions.

1968   *Couples* is published and becomes a best-seller. Updike is featured on the cover of the 26 April *Time,* and in Ipswich he writes and performs in the Seventeenth-century Day Pageant, *Three Texts from Early Ipswich.*

1969   In *Midpoint and Other Poems*, he offers his philosophies of life in poetic form.

1970   Updike's alter-ego emerges in *Bech: A Book,* while *Rabbit, Run* is made into a movie. Travels to Japan and Korea with daughter Elizabeth. The Updikes move to a house on Labor-in-Vain Rd., Ipswich.

1971   *Rabbit Redux* is published.

1972   Updike is appointed Honorary Consultant in American Letters to the Library of Congress for a three-year term. From 8–14 March he lectures in Venezuela as the guest of the Centro Venezolano Americano.

1973   With Mary, he travels to Africa and lectures in Ghana, Nigeria, Tanzania, Kenya, and Ethiopia on a Lincoln Lectureship from the Fulbright Board of Foreign Scholarships.

1974   In September, he separates from Mary and moves to an apartment on Beacon St., in Boston. With John Cheever, Arthur Miller, and Richard Wilbur, Updike composes an open letter to U.S.S.R. Ambassador Anatoly Dobrinin to cease the official harrassment of Soviet writer Alexander Solzhenitsyn.

1975   *A Month of Sundays,* the first volume in Updike's *Scarlet Letter* trilogy, is published.

1976   In March, Updike and his wife of 22 years file for "no-fault" divorce. That June, he moves, with Martha Bernhard and her three sons, into a nineteenth-century house at 58 W. Main St. in nearby Georgetown, Mass. On 29 April, *Buchanan Dying* premieres at the Green Room Theater at Franklin and Marshall College (Lancaster, Pa.). *Marry Me: A Romance* is published, and Updike is elected to the fifty-member Academy within the National Institute of Arts and Letters.

1977   His divorce final, Updike marries Martha Bernhard on 30 September.

1978   Asked to testify in Boston before the Subcommittee on Select Education of the House of Representatives Commit-tee on Education and Labor, Updike speaks against govern-ment support for the arts. *The Coup* is published and hailed as an energetic departure from Updike's suburban novels.

1979   *Too Far to Go: The Maples Stories* is published and pro-duced for television as an NBC two-hour movie.

1980   "The Music School" is produced for public television, and broadcast the week of 28 April as part of "The American Short Story" series.

1981   Updike is awarded the Edward MacDowell Medal for litera-ture. The subject of a BBC documentary, "What Makes Rabbit Run?", he embarks on a nostalgic October journey to Ipswich and Berks County, Pa., with a British film crew. *Rabbit Is Rich* is published and receives a National Book Critics Circle Award for Fiction.

1982   Updike is awarded the Pulitzer Prize for Fiction and the American Book Award for *Rabbit Is Rich*. In May, he moves with Martha to Beverly Farms, Massachusetts. For his fiftieth birthday, Knopf reissues Updike's first book, *The Carpentered Hen,* and he is featured on the cover of the 18 October *Time. Bech Is Back* is published.

1983   In May, Updike travels to Harrisburg, Pa., to receive the
            fourth Distinguished Pennsylvania Artist award from Gover-
            nor Thornburgh.

1984   Updike is awarded the National Arts Club Medal of Honor,
            and *Hugging the Shore* (1983) receives the National Book
            Critics Circle Award for Criticism. *The Witches of Eastwick*
            is published.

1986   *Roger's Version* continues the *Scarlet Letter* trilogy.

1987   *The Witches of Eastwick* is made into a movie, with an all-
            star cast (Jack Nicholson, Cher, Susan Sarandon, Michelle
            Pfeiffer).

1988   *S.* completes the *Scarlet Letter* trilogy. In October, Updike
            gives the first Annual PEN/Malamud Memorial Reading at
            the Folger Shakespeare Library in Washington, D.C.

1989   Updike receives the National Medal of Arts from President
            Bush in a 17 November ceremony at the White House.

1990   *Rabbit at Rest* is published, fourth and final volume in the
            saga of Harry Angstrom. Updike returns to Pennsylvania to
            talk about his childhood and "Rabbit" books with a film
            crew from the *South Bank Show* (London Weekend Tele-
            vision).

1991   He receives Italy's Scanno Prize for *Trust Me,* as well as the
            National Book Critics Circle Award and a second Pulitzer
            Prize for *Rabbit at Rest*—making him only the third Amer-
            ican to win the Pulitzer Prize for fiction on two occasions.
            "A Sandstone Farmhouse" is awarded the First O. Henry
            Prize—Updike's second.

1993   His fortieth book with Knopf is published: *Collected Poems
            1953–1993.* In July, Updike travels to Key West, Fla., to
            accept the second Conch Republic Prize for Literature.

Conversations with John Updike

New Creative Writers: Another Noteworthy Beginning

Judith Serebnick/1959

From *Library Journal* 84 (1 February 1959), 499. Copyright © 1959 by Reed Publishing, USA. Reprinted by permission of *Library Journal* and Judith Serebnick. Conducted by mail in January, 1959.

We can think of no better way to start this year than with John Updike's *The Poorhouse Fair* (Knopf—January). Due to the lack of a definite publication date, this first novel did not appear in our last article; we would like to correct that grave omission now.

The novel is concerned with the activities in a New Jersey poorhouse on the day of the annual fair. Mr. Updike can remember the impetus for the novel: "I was home in Pennsylvania in March of 1957, having completed a 600-page novel which I had just decided not to rewrite, but to chalk up to practice. . . . At the end of the street where I had lived in Shillington, there had been an enormous poorhouse, complete with farmland, pigstys, etc., which was being torn down to make way for a lot of little houses. I suddenly wished to write a memorial to it, a book about America changing. I had lived with two grandparents while growing up, and I had no fear of writing about old people; also I thought it would be good to have a first novel (wretched genre) so obviously un-a-clef. I wrote it in Ipswich [Massachusetts; where Mr. Updike now lives], in three summer months; and rewrote it in three fall months."

As for what he was trying to do or show in his novel, his reply: "As you say, this is impossible to answer without seeming foolish. I was trying to do any number of things, some of which I've forgotten. I was trying to say something about what I felt the condition of America was in 1957. I was personifying, and in a way purging, some personal emotions of my own. I was trying to make an oblique monument to my grandfather, who in the guise of Hook I wished to treat with a tenderness I had never shown the old man himself. I was trying to write well, in a way I hadn't written before, making syntax and punctuation my own, rather than have them, to an extent, manipulate *me*. I was trying to write a first novel which would serve, in its breadth, as a base for further novels." To Mr. Updike, who has supported himself by writing since the age of 23 (he now has two children), the writer's life to imitate is Shakespeare's: "a steady, abundant, and varied output, with the author himself completely invisible."

He believes that "librarians are the cornerstone of our literary establishment, its least corruptible elements; I remember well the kindness of a Miss Ruth in Reading, Pa., and the wonderful haven and palace that library was."

Updike Is Uneasy about Literary Prizes

Edgar J. Driscoll, Jr./1964

From *The Boston Globe*, 17 March 1964. Reprinted courtesy of *The Boston Globe*.

The firmly packed snowball sped straight to its mark, smacking dead center on the big red STOP sign at the corner of East St., Ipswich.

"Nice shot, John," called an elderly neighbor, parcels in hand, as she made her way home from market.

"Thanks, Mrs. Merson," said the marksman, better known to the world outside for a different kind of smash success.

He's 32-year-old John Updike, young lion of the literary set, whose compelling novel, *The Centaur*, carried off the National Book Committee's 1963 prize for fiction only a few days ago.

Author also of two widely heralded earlier works, *The Poorhouse Fair* and *Rabbit, Run*, Updike was winging his daily dozen, snow conditions permitting, from the high-rise steps of his charming, old 17th century clapboard house in what might be called downtown Ipswich.

Clustered at the windows, egging him on, were three of his four young children, David, 7, Michael, 4, and Miranda, a tow-headed muffin of three. Elizabeth, 8, was at a meeting of her "Brownie" Scout troop.

The time was 3 o'clock on a Thursday afternoon. Updike was returning home from his daily stint of writing in a small back office over a restaurant in the business center of town. He spends an average of five hours a day there, and $1000 prize or not, there was no time out for a holiday.

Greeting him at the door was his friendly, attractive wife, trim in black cashmere sweater and black slacks. She's the daughter of Rev. and Mrs. Leslie T. Pennington of Chicago, where he is minister of the First Unitarian Church.

The Updikes have been living in this typical North Shore town for the past seven years, after he quit writing full time for *The New Yorker*'s "Talk of the Town." He still contributes to the magazine, however.

5

Why Ipswich? Well, the couple was married in Cambridge, where Mary grew up, and spent a couple of days on their honeymoon here.

After living in the heart of Manhattan, "we wanted to get far enough away so that we wouldn't be tempted to commute. We thought of Ipswich as being completely rural, and wanted the children to grow up in a small town. Only now," Mary exclaims, "we've found it isn't really rural at all—actually it's a commuting town."

The Updikes, however, confine their commuting to two trips to Boston every two weeks or so, to take in the movies, the theater or visit friends. They like it fine where they are.

"I'm extremely fond of Doris Day, the late Errol Flynn, Ingmar Bergman movies, and the folk songs of Joan Baez," the tall, lanky author with a shock of unruly brown hair says with a gleam in his eyes.

Evenings at home in the rambling 11-room house ("I think there are 11, though I've never really counted them") are spent by the huge old fireplace in the living room, comfortably furnished with modern sofa and chairs, or, in a book-lined study, upright piano at one end, guitar, sheet music and recorders on top.

He likes to read old books, "books that won't upset me." She reads contemporary fiction "avidly."

Both also try their hand at painting. In fact, his office has several Updikes on the wall. Good, too, reflecting training he had at Oxford, where he studied art for a year on a Knox Fellowship. This was after graduating summa cum laude from Harvard, class of '54.

Mary, in turn was a fine-arts major at Radcliffe, class of '52. She prepared at Buckingham School in Cambridge. She has taught ceramics and painting at Browne & Nichols School there and the work of the young Updikes reflects her interest. Lively paintings by them decorate the kitchen bulletin board.

Ipswich's famous author, whose parents still live near the town of Shillington, Pa., where he was brought up, says he doesn't know what he'll do with the prize money. "Bank it, spend it, who knows?" he says with a shrug. "We need rugs"—this said eyeing the wide-wide floor boards on the friendly old house. "And we need a new car"— motioning out the window to the family's 10-year-old sedan.

What do his fellow townsmen think of his success? "People are very polite around here. The town is very nice about it, they take it in stride," says the man whose work is considered by many to be the most delicately woven, shamelessly artful prose now being crafted by any American writer.

And he? Standing in the kitchen, with the young Updikes and their neighborhood friends whooping it up around him, he seemed a little afraid of it.

"I feel sort of uneasy about literary prizes," the shy, self-effacing author said. "Just look over the list. The wrong people tend to get them. I hope I'm not one of them.

"Take Tolstoy, he never won a Nobel Prize in his day, nor did one ever go to Joyce or Proust. But perhaps this feeling is less true now than it used to be.

"Personally, I think any success is discouraging to an American writer, it smacks of a curse. Failure is the only lasting success. . . ."

Success or failure notwithstanding, the youthful writer intends to keep right on writing. And getting published, too (which in his case no longer presents any great problems).

For to a writer, "the sensation of being in print is terribly important. I don't understand these writers who don't want to be published. And there are lots of them. Why? Because they're not sure they are good enough. But what sort of attitude is that? No one is ever sure enough.

"It's like wanting to be pregnant without having a baby."

Updike attributes much of his early success to practical experience on the *Lampoon* at Harvard. He started out as a cartoonist with them, then shifted to poetry and prose. He ended up successively as Narthex, Ibis and President, honoraria of which, "coming from a small Pennsylvania town," he was very proud.

Does he draw from the Ipswich people around him for his more recent works—a natural question for townspeople living in a famous writer's midst?

"No, not really. I don't know them that well," he says. Is his work autobiographical? "That's not really for me to say. But I would say not especially. And certainly not extraordinarily so, as things go nowadays."

Updike, who limits himself to polishing no more than 300 words a day, is currently working on some new short stories. Maybe there's even a new novel on the way. But when he closes shop, he keeps thinking of his words. "I even write notes to myself," he explains.

There also are two new Updike writing talents on the way. Both Elizabeth and David, who attend the local elementary school, are mad about writing at this point and want to be writers when they grow up.

In this lively, informal household ("we think the living room was once a tavern; you can smell the malt on a really damp day") the gifts seem only natural.

Yet the Updike interests are varied, too. They are active members of the town's Fair Housing Committee; are members of a recorder group; and take keen interest in Congregational Church affairs, where he serves as chairman of its Historical Society.

Summers they soak up the sun on Crane Beach, winters they ski. Updike also enjoys golf with a local pediatrician, druggist and Episcopal minister when weather permits.

In short, life is never dull at 26 East St. And as Updike fans well know, neither are his writings.

Can a Nice Novelist Finish First?

Jane Howard/1966

From *Life Magazine* 61 (4 November 1966), 74, 74A, 74C–74D, 76, 79–82. Reprinted by permission of Jane Howard and *Life Magazine*, copyright Time Warner.

John Updike thinks he might, if he weren't a writer, be in character as a turtle, a housewife, or as Errol Flynn—"Errol Flynn," he is quick to add, "as Robin Hood."

His reasons are specific. "Turtles," he says, "live quite long and can retreat immediately, and live very close to the grass, the smell of which I've always liked. I also like the sound of rain on a roof, which a turtle must get quite a lot of." As for housewives, he has great sympathy for their "devastating sense of emptiness—their ear is somehow held closer than most ears to the steady ticking of time." And as for Errol Flynn, Updike admires the ability that late and eminent swashbuckler had to "move through life sideways, very quickly and effectively, quite gracefully, able to do everything well."

Updike can do a number of things well himself. He is expert, for example, at juggling apples and oranges and even better at juggling the writing of novels, short stories, essays, children's books and light verse. His newest work, a collection of 20 short stories called *The Music School* (Knopf), is his 11th book—a number that would be respectable if achieved by an octogenarian writer and is truly phenomenal for the 34-year-old possessor of so boyish a shaggy haircut and so recent (1954) a diploma from Harvard.

Apart from the sheer volume of it, Updike's work is distinguished by lyrical language. The people he writes about are commonplace, their lives mundane, but the way he describes them is dazzling—so dazzling, some critics think, that it blinds. Even those who agree with reviewer Robert Martin Adams in the New York *Times* that *The Music School* is "a beautifully written, an exquisitely artful book" complain publicly, as Stanley Kauffman has just done in the *New Republic*, that Updike is "a lesser, latter-day Emily Dickinson" who "reaches out the front door and grabs a couple of people and pulls them inside for inspection."

The argument has raged for years. Many thought *The Poorhouse
Fair*, Updike's first novel, about an old people's home, pretentious for
a 27-year-old; others were enraptured. To some the juxtaposition of old
myth with modern reality in *The Centaur* (his 1963 novel about a
Pennsylvania high-school science teacher who kept turning into a horse
and back to a teacher again) seemed gratuitous and show-offy. But the
National Book Award Committee voted it that year's best novel. A
number of critics swore they couldn't even bring themselves to finish
Rabbit, Run, Updike's 1960 novel about a superannuated high-school
basketball star who found the dilemmas of adult life considerably more
perplexing than those of the locker room. But others took the occasion
to hail Updike as a direct spiritual descendant of Jane Austen.

Of the Farm, last year's novel, found wide favor, but not from John
Aldridge, who concluded his *Book Week* review with the scathing
statement that "Mr. Updike has nothing to say."

The literary destiny of this gifted young writer, who looks so nice
and modest on his book jacket photographs, is bound to be argued
even more hotly as each new book appears. Will he ever write a really
big, good, enduring book—a book as important as his talent? In other
words, can a nice novelist finish first? An impossible question to answer, maybe, but interesting to consider.

Updike's approach to writing is curiously, though not intentionally,
attuned to the Pop Art movement. "There is," he thinks, "a great
deal to be said about almost anything. Everything can be as interesting
as every other thing. An old milk carton is worth a rose; a trolley car
has as much right to be there, in terms of esthetics, as a tree." He
thinks every person is just as interesting as every other, too. "The idea
of a hero," he says, "is aristocratic. As aristocracies have faded, so
have heroes. You cared about Oedipus and Hamlet because they were
noble and you were a groundling. Now either nobody is a hero or
everyone is. I vote for everyone."

Thus Updike's manicurists are as carefully drawn as his graduate
students, and his secondhand cars are described no less poetically than
his rhododendron borders. He lavishes extravagant detail on accounts
of the way a janitor sweeps up debris from a school corridor, how a
man reaches for a paper napkin at a luncheonette counter, and the re-
flections cast on ceilings by nighttime traffic to bemuse an insomniac.

This is all very well, say the critics. Wise minds from the time of the 139th Psalm to Gerard Manley Hopkins to Rachel Carson have endorsed a Sense of Wonder. But where does Updike's hyperdeveloped Sense of Wonder get him or us? Is he capable, to paraphrase an early reviewer, of "thought rather than language"? Does he indeed, as another accuses, "shun the major sorrows and calamities"?

Indeed, Updike people do not go around killing themselves or (with one poignant and accidental exception) each other. "They go back to work," says Updike; "that's the *real* way that people die." Furthermore, they go back to work not much bothered about civil rights or Southeast Asia or the Peace Corps or mass murder. They don't experiment with LSD or have abortions or run for Congress; they aren't pederasts or Lesbians; they don't even divorce each other—though they think about it. Should Updike then, as a reader suggests, "have lived in the early 18th century when everything was settled and important ideas need not apply"? Do his people just walk around their reasonably comfortable homes (in all-white neighborhoods), fretting about nuances and paying too much attention to the textures and sounds of things because their creator cannot think of anything more monumental for them to do?

"My subject," Updike replies to this, "is the American Protestant small-town middle class. I like middles. It is in middles that extremes clash, where ambiguity restlessly rules. Something quite intricate and fierce occurs in homes, and it seems to me without doubt worthwhile to examine what it is." As for the mid-20th century as against other junctures in history, Updike says, "It's true that we live on the verge of catastrophe—not worldwide annihilation, perhaps, but surely something drastic. Still, since 1945 our little dramas have generally been played out somewhat short of catastrophe. We do survive every moment, after all, except the last one."

What arrests him about many thousands of those passing, survived moments is what he calls "the despair of the daily. . . . One suspects," he says, "that it's good to be alive, that there is much more beauty around us than we ever notice, that existence is charged with goodness. Yet even though one isn't willing to die, life still, day by day, often seems monotonous and long. Our goals, once we reach them, bore us."

Updike's "us," as he once delineated it in a story in his collection *Pigeon Feathers*, refers to "the docile Titans—guileless, competent, mildly earnest—that we have fattened, an ocean removed from the

slimming Latin passions and Nordic anxieties of Europe, on our unprecedented abundance of milk and honey, vitamins and protein."

He comes of docile Titan stock himself. He was born in 1932 to an
impoverished but well-read eastern Pennsylvania couple who came of
Dutch, Irish and German ancestors. They and his grandparents raised
him in Shillington (fictionally he renames it Olinger) and on a farm
outside another small town called Plowville. His household was Lutheran and Democratic and inclined, Updike once recalled, to laugh a
lot and "examine everything for God's fingerprints." Groping through
an adolescence in which, to judge by what he writes of it, he must
have been far more shy and less sure than he is now, he too grew up
funny and devout. He also got to be oddly good-looking, with an arresting hooked nose, sea-captainish crinkled eyes and what a colleague
now calls "a prehensile face." He further absorbed what he terms "a
Depression mentality," which helps to explain his prodigious literary
output. "My father was always afraid he'd have to go to the poorhouse
any minute," Updike says, "and I guess I work hard because I have
the same fear."

Updike reports six mornings a week to his office a flight above the
Dolphin Restaurant on South Main Street in downtown Ipswich, Mass.
There he types his short stories, writes his novels in longhand and
works just as industriously as his more conventional neighbors who are
lawyers, drycleaners and vendors of fried clams. The results of his la-
bors equip Updike and his wife and their four children with a 17th century house with enough rooms for everyone to get lost, a remodeled
kitchen, a piano, splashes of blue-and-green Design Research uphol-
stery fabrics, good paintings, many plants, myriad books. They also
have a station wagon, a convertible, and vacations in Martha's Vineyard and the Caribbean.

His prosperity derives largely from what Updike calls "my parasitic
relationship with Steuben Glass," by which he means the advertising
revenues of *The New Yorker* magazine. *The New Yorker*, which still
gets first look at his stories and publishes most of them, started matter-
ing to him in his 11th year, when an aunt sent him a subscription and
he decided "my sole ambition in the world was to make *The New Yorker* myself." At that point he aspired to make it as a cartoonist. The reason he took a scholarship to Harvard (instead of one to Cornell) was
that he wanted to do cartoons for the famous *Lampoon*, which had nur-

tured Robert Benchley and other of his idols. An additional reason was
that his mother methodically made a list of the alma maters of all the
writers in Whit Burnett's prize short story anthology, and saw how impressive a percentage were Harvard men. Mrs. Updike's interest in this
matter was not just maternal or vicarious: she was taking correspon-
dence courses in writing herself those years, and lately has had some of
her own stories published in *The New Yorker*, signed with her maiden
name, Linda Grace Hoyer.

Her son became the most vivid and prolific talent of his era on the
Lampoon. He still flips with proud nostalgia through bound volumes
of issues from those years, which have an astonishing number of cartoons, poems and essays signed "JHU" (the H is for Hoyer). He kept
sending things to *The New Yorker* and getting them back. Rejection,
however, did not discourage young JHU, who as the semesters went by
was acquiring a proper Harvard ego—a Kennedyish ebullience and an
elaborately diffident habit of saying "sort of" and "kind of" and "in
a funny way" oftener than most people do. He also acquired, even before graduation, a wife. His path and that of Mary Pennington first
crossed in the Fogg Museum, where she went as a Radcliffe fine-arts
major and he to check a rumor that fine-arts girls were prettier than
English-major girls. Apparently he found it so.

Four-F because of psoriasis, Updike went to Oxford on a fellowship
to study art for a year—a glittering year in which *The New Yorker*
bought four stories and ten poems and offered him a job as "Talk of
the Town" reporter. This alluring prospect squelched any thoughts Updike had of lingering abroad. He and Mary soon thrived in Manhattan,
and he loved his job. "The 'Talk,'" he says, "was my real genre—I
never had a failure there." But when their second child arrived they
decided they had to move. Not to Pennsylvania, except for short visits
and in fiction: "My face might blend into the landscape better there,"
Updike says, "but there I'd always be thought of as my father's son,
and there the pollen gives me hay fever. I'm less singular here in New
England, where the air is so clear that everything sticks out more."

Although there is a small, skeptical old guard in Ipswich, at least
one of whose members refers to Updike as "Carveup or Checkup or
whatever-his-name-is," most of the town's 10,000 people take his presence for granted. Short of joining the Benevolent and Protective Order
of Elks, in fact, he could scarcely be more enmeshed than he is in the

life of the town. He is a member of the rebuilding committee of the burnt-down Congregational Church and of the town Democratic committee, a participant in golf, poker and touch football games, and plays the recorder in a group that meets on alternate Wednesday evenings. He and his wife also give and go to a fair number of parties, which he thinks are by no means the frivolous affairs most people consider them. "Parties are somehow deadly serious," Updike says. "To say no to one is to say no to life."

For someone who protests, as Updike does, that "I'm so way out I'm almost in," these are unlikely affiliations. Profound young artists, after all, do not traditionally join hands with the reigning bourgeoisie. These days profound young artists are more likely to organize marches, sign anti-Vietnam war petitions, and boycott White House parties (one of which Updike went to). His views are always surprising his peers.

What particularly surprises Updike's peers, most of whom ceased being practicing Protestants somewhere during their years in high-school Young People's groups, is his churchgoing. He really goes; he actively believes. For this he has many reasons, most deriving from his intellectual heroes Soren Kierkegaard and the Swiss theologian Karl Barth, whom he quotes as having said that "a drowning man cannot pull himself out by his own hair." Updike interprets this to mean "there is no help from within—without the supernatural the natural is a pit of horror. I believe that all problems are basically insoluble and that faith is a leap out of total despair.

"I've touched a kind of bottom," he says, "when I've felt that existence itself was an affront to be forgiven. I've felt in myself and in those around me a failure of nerve—a sense of doubt as to the worth of any action. At such times one has nothing but the ancient assertions of Christianity to give one the will to act, even if the act is only the bringing in of the milk bottles off the front porch."

Great as is Updike's esteem for Barth, he has no wish to meet him, nor other figures he admires exceedingly, like Ted Williams and Doris Day. "The whole business of meeting people is so questionable," he says. "When it happens there's always the big, unspoken 'So what?'" A lot of people, however, go out of their way to meet Updike. He is almost as famous, though he denies it, as any living American male writer. The other afternoon a senior from a college in Kansas appeared on his doorstep, having come all that way by bus and train to have his

Updike paperbacks autographed. The next day a lady the author had never seen before stopped him to introduce her small children, so that when they were old and literate they could say they had met him. In practically every mail he is invited to address a convocation or forum on "What Is Man?" or some such topic, and he is periodically asked to be a writer-in-residence at colleges.

Such invitations are usually declined. "Teaching, as I tried to say in a novel I once wrote, consumes energy," he says. "My father taught, my maternal grandfather taught, and I thought I'd try not to. As for speaking, a writer shouldn't take himself too seriously. I don't think it's a very fruitful state of mind for him to consider himself any sort of spokesman." He has made a few official appearances, though. One was a State Department cultural exchange visit to Russia, which he loved. "There I was everything I'm not here," he says, "a public figure, toasting this and that all the time. Russia is so Russian—that flat, gentle, virginal, birchy land, and their *mud*. They've got mud to burn; they're definitely ahead in the mud race."

Eventually Updike wants to write a play about, of all unsung heroes, President James Buchanan, and possibly to do some work in the movies. "I originally wrote *Rabbit, Run* in the present tense, in a sort of cinematic way," he says. "I thought of it as *Rabbit, Run: a Movie*. Novels are descended from chronicles of what has long ago happened, but movies happen to you in the present, as you sit there." His present project is a novel, by far his longest to date, about a town "in darkest New England" called Tarbox. Tarbox, as already introduced in a story in *The Music School*, sounds remarkably like Ipswich. The novel has been hard going. "I have no faith in myself as a novelist," Updike says. "There seems no science to it. Novels are so endless—you have the feeling of being digested in the belly of a big thing. You forget your characters' middle names and the color of their children's hair. You begin with some haptic idea of its shape in your head and the ending firmly in mind, and then you just set forth, as bravely as you can."

Very often, nearly as often as in the work of J.D. Salinger, Updike's writing concerns children. "I'm still running on energy laid down in childhood," he says. "Writing is a way of keeping up that childhood."

The present national preoccupation with sex does not seem particularly menacing to Updike. On the contrary, his characters lead rich (and richly described) sex lives, so much so that one critic complains

"I *do* wish he'd get his mind off girls' thighs." He probably won't, though. "I do buy Freud's notion about the radical centrality of sex," Updike says. "It's somehow so, isn't it? All kinds of activity, all the getting of money, are a forum of preening. Look at all those cars out there now, all moving people from one tryst to another."

What really has "radical centrality" for Updike, however, is not sex but work—his own and that of his characters. "My novels are all about the search for useful work," he says. "So many people these days have to sell things they don't believe in and have jobs that defy describing. It's so different from the time when men even took their names from the work they did—Carpenter, Farmer, Fisher. A man has to build his life outward from a job he can do. Once he finds one he's got eight hours of the day licked, and if he sleeps eight more, he's two-thirds golden."

It saddens Updike some that the work he does himself for three arduous hours daily (three solid writing hours surely being equivalent to eight in an office) is greeted with such tempered praise. "There's a 'yes-but' quality about my writing," he says, "that evades entirely pleasing anybody. It seems to me that critics get increasingly querulous and impatient for madder music and stronger wine, when what we need is a greater respect for reality, its secrecy, its music. Too many people are studying maps and not enough are visiting places."

For himself, as he once wrote, "I will try not to panic, to keep my standard of living modest, and to work steadily, even shyly, in the spirit of those medieval carvers who so fondly sculpted the undersides of choir seats."

Updike on other writers

John O'Hara has more genius than talent. Very little censoring goes on in his head, but his best stories have the flowing ease and surprisingness of poems. He does create beautiful women. His women are really there; you get a feeling of their fatigue.

Black humor today strikes me as being thin—paper-thin, and printed hastily. Joyce's black humor is fine; it is etched upon an enormous, solid surface. He really listened to conversations, and tried to curve sentences around things, so that by the time his wacky sections come up, you trust him, in a way you don't trust, say, Pynchon. Reading Pynchon is like reading a very long Popeye strip, without the spinach.

Salinger's early stories were a real technical breakthrough, and I still hope he will emerge safe on the other side of the Glass stories. His silence is of course a religious lesson for all of us. He has become the sound of one hand clapping.

Mailer has energy and candor, and cares about what he thinks of as important things, but has quite abandoned fiction as a form of truth-seeking. He's become a pamphleteer. In a funny way I have more affection for Jack Kerouac, who, however unreadably, has kept faith with fiction. I found *On the Road* liberating; it had a contagious love for American actuality. Mailer's egotism is less appealing. He cares more about power than words. Maybe a European country like France would make better use of him. Our attempts here to institutionalize and propagandize the arts fall flat. The national instinct is to keep art a cottage industry, produced by isolated cranks. Mailer wants to be a crank surrounded by applauding people.

In 19th century American novels, up to Henry James, you find a sureness of style that's been lost. Hawthorne, Melville, and Thoreau had access to a dignified, workable English; they wrote their books and their letters with the same pen.

Nobody's style now seems totally finished. Malamud's noble simplicity excludes something; Bellow's soft, nervous, open style keeps picking up lint. Dandy lint, of course. Bellow and Cheever have kept a nice roughness, as if they're slightly dazzled, or about to change direction. I've never met anyone quicker on his feet, both fictional and real, than Cheever.

John Updike Works Three Hours
and Poses as a Vacationer

Sally Reston/1968

From the *Vineyard Gazette*, 3 May 1968, 1, 5. Copyright © 1968
Vineyard Gazette, Inc. Reprinted by permission.

John Updike wrote and revised much of his successful novel, *Couples*,
on Martha's Vineyard. He has spent the last three summers up-Island
and will be in Chilmark again this summer.

"I remember writing all of Foxy's letters" (Foxy is the main female
character in the book) "on a Menemsha Beach," he told the *Gazette*
the other day. But Updike had no idea then where the book would lead
him—how it would change his life; what questions it would raise
about his career, purpose, and philosophy.

Time magazine put him on its cover, looking like a troubled modern
gypsy in a green turtleneck sweater. Hollywood bought the movie
rights to the novel for half a million dollars, most of which will go to
the Internal Revenue Bureau.

But the spectacular national picture of Updike as the successful ped-
dler of sex, while justified by his novel of wife-swapping in a Boston
suburb, could be a caricature. He is a talented moralist, who portrays
the casual bed-hopping of affluent suburbanites not to celebrate but to
condemn them. And personally, he does not fit the popular conception
of a cynical, modern novelist.

At first glance, he is cheerful, relaxed, friendly, and modest. He
wears his cinnamon-colored hair short in front, a bit long over the ears
and nape of the neck, and dresses (at least in Boston) in a neat brown
suit, white shirt, heather-colored socks, and well-polished loafers. His
bushy brows, his big nose reddened in the Sunday sun, his laughter,
grunting and rumbling underneath his comfortable conversation, give
the impression of plain and open candor men respect.

He talked freely about his writing, his family, his background, his
life on the Vineyard, and his plans for the future:

How did he start as a writer? "I began supporting myself by writing when I was 22," he said. Maybe it would have been better to be a sea captain first. All that experience would have been helpful before starting to write.

"Also, there's a screen around the writer. It's not only made by other people. The writer makes it himself. Somehow it's harder for suffering to break through. Maybe having been a failure when young would be a help."

How would he advise young writers starting out today? "Perhaps I'm not a very good person to talk about that," Updike replied. "The young today are different. When I was young" (he is only 36 now) "I used to want to go to the wilderness of the Rockies. Now the wilderness of the city is more available to them and in a way it's just as open-ended. No questions asked. . . . They can be alone."

Updike talked about writing at home and writing away from home. He lives in Ipswich with his wife, Mary, the daughter of a Unitarian minister, and his four children. He has an office over a restaurant in the village, and he talked about the advantages of leaving there and writing elsewhere.

"A change of scene restores you to yourself," he said. "I find I can leave some of the furniture of my life behind . . . I can get up earlier on the Vineyard. About three hours writing a day is the most I can do. The rest of the time I pose as a vacationist."

What sort of materials did he need when he was writing away from home?

"I travel light as a writer. There is something intimate about pen and paper. My short stories, though, are always typed, but *Couples*, though it's a long book—too long, I didn't really mean to make it that long—I wrote in pencil on the back of old manuscripts.

"When I travel I have to stay away a while before I can produce. The first two days in a new place, I always want to be running out all the time to see what's going on—afraid I'm missing something. That's my definition of a writer: somebody who's always missing something."

Updike talked about good and evil. Last summer, while finishing *Couples* on the Vineyard, he was also reviewing French novels for *The New Yorker*. "I seem to get all the religious ones or the dirty ones," he said. "Somehow the two go together: they are the ultimates of life."

He said this rather casually. He seemed vaguely puzzled and maybe even irritated by the question of why he wrote about immorality in order to prove a moral point, instead of writing about goodness to prove that it was its own reward. And this led to a discussion of these "ultimates of life," which is the theme of his book.

Couples has been criticized as merely an "uptown *Peyton Place*," as "sex and sex alone," and it's true that Mr. Updike's reporting of extramarital adventures is almost painfully explicit.

Among the 10 intertwining couples in the book, the two Applebys and two Smiths are so often in each others' beds that the group refers to them as the "Applesmiths." Similarly, the two Saltzes and the two Constantines merge into the "Saltines." Mr. Updike leaves nothing to the imagination.

Why had he done this? What was he trying to say?

"Well," he replied, "I may be personally Puritan, but I don't judge others. It seems to me these people (in *Couples*) do the best they can given the culture they come from. In Pennsylvania, I was raised a Lutheran. Lutherans believe doctrine—faith—is important, but not deeds, because we are all mired in sin.

"It's funny," he said, "but when I try to talk about this, it comes out kind of dumb. My view is very primitive. I tend to see everything poised between heaven and hell.

"I guess I hope to show in fiction that goodness and evil are mixed. My instinct is to show the other side—the 'Yes' and 'No' of circumstances, the comic incongruities of life.

"I have done some studies of saintliness. The central figure of my novel, *The Centaur*" (his 68 year-old-father, formerly a math teacher in Shillington, Pa.), "was meant to be a good man. But irrepressible goodness is out of phase in the world today. . . ."

Would these people in *Couples* have been different 30 or 40 years ago? Mr. Updike was asked. "Oh, yes," he replied. "In the Depression they'd have been concerned only with getting jobs and money. This book deals with the contemporary world—with people living in the atmosphere of economic affluence and the Cold War. This period has made work less serious. . . . Today, work is available and people want to do it with their left hand. They don't believe in the importance of vocation but of varying degrees of 'friendship.' Life in bed and around the table is what they care most about.

"The eight-hour day does create the kind of recreational opportu-

nities that belonged formerly to a tiny minority of aristocrats. Now
those opportunities are available to all.

"I guess," he concluded, "I must feel this is bad or dangerous."

What's next? "As a matter of fact, I've just done a libretto for a
children's opera, and I've agreed to write a pageant for my home town.
In Ipswich, where I live, there are a lot of 17th century houses, and
every summer they celebrate the town in a '17th Century Day.' There
are 12,000 people there, and I've agreed to help. I don't know anything
about the pageant form. I've never really seen one, and when I try to
imagine what a pageant is like, all I can see are drum majorettes . . .
But I'm going to try. . . ."

What else? "Eventually," he said, "I'd like to aspire to the proud
title of poet. I'm trying to write a long poem, vague in my mind as
yet. In the past, I've written what they call light verse, though I
thought a lot of it was serious. I hope also to have a new book of
poems by the end of the summer.

"But I want the long poem to be a series of meditations. The other
day I read something in a science magazine about atomic configura-
tions. I'm thinking about dividing my poem into the seven dances of
the solids, described in Spencerian stanzas.

"It's an awful idea," he laughed apologetically, "but at least it *is* an
idea."

Mr. Updike is obviously interested in contemporary politics, and
particularly in the current arguments over the Vietnam war, the cities
and the riots, but he says he is not interested in these things as topics
for books.

"I do someday want to write about Buchanan, Pennsylvania's only
president," he said. "He interests me. Nobody much cared about
him. He found himself on a hot spot and did the best he could. He
was lost in the White House—a little chocolate in a big box. On the
whole, he was a big bore, but he had the love of America in his
head."

It's a long way from Foxy and the *Couples* to Buchanan and the
White House, but we hope he makes it.

The Art of Fiction XLIII: John Updike

Charles Thomas Samuels/1968

From *Writers at Work, Fourth Series* by George A. Plimpton, Editor. New York: Viking Press, 1976, 425–454. Copyright 1974, 1976 by *The Paris Review*. Used by permission of Viking Penguin, a division of Penguin Books USA Inc. First published in *The Paris Review* 45 (Winter 1968), 84–117.

In 1966, when John Updike was first asked to do a *Paris Review* interview, he refused: "Perhaps I have written fiction because everything unambiguously expressed seems somehow crass to me; and when the subject is myself, I want to jeer and weep. Also, I really don't have a great deal to tell interviewers; the little I learned about life and the art of fiction I try to express in my work."

The following year, a second request won acceptance, but Updike's apprehension caused further delay. Should there be a meeting followed by an exchange of written questions and answers, or should this procedure be reversed? Need there be any meeting at all? (Updike fears becoming, even for a moment, "one more gassy monologist.") In the end, during the summer of 1967, written questions were submitted to him, and afterward, he was interviewed on Martha's Vineyard, where he and his family take their vacation.

A first view of Updike revealed a jauntiness of manner surprising in a writer of such craft and sensibility. After barreling down Edgartown's narrow main street, the author appeared from his beat-up Corvair—a barefoot, tousle-haired young man dressed in khaki Bermudas and a sweatshirt.

Updike is a fluent talker, but obviously not a man who expects talk to bridge the distance between others and his inner life. Therefore, the final stage of this interview was his revision of the spoken comments to bring them into line with the style of his written answers. The result is a fabricated interview—in its modest way, a work of art, and thus appropriate to a man who believes that only art can track the nuances of experience.

22

Interviewer: You've treated your early years fictionally and have discussed them in interviews, but you haven't said much about your time at Harvard. I wonder what effect you think it had.

Updike: My time at Harvard, once I got by the compression bends of the freshman year, was idyllic enough, and as they say, successful; but I felt toward those years, while they were happening, the resentment a caterpillar must feel while his somatic cells are shifting all around to make him a butterfly. I remember the glow of the Fogg Museum windows, and my wife-to-be pushing her singing bicycle through the snowy Yard, and the smell of wet old magazines that arose from the cellar of the *Lampoon* and hit your nostrils when you entered the narthex, and numerous pleasant revelations in classrooms—all of it haunted, though, by knowledge of the many others who had passed this way, and felt the venerable glory of it all a shade keener than I, and written sufficiently about it. All that I seem able to preserve of the Harvard experience is in one short story, "The Christian Roommates." There was another, "Homage to Paul Klee," that has been printed in *The Liberal Context* but not in a book. Foxy Whitman, in *Couples*, remembers some of the things I do. Like me, she feels obscurely hoodwinked, pacified, by the process of becoming nice. I distrust, perhaps, hallowed, very O.K. places. Harvard has enough panegyrists without me.

Interviewer: Did you learn much writing for the *Lampoon?*

Updike: The *Lampoon* was very kind to me. I was given, beside the snug pleasures of club solidarity, carte blanche as far as the magazine went—I began as a cartoonist, did a lot of light verse, and more and more prose. There was always lots of space to fill. Also, I do have a romantic weakness for gags—we called ourselves, the term itself a gag, gagsters. My own speciality was Chinese jokes. A little birthday party, and the children singing to the blushing center of attention, "Happy Birthday, Tu Yu." Or coolies listening to an agitator and asking each other, "Why *shouldn't* we work for coolie wages?" Or—another cartoon—a fairy princess in a tower, her hair hanging to the ground and labeled Fire Exit. And I remember Bink Young, now an Episcopal priest, solemnly plotting, his tattered sneakers up on a desk, how to steal a battleship from Boston Harbor. Maybe, as an imperfectly metamorphosed caterpillar, I was grateful for the company of true butterflies.

Interviewer: Have you given up drawing entirely? I noticed that your recent "Letter from Anguilla" was illustrated by you.

Updike: You're nice to have noticed. For years I wanted to get a drawing into *The New Yorker*, and at last I did. My first ambition was to be an animator for Walt Disney. Then I wanted to be a magazine cartoonist. Newly married, I used to draw Mary and the children, and did have that year in art school, but of late I don't draw at all, don't even doodle beside the telephone. It's a loss, a sadness for me. I'm interested in concrete poetry, in some attempt to return to the manuscript page, to *use* the page space, and the technical possibilities. My new book, a long poem called *Midpoint*, tries to do something of this. Since we write for the eye, why not really write for it—give it a treat? Letters are originally little pictures, so let's combine graphic imagery, photographic imagery, with words. I mean *mesh* them. Saying this, I think of Pound's Chinese characters, and of course Apollinaire; and of my own poems, "Nutcracker," with the word "nut" in bold face, seems to me as good as George Herbert's angel-wings.

Interviewer: After graduating from Harvard, you served as a *New Yorker* staff writer for two years. What sort of work did you do?

Updike: I was a "Talk of the Town" writer, which means that I both did the legwork and the finished product. An exalted position! It was playful work that opened the city to me. I was the man who went to boating or electronic exhibits in the Coliseum and tried to make impressionist poems of the objects and overheard conversations.

Interviewer: Why did you quit?

Updike: After two years I doubted that I was expanding the *genre*. When my wife and I had a second child and needed a larger apartment, the best course abruptly seemed to leave the city, and with it the job. They still keep my name on the staff sheet, and I still contribute Notes and Comments, and I take much comfort from having a kind of professional home where they consider me somehow competent. America in general doesn't expect competence from writers. Other things, yes; competence, no.

Interviewer: How do you feel about being associated with that magazine for so many years?

Updike: Very happy. From the age of twelve when my aunt gave us a subscription for Christmas, *The New Yorker* has seemed to me the best of possible magazines, and their acceptance of a poem and a story by me in June of 1954 remains the ecstatic breakthrough of my literary life. Their editorial care and their gratitude for a piece of work they like are incomparable. And I love the format—the signature at the end, everybody the same size, and the battered title type, evocative of the twenties and Persia and the future all at once.

Interviewer: You seem to shun literary society. Why?

Updike: I don't, do I? Here I am, talking to you. In leaving New York in 1957, I did leave without regret the literary demimonde of agents and would-be's and with-it nonparticipants; this world seemed unnutritious and interfering. Hemingway described literary New York as a bottle full of tapeworms trying to feed on each other. When I write, I aim in my mind not toward New York but toward a vague spot a little to the east of Kansas. I think of the books on library shelves, without their jackets, years old, and a countryish teen-aged boy finding them, and having them speak to him. The reviews, the stacks in Brentano's, are just hurdles to get over, to place the books on that shelf. Anyway, in 1957, I was full of a Pennsylvania thing I wanted to say, and Ipswich gave me the space in which to say it, and in which to live modestly, raise my children, and have friends on the basis of what I did in person rather than what I did in print.

Interviewer: Do your neighbors—present in Ipswich, past in Shillington—get upset when they fancy they've found themselves in your pages?

Updike: I would say not. I count on people to know the difference between flesh and paper, and generally they do. As to Shillington, I've been long away from the town, and there is a greater element of distortion or suppression than may appear; there are rather few characters in those Olinger stories that could even remotely take offense. Ipswich I've not written too much about. Somewhat of the marsh geography peeps through in *Couples*, but the couples themselves are more or less adults who could be encountered anywhere in the East. The town, although it was a little startled at first by the book, was reassured, I think, by reading it. The week after its publication, when the Boston papers were whooping it up in high tabloid style, and the *Atlantic* ran a banshee cry of indignation from Diana Trilling, people like the gas station attendant and a strange woman on the golf course would stop me and say something soothing, complimentary. I work downtown, above a restaurant, and can be seen plodding up to my office most mornings, and I think Ipswich pretty much feels sorry for me, trying to make a living at such a plainly unprofitable chore. Also, I do participate in local affairs—I'm on the Congregational church building committee and the Democratic town committee, and while the *Couples* fuss was in progress, capped by that snaggle-toothed cover on *Time*, I was writing a pageant for our Seventeenth-century Day. Both towns in my mind are not so much themselves as places I've happened to be in when I was a child and then an adult. The difference between Olinger and Tarbox is much more the difference between childhood and adulthood than the difference between two geographical locations. They are stages on my pilgrim's progress, not spots on the map.

Interviewer: What about your parents? They seem to appear often in your work. Have their reactions to earlier versions had an effect on later ones?

Updike: My parents should not be held to the letter of any of the fictional fathers and mothers. But I don't mind admitting that George Caldwell was assembled from certain vivid gestures and plights characteristic of Wesley Updike; once, returning to Plowville after *The Centaur* came out, I was upbraided by a Sunday-school pupil of my father's for my outrageous portrait, and my father, with typical sanctity, interceded, saying, "No, it's the truth. The kid got me right." My mother, a different style of saint, is an ideal reader and an ideally permissive writer's mother. They both have a rather un-middleclass appetite for the jubilant horrible truth, and after filling my childhood with warmth and color, they have let me make my adult way without interference and been never other than encouraging, even when old wounds were my topic, and a child's vision of things has been lent the undue authority of print. I have written free from any fear of forfeiting their love.

Interviewer: Most of your work takes place in a common locale: Olinger. So it was interesting to see you say farewell to that world in your preface to the *Olinger Stories*. Yet in the following year you published *Of the Farm*. Why do you feel so drawn to this material?

Updike: But *Of the Farm* was about Firetown; they only visit the Olinger supermarket. I am drawn to southeastern Pennsylvania because I know how things happen there, or at least how they used to happen. Once you have in your bones the fundamental feasibilities of a place, you can imagine there freely.

Interviewer: That's not what I mean. What I meant to ask is not why you keep writing about Olinger per se, but why you write so much about what most people take to be your own adolescence and family. Numerous critics, for example, have pointed to similarities between *Of the Farm*, *The Centaur*, and stories like "My Grandmother's Thimble." "Flight," for example, seems an earlier version of *Of the Farm*.

Updike: I suppose there's no avoiding it—my adolescence seemed interesting to me. In a sense my mother and father, considerable actors both, were dramatizing my youth as I was having it so that I arrived as an adult with some burden of material already half formed. There is, true, a submerged thread connecting certain of the fictions, and I guess the submerged thread is the autobiography. That is, in *Of the Farm*, although the last name is not the name of the people in *The Centaur*, the geography is not appreciably changed, and the man in each case is called George. *Of the Farm* was in part a look at the world of *The Centaur* after the centaur had indeed died. By the way, I must repeat that I didn't mean Caldwell to die in *The Centaur*; he dies in the sense of living, of going back to work, of being a shelter for his son. But by the time Joey Robinson is thirty-five, his father is dead. Also, there's the curious touch of the Running Horse River in *Rabbit, Run* which returns in the Alton of *The Centaur*. And somehow that Running Horse bridges both the books, connects them. When I was little, I used to draw disparate objects on a piece of paper—toasters, baseballs, flowers, whatnot—and connect them with lines. But every story, really, is a fresh start for me, and these little connections—recurrences of names, or the way, say, that Piet Hanema's insomnia takes him back into the same high school that John Nordholm, and David Kern, and Allen Dow sat in—are in there as a kind of running, oblique coherence. Once I've coined a name, by the way, I feel utterly hidden behind that mask, and what I remember and what I imagine become indistinguishable. I feel no obligation to the remembered past; what I create on paper must, and for me does, soar free of whatever the facts were. Do I make any sense?

Interviewer: Some.

Updike: In others words, I disavow any essential connection between my life and whatever I write. I think it's a morbid and inappropriate area of concern, though natural enough—a lot of morbid concerns are natural. But the work, the words on the paper, must stand apart from our living presences; we sit down at the desk and become nothing but the excuse for these husks we cast off. But aside from the somewhat teasing little connections, there is in these three novels and the short stories of *Pigeon Feathers* a central image of flight or escape or loss, the way we flee from the past, a sense of guilt which I tried to express in the story, the triptych with the long title, "The Blessed Man of Boston, My Grandmother's Thimble, and Fanning Island," wherein the narrator becomes a Polynesian pushing off into a void. The sense that in time as well as space we leave people as if by volition and thereby incur guilt and thereby owe them, the dead, the forsaken, at least the homage of rendering them. The trauma or message that I acquired in Olinger had to do with suppressed pain, with the amount of sacrifice I suppose that middle-class life demands, and by that I guess I mean civilized life. The father, whatever his name, is sacrificing freedom of motion, and the mother is sacrificing in a way—oh, sexual richness, I guess; they're all stuck, and when I think back over these stories (and you know, they *are* dear to me, and if I had to give anybody one book of me it would be the Vintage *Olinger Stories*), I think especially of that moment in "Flight" when the boy, chafing to escape, fresh from his encounter with Molly Bingaman and a bit more of a man but not enough quite, finds the mother lying there buried in her own peculiar messages from far away, the New Orleans jazz, and then the grandfather's voice comes tumbling down the stairs singing, "There is a happy land far far away." This is the way it was, is. There has never been anything in my life quite as compressed, simultaneously as communicative to me of my own power and worth and of the irremediable grief in just living, in just going on.

I really don't think I'm alone among writers in caring about what they experienced in the first eighteen years of their life. Hemingway cherished the Michigan stories out of proportion, I would think, to their merit. Look at Twain. Look at Joyce. Nothing that happens to us after twenty is as free from self-consciousness because by then we have the vocation to write. Writers' lives break into two halves. At the point where you get your writerly vocation you diminish your receptivity to experience. Being able to write becomes a kind of shield, a way of hiding, a way of too instantly transforming pain into honey—

whereas when you're young, you're so impotent you cannot help but strive and observe and feel.

Interviewer: How does Mrs. Updike react to your work? *Time* quotes you as having said she never entirely approves of your novels.

Updike: Mary is a pricelessly sensitive reader. She is really always right, and if I sometimes, notably in the novels, persevere without her unqualified blessing, it is because somebody in me—the gagster, the fanatic, the boor—must be allowed to have his say. I usually don't show her anything until I am finished, or stuck. I never disregard her remarks, and she is tactful in advancing them.

Interviewer: In your review of James Agee's *Letters to Father Flye,* you defend professionalism. Even so, are you bothered by having to write for a living?

Updike: No, I always wanted to draw or write for a living. Teaching, the customary alternative, seemed truly depleting and corrupting. I have been able to support myself by and large with the more respectable forms—poetry, short stories, novels—but what journalism I have done has been useful. I would write ads for deodorants or labels for catsup bottles if I had to. The miracle of turning inklings into thoughts and thoughts into words and words into metal and print and ink never palls for me; the technical aspects of bookmaking, from type font to binding glue, interest me. The distinction between a thing well done and a thing done ill obtains everywhere—in all circles of Paradise and Inferno.

Interviewer: You write a fair amount of literary criticism. Why?

Updike: I do it (a) when some author, like Spark or Borges, excites me and I want to share the good news, (b) when I want to write an essay, as on romantic love, or Barth's theology, (c) when I feel ignorant of something, like modern French fiction, and accepting a review assignment will compel me to read and learn.

Interviewer: Do you find it helpful in your fiction?

Updike: I think it good for an author, baffled by obtuse reviews of himself, to discover what a recalcitrant art reviewing is, how hard it is to keep the plot straight in summary, let alone to sort out one's honest responses. But reviewing should not become a habit. It encourages a writer to think of himself as a pundit, of fiction as a collective enterprise and species of expertise, and of the imagination as a cerebral and social activity—all pernicious illusions.

Interviewer: I'd like to ask a bit about your work habits if I may. What sort of schedule do you follow?

Updike: I write every weekday morning. I try to vary what I am doing, and my verse, or poetry, is a help here. Embarked on a long project, I try to stay with it even on dull days. For every novel, however, that I have published, there has been one unfinished or scrapped. Some short stories—I think offhand of "Lifeguard," "The Taste of Metal," "My Grandmother's Thimble"—are fragments salvaged and reshaped. Most came right the first time—rode on their own melting, as Frost said of his poems. If there is no melting, if the story keeps sticking, better stop and look around. In the execution there has to be a "happiness" that can't be willed or foreordained. It has to sing, click, something. I try instantly to set in motion a certain forward tilt of suspense or curiosity, and at the end of the story or novel to rectify the tilt, to complete the motion.

Interviewer: When your workday is through, are you able to leave it behind, or does your writing haunt your afternoons and echo your experience?

Updike: Well, I think the subconscious picks at it, and occasionally a worrisome sentence or image will straighten itself out, and then you make a note of it. If I'm stuck, I try to get myself unstuck before I sit down again because moving through the day surrounded by people and music and air, it is easier to make major motions in your mind than it is sitting at the typewriter in a slightly claustrophobic room. It's hard to hold a manuscript in your mind, of course. You get down to the desk and discover that the solution you had arrived at while having insomnia doesn't really fit. I guess I'm never unconscious of myself as a writer and of my present project. A few places are specially conducive to inspiration—automobiles, church—private places. I plotted *Couples* almost entirely in church—little shivers and urgencies I would note down on the program and carry down to the office Monday.

Interviewer: Well, you're not only a writer but a famous one. Are you experiencing any disadvantages in being famous?

Updike: I'm interviewed too much. I fight them off, but even one is too many. However hard you try to be honest or full, they are intrinsically phony. There is something terribly wrong about committing myself to this machine and to your version of what you get out of the machine—you may be deaf for all I know, and the machine may be faulty. All the stuff comes out attached to my name, and it's not really me at all. My relationship to you and my linear way of coping out loud are distortive. In any interview, you do say more or less than you mean. You leave the proper ground of your strength and become one more gassy monologist. Unlike Mailer and Bellow, I don't have much itch to pronounce on great matters, to reform the country, to get elected mayor of New York, or minister to the world with laughter like the hero of *The Last Analysis*. My life is, in a sense, trash; my life is only that of which the residue is my writing. The person who appears on the cover of *Time* or whose monologue will be printed in *The Paris Review* is neither the me who exists physically and socially or the me who signs the fiction and poetry. That is, everything is infinitely fine, and any opinion is somehow coarser than the texture of the real thing.

I find it hard to have opinions. Theologically, I favor Karl Barth; politically, I favor the Democrats. But I treasure a remark John Cage made, that not judgingness but openness and curiosity are our proper business. To speak on matters where you're ignorant dulls the voice for speaking on matters where you do know something.

Interviewer: One of the things I've always thought would be difficult for famous writers is being constantly sent manuscripts by aspiring amateurs. Do you experience this, and if so, how do you treat them?

Updike: I tend to lose them. The manuscripts. I remember myself as an aspiring writer, and you know, I never did this. I assumed that published writers had worked at it until they became worth publishing, and I assumed that that's the only way to do it, and I'm a little puzzled by young men who write me charming letters suggesting that I conduct an impromptu writing course. Evidently, I've become part of the Establishment that's expected to serve youth—like college presidents and the police. I'm still trying to educate myself. I want to read only what will help me unpack my own bag.

Interviewer: While we're on the subject of your public role, I wonder how you react to the growing use of your fiction in college courses?

Updike: Oh, is it? Do they use it?

Interviewer: I use it a great deal. What do you think about it, as a writer? Do you think that it's going to interfere with the reader's comprehension or feeling for your work? I mean, do you go along with Trilling's idea, for example, that modern literature is somehow diluted by appearing in the social context of the classroom, or are you not concerned about this?

Updike: No. Looking back on my own college experience, the college course is just a way of delivering you to the books, and once you're delivered, the writer-reader relationship is there. I read Dostoevsky for a college course and wept.

If what you say is true, I'm delighted. I do think it difficult to teach, as is done so much now, courses in truly contemporary writing. (At Oxford, they used to stop with Tennyson.) Of course, maybe I'm not so contemporary anymore; maybe I'm sort of like Eisenhower or—

Interviewer: You're over thirty—you're over the hill.

Updike: Don't laugh—most American writers *are* over the hill by thirty. Maybe I'm like Sherman Adams and Fats Domino and other, you know, *semi*-remote figures who have acquired a certain historical interest. We're anxious in America to package our things quickly, and the writer can become a package before he's ready to have the coffin lid nailed down.

Interviewer: Well, let's think of another package now—not the package by time but by country. Are you conscious of belonging to a definable American literary tradition? Would you describe yourself as part of an American tradition?

Updike: I must be. I've hardly ever been out of the country.

Interviewer: Specifically, do you feel that you've learned important things or felt spiritual affinities with classic American writers such as Hawthorne, Melville, James, people of this sort?

Updike: I love Melville and like James, but I tend to learn more from Europeans because I think they have strengths that reach back past Puritanism, that don't equate truth with intuition—

Interviewer: In other words, you want to be nourished by the thing that you don't feel is inherently your tradition.

Updike: Right. I'm not saying I can write like Melville or James, but that the kind of passion and bias that they show is already in my bones. I don't think you need to keep rehearsing your instincts. Far better to seek out models of what you *can't* do. American fiction is notoriously thin on women, and I *have* attempted a number of portraits of women, and we may have reached that point of civilization, or decadence, where we *can* look at women. I'm not sure Mark Twain *was* able to.

Interviewer: Let's get into your work now. In an interview you gave *Life* you expressed some regret at the "yes, but" attitude critics have taken toward it. Did the common complaint that you had ducked large subjects lead to the writing of *Couples*?

Updike: No, I meant my *work* says, "Yes, but." Yes, in *Rabbit, Run*, to our inner urgent whispers, but—the social fabric collapses murderously. Yes, in *The Centaur*, to self-sacrifice and duty, but—what of a man's private agony and dwindling? No, in *The Poorhouse Fair*, to social homogenization and loss of faith, but—listen to the voices, the joy of persistent existence. No, in *Couples*, to a religious community founded on physical and psychical interpenetration, but—what else shall we do, as God destroys our churches? I cannot greatly care what critics say of my work; if it is good, it will come to the surface in a generation or two and float, and if not, it will sink, having in the meantime provided me with a living, the opportunities of leisure, and a craftsman's intimate satisfactions. I wrote *Couples* because the rhythm of my life and my oeuvre demanded it, not to placate hallucinatory critical voices.

Interviewer: What do you mean by attributing the setting up of religious communities in *Couples* to God's destruction of our churches?

Updike: I guess the noun "God" reappears in two totally different senses, the god in the first instance being the god worshipped within this nice white church, the more or less watered-down Puritan god; and then god in the second sense means ultimate power. I've never really understood theologies which would absolve God of earthquakes and typhoons, of children starving. A god who is not God the Creator is not very real to me, so that, yes, it certainly *is* God who throws the lightning bolt, and this God is above the nice god, above the god we can worship and empathize with. I guess I'm saying there's a fierce God above the kind God, and he's the one Piet believes in. At any rate, when the church is burned, Piet is relieved of morality and can choose Foxy—or can accept the choice made for him by Foxy and Angela operating in unison—can move out of the paralysis of guilt into what after all is a kind of freedom. He divorces the supernatural to marry the natural. I wanted the loss of Angela to be felt as a real loss—Angela is nicer than Foxy—nevertheless it is Foxy that he most deeply wants, it is Foxy who in some obscure way was turned on the lathe for him. So that the book does have a happy ending. There's also a way, though, I should say (speaking of "yes, but") in which, with the destruction of the church, with the removal of his guilt, he becomes insignificant. He becomes merely a name in the last paragraph: he becomes a satisfied person and in a sense dies. In other words, a person who has what he wants, a satisfied person, a content person, ceases to be a person. Unfallen Adam is an ape. Yes, I guess I do feel that. I feel that to be a person is to be in a situation of tension, is to be in a dialectical situation. A truly adjusted person is not a person at all—just an animal with clothes on or a statistic. So that it's a happy ending, with this "but" at the end.

Interviewer: I was impressed by the contrast between the presentation of oral-genital contacts in *Couples* and its single appearance in *Rabbit, Run*. Rabbit's insistence that Ruth perform the act is the cause of their breakup.

Updike: No. Janice's having the baby is.

Interviewer: If you say so; but I'd still like to know why an act that is treated so neutrally in the later book is so significant in the earlier one.

Updike: Well, *Couples*, in part, is about the change in sexual deportment that has occurred since the publication of *Rabbit, Run*, which came out late in '59; shortly thereafter, we had *Lady Chatterley* and the first Henry Miller books, and now you can't walk into a grocery store without seeing pornography on the rack. Remember Piet lying in Freddy's bed admiring Freddy's collection of Grove Press books? In *Rabbit, Run* what is demanded, in *Couples* is freely given. What else? It's a way of eating, eating the apple, of knowing. It's nostalgic for them, for Piet of Annabelle Vojt and for Foxy of her Jewish boyfriend. In de Rougemont's book on Tristan and Iseult he speaks of the sterility of the lovers, and Piet and Foxy are sterile vis-à-vis each other. Lastly, I was struck, talking to a biochemist friend of mine, how he emphasized not only the chemical composition of enzymes but their structure; it matters, among my humans, not only what they're made of but exactly how they attach to each other. So much for oral-genital contacts.

About sex in general, by all means let's have it in fiction, as detailed as needs be, but real, real in its social and psychological connections. Let's take coitus out of the closet and off the altar and put it on the continuum of human behavior. There are episodes in Henry Miller that have their human resonance; the sex in *Lolita*, behind the madman's cuteness, rings true; and I find the sex in D.H. Lawrence done from the woman's point of view convincing enough. In the microcosm of the individual consciousness, sexual events are huge but not all eclipsing; let's try to give them their size.

Interviewer: I'd like to move on to *The Centaur* now. If I'm right in regarding it as formally uncharacteristic, I wonder why you prefer it to your other novels?

Updike: Well, it seems in memory my gayest and truest book; I pick it up, and read a few pages, in which Caldwell is insisting on flattering a moth-eaten bum, who is really the god Dionysius, and I begin laughing.

Interviewer: What made you decide to employ a mythic parallel?

Updike: I was moved, first, by the Chiron variant of the Hercules myth—one of the few classic instances of self-sacrifice, and the name oddly close to Christ. The book began as an attempt to publicize this myth. The mythology operated in a number of ways: a correlative of the enlarging effect of Peter's nostalgia, a dramatization of Caldwell's sense of exclusion and mysteriousness around him, a counterpoint of ideality to the drab real level, an excuse for a number of jokes, a serious expression of my sensation that the people we meet are *guises*, do conceal something mythic, perhaps prototypes or longings in our minds. We love some women more than others by predetermination, it seems to me.

Interviewer: Why haven't you done more work in this mode?

Updike: But I have worked elsewhere in a mythic mode. Apart from my short story about Tristan and Iseult, there is the St. Stephen story underlying *The Poorhouse Fair*, and Peter Rabbit under *Rabbit, Run*. Sometimes it is semiconscious; for example, only lately do I see that Brewer, the city of brick painted the color of flowerpots, is the flowerpot that Mr. McGregor slips over Peter Rabbit. And in *Couples*, Piet is not only Hanema/anima/Life, he is Lot, the man with two virgin daughters, who flees Sodom and leaves his wife behind.

Interviewer: Yes, of course, the Tristan story is like *The Centaur*, but even if your other novels have underlying mythological or scriptural subjects, they don't obtrude as they do in *The Centaur*. So let me rephrase my question. Why *didn't* you make the parallels more obvious in the other books?

Updike: Oh—I don't think basically that such parallels should be obvious. I think books should have secrets, like people do. I think they should be there as a bonus for the sensitive reader or there as a kind of subliminal quavering. I don't think that the duty of the twentieth-century fiction writer is to retell old stories only. I've often wondered what Eliot meant in his famous essay on *Ulysses*. Does he mean that we are ourselves so depleted of psychic energy, of spiritual and primitive force, that we can do little but retell old stories? Does he mean that human events, love, death, wandering, certain challenges overcome or certain challenges which sweep us under, have already attained classic narrative form? I don't quite know what Eliot meant. I do know that there is certainly for all of us some attraction in old stories. Mine is a generation not raised on the Bible. The Greek stories seem to be more universal coin, and they certainly have served to finance more modern creations than the Hebrew stories. (Although do read sometime Kierkegaard's splendid retelling of Abraham and Isaac in *Fear and Trembling*.) Freud, for one, named a number of states of mind after them.

I have read old sagas—*Beowulf*, the *Mabinogion*—trying to find the story in its most rudimentary form, searching for what a story *is*— Why did these people enjoy hearing them? Are they a kind of disguised history? Or, more likely I guess, are they ways of relieving anxiety, of transferring it outwards upon an invented tale and purging it through catharsis? In any case, I feel the need for this kind of recourse to the springs of narrative, and maybe my little buried allusions are admissions of it. It's funny, the things you don't know you're doing; I was aware of Piet as Lot and I was aware of Piet and Foxy as being somehow Tristan and Iseult, but I was not aware of him as Don Juan. The other day I got a long, brilliant letter from a man at Wesleyan describing the book in terms of the Don Juan legend, pointing out numerous illuminating analogies. He thinks that Don Juans, historically, appear in the imperialist countries just as the tide turns: the classic Don Juan appears in Spain just as Spain has lost the Netherlands, and so Piet's activity somehow coincides with our frustration in Vietnam. All this is news to me, but, once said, it sounds right. I'll have to read the letter again. It elicited for me certain basic harmonies, certain congruences with prototypes in the Western consciousness that I'm happy to accept.

Interviewer: Let's turn from myth to history. You have indicated a desire to write about President Buchanan. Yet, so far as I can see, American history is normally absent from your work.

Updike: Not so; quite the contrary. In each of my novels, a precise year is given and a President reigns; *The Centaur* is distinctly a Truman book, and *Rabbit, Run* an Eisenhower one. *Couples* could have taken place only under Kennedy; the social currents it traces are as specific to those years as flowers in a meadow are to their moment of summer. Even *The Poorhouse Fair* has a President, President Lowenstein, and if one is not named in *Of the Farm*, it may be because that book, in an odd way, also takes place in the future, though a future only a year or so in advance of the writing—a future now in the past. Hook, Caldwell, the Applesmiths, all talk about history, and the quotidian is littered with newspaper headlines, striking the consciousness of the characters obliquely and subliminally but firmly enough: Piet's first step at seducing Foxy is clearly in part motivated by the death of the Kennedy infant. And the atmosphere of fright permeating *The Centaur* is to an indicated extent early cold-war nerves. My fiction about the daily doings of ordinary people has more history in it than history books, just as there is more breathing history in archeology than in a list of declared wars and changes in government.

Interviewer: What about violence? Many critics complain that this is absent from your work—reprehensibly, because it is so present in the world. Why is there so little in your pages?

Updike: There has been so little in my life. I have fought in no wars and engaged in few fistfights. I do not think a man pacifist in his life should pretend to violence in fiction; Nabokov's bloody deeds, for example, seem more literary than lived to me. Muriel Spark's have the quality of the assassinations we commit in our minds. Mailer's recent violence is trumpery, just like Leslie Fiedler's cry for more, more. I feel a tenderness toward my characters that forbids making violent use of them. In general, the North American continent in this century has been a place where catastrophe has held off, and likewise the lives I have witnessed have staved off real death. All my novels end with a false death, partial death. If, as may be, the holocausts at the rim of possibility do soon visit us, I am confident my capacities for expression can rise, if I live, to the occasion. In the meantime let's all of us with some access to a printing press not abuse our privilege with fashionable fantasies.

Interviewer: Well, one thing I'm sure must impress everyone about your fiction: the factual accuracy. The way, for example, you can provide data for Ken Whitman's talk on photosynthesis as well as Piet's on architectural restoration. Do you actively research such material, or do you rely on what you already know?

Updike: Well, a bit of both, and I'm glad you do find it convincing. I'm never sure it is. A man whose life is spent in biochemistry or in building houses, his brain is tipped in a certain way. It's terribly hard, I think, for specialists to convey to me, as I ask them more or less intelligent questions, the right nuance—it's hard for me to reconstruct in my own mind the mind of a man who has spent twenty years with his field. I think the attempt should be made, however. There is a thinness in contemporary fiction about the way the world operates, except the academic world. I do try, especially in this novel, to give characters professions. Shaw's plays have a wonderful wealth of professional types. Shaw's sense of economic process, I guess, helped him (a) to care and (b) to convey, to plunge into the mystery of being a chimneysweep or a minister. One of the minimal obligations a book has to a reader is to be factually right, as to be typographically pleasant and more or less correctly proofread. Elementary author ethics dictate that you do at least *attempt* to imagine technical detail as well as emotions and dialogue.

Interviewer: I'd like to ask a question about *The Poorhouse Fair*. Many people have been bothered in that book by Conner's foolishness. He seems a bit easy as the butt of satire. Do you think there is much justification in that charge?

Updike: I'd have to reread the book to know. It could be that I was too little in sympathy with what I imagine him to be standing for. Of course a writer is in no position to alter a reader's reaction. Performance is all, and if I didn't really give you flesh and blood, then nothing I can say now will substitute. But it occurs to me that Conner was a preliminary study for Caldwell in *The Centaur*: the bulging upper lip and a certain Irishness, a certain tenacity, a certain —they're both poor disciplinarians, I notice in thinking about them. I wasn't satirical in my purpose. I may have been negative, but satire, no. I'm not conscious of any piece of fiction of mine which has even the slightest taint of satirical attempt. You can't be satirical at the expense of fictional characters, because they're your creatures. You must only love them, and I think that once I'd set Conner in motion I did to the best of my ability try to love him and let his mind and heart beat.

Interviewer: Isn't "The Doctor's Wife" an exception to your statement that you never satirize one of your characters?

Updike: You think I'm satirizing the doctor's wife? I'm *criticizing* the doctor's wife. Yes, I do feel that in some way she is a racist, but I don't think I'm trying to make her funny because she's a racist.

Interviewer: There's some satire in your poetry, isn't there? But I wonder why, with few exceptions, you only write light verse.

Updike: I began with light verse, a kind of cartooning in print, and except for one stretch of a few years, in which I wrote most of the serious poems in *Telephone Poles*, I feel uncertain away from rhyme to which something comic adheres. Bergson's mechanical encrusted upon the organic. But the light verse poems putting into rhyme and jaunty metrics some scientific discovery have a serious point—the universe science discloses to us is farcically unrelated to what our primitive senses report—and I have, when such poems go well, a pleasure and satisfaction not lower than in any other form of literary activity.

Interviewer: You've published work in all the literary forms except drama. Why haven't you worked in this form?

Updike: I've never much enjoyed going to plays myself; they always seem one act too long, and I often can't hear. The last play I went to, I remember, was *A Delicate Balance*; I sat next to the wall, and trucks kept shifting gears on the other side of it, and I missed most of the dialogue. The unreality of painted people standing on a platform saying things they've said to each other for months is more than I can overlook. Also, I think the theater is a quicksand of money and people with push. Harold Brodkey, a splendid writer my age, disappeared for five years into a play that was never produced. From Twain and James to Faulkner and Bellow, the history of novelists as playwrights is a sad one. A novelist is no more prepared to write for the stage than a good distance runner is equipped for ballet. A play is verbal ballet, and I mean to include in that equation some strong reservations about ballet. Less than perfectly done, it's very tiresome. A play's capacity for mimesis is a fraction of a novel's. Shakespeare, and to a lesser extent Shaw, wrote their plays as "turns" and exercises for actors they knew—without Will Kempe, no Falstaff. Without this kind of intimacy, the chances of life creeping into a play are slight. On both sides

of the footlights, I think the present American theater mainly an excuse for being sociable.

Interviewer: But if I'm not mistaken, you once expressed a desire
to write for the films and I think *Rabbit, Run*, in particular, is quite a
cinematic novel. Do you have any such plans now?

Updike: *Rabbit, Run* was subtitled originally, "A Movie." The present tense was in part meant to be an equivalent of the cinematic mode
of narration. The opening bit of the boys playing basketball was visu-
alized to be taking place under the titles and credits. This doesn't
mean, though, that I really wanted to write for the movies. It meant I
wanted to make a movie. I could come closer by writing it in my own
book than by attempting to get through to Hollywood.

Interviewer: Do you think the film has much to teach the novelist?

Updike: I'm not sure. I think that we live in an eye-oriented era and
that both the movies and the graphic arts, the painterly arts, haunt us,
haunt word people quite a lot. I've written about our jealousy in my
review of Robbe-Grillet and his theories. In brief, we're jealous because the visual arts have captured all the glamorous people—the rich
and the young.

Interviewer: Do you think there is a possibility of the novelist feeling at a disadvantage, that the instantaneousness and completeness of
the image is making him somehow have to run to catch up? Have you
ever felt that?

Updike: Oh, sure. I think we are covetous of the success, the
breadth of appeal. A movie does not really require much work. It
pours into us, it fills us like milk being poured into a glass, whereas
there is some cerebral effort needed to turn a bunch of mechanical
marks on a page into moving living images. So that, yes, the power of
the cinema, the awful power of it, the way from moron to genius it
captivates us, it hypnotizes us. . . . What I don't know is how relevant
attempts to imitate this instantaneity, this shuffle of images, are to the
novelist's art. I think that the novel is descended from two sources,
historical accounts and letters. The personal letters, the epistolary novel, the novel of Richardson, which is revived now only as a *tour de
force*, does have this cinematic instantaneity; the time is occurring on
the page. But this is a minority current in the contemporary novel; we
are held captive to the novel as history, as an account of things once
done. The account of things done minus the presiding, talkative, con-

fiding, and pedagogic author may be a somewhat dead convention; that is, like anybody who takes any writing courses, I was told how stale and awful it is when authors begin to signal, as Dickens did, over the heads of the characters to the reader. Yet I feel that something has been lost with this authority, with this sense of an author as God, as a speaking god, as a chatty God, filling the universe of the book. Now we have the past tense, a kind of a noncommittal deadness: God paring his fingernails. We may be getting the worst of both worlds.

Couples was in some ways an old-fashioned novel; I found the last thirty pages—the rounding up, the administering of fortunes—curiously satisfying, pleasant. Going from character to character, I had myself the sensation of flying, of conquering space. In *Rabbit, Run* I liked writing in the present tense. You can move between minds, between thoughts and objects and events with a curious ease not available to the past tense. I'm not sure it's as clear to the reader as it is to the person writing, but there are kinds of poetry, kinds of music you can strike off in the present tense. I don't know why I've not done a full-length novel in it again. I began tentatively, but one page deep into the book, it seemed very natural and congenial, so much so that while doing *The Centaur* I was haunted by the present tense and finally wrote a whole chapter in it.

Interviewer: You speak with some regret about the present authorial disinclination to signal above the heads of the characters. I am interested in your evaluation of the success of three contemporary writers who seem to me to have maintained this willingness to signal to the reader directly. The first one I'd like to mention and get your reaction to is Robert Penn Warren.

Updike: I'm sorry. I don't know Penn Warren's prose well enough to comment.

Interviewer: How about Barth?

Updike: Barth I know imperfectly, but I have read the first two novels and parts of the last two and some of the short stories. I also know Barth personally and find him a most likable and engaging and modest man. He and I are near the same age and born not too far from each other, he in Maryland and I in southeastern Pennsylvania. His work is partly familiar and partly repellent; I feel he hit the floor of nihilism hard and returns to us covered with coal dust. We are very close to an abyss as we traverse Barth's rolling periods and curiously elevated point of view. I guess my favorite book of his is *The Floating Opera*, which is like *The Poorhouse Fair* in ending with a kind of carnival, a brainless celebration of the fact of existence. As it stands now, Barth seems to me a very strongminded and inventive and powerful voice from another planet; there is something otherworldly about his fiction that makes it both fascinating and barren, at least for me. I'd rather visit Uranus than read through *Giles Goat-Boy*.

Interviewer: What about Bellow?

Updike: There is in Bellow a kind of little professor, a professor-elf, who keeps fluttering around the characters, and I'm not sure he's my favorite Bellow character, this voice. He's almost always there, putting exclamatory marks after sentences, making little utterances and in general inviting us to participate in moral decisions. This person—whom I take to be the author—contributes to the soft focus of Bellow's endings. The middles are so rich with detail, with charm and love of life; I think how in *Henderson the Rain King* he remembers rubbing oil into his pregnant wife's stomach to ease the stretch marks. It's this professor, this earnest sociological man who somehow wants us to be better than we are, who muddles the endings, not exactly happy endings, but they are endings which would *point the way*. He cares so—the way Bellow can conjure up a minor character and set him tumbling across the paragraph.

But the general question of authorial presence—I find it irksome when an author is there as a celebrity. In Salinger's later works and most of Mailer's work the author appears as somebody who counts, somebody who has an audience of teen-agers out there waiting to hear from him. This kind of return to before Chekhov I don't find useful, although authorial invisibility is also a pose. The proper pose may be the Homeric bard's one—he is there, but unimportantly there, there by sufferance of the king.

Interviewer: What about the cultivation of pretense—playing around with it. I mean, what do you think of a writer like Barthelme?

Updike: He was an art director of some sort and, just as Kerouac's work was a kind of action writing to answer action painting, so Barthelme's short stories and the one novelette seem to me to be an attempt to bring over into prose something Pop. I think, you know, on the one hand of Andy Warhol's Campbell's soup cans and on the other of the Chinese baby food that the Seven Dwarfs in *Snow White* are making. Then again you do get a hard-edge writing in a way. In one of his short stories he says that the hard nut-brown word has enough aesthetic satisfaction for anybody but a fool. I also think his stories are important for what they don't say, for the things that don't happen in them, that stand revealed as clichés.

Yes—I think he's interesting, but more interesting as an operator within a cultural scene than as a—oh, as a singer to my spirit. A quaint phrase that possibly betrays me.

Interviewer: What of writers who've influenced you. Salinger? Nabokov?

Updike: I learned a lot from Salinger's short stories; he did remove the short narrative from the wise-guy, slice-of-life stories of the thirties and forties. Like most innovative artists, he made new room for shapelessness, for life as it is lived. I'm thinking of a story like "Just Before the War with the Eskimos" not "For Esmé," which already shows signs of emotional overkill. Nabokov, I admire but would emulate only his high dedication to the business of making books that are not sloppy, that can be reread. I think his aesthetic models, chess puzzles, and protective colorations in Lepidoptera, are rather special.

Interviewer: Henry Green? O'Hara?

Updike: Green's tone, his touch of truth, his air of peddling nothing and knowing everything, I would gladly attain to, if I could. For sheer transparence of eye and ear he seems to me unmatched among living writers. Alas, for a decade he has refused to write, showing I suppose his ultimate allegiance to life itself. Some of O'Hara's short stories also show a very rare transparence, freshness, and unexpectedness. Good works of art direct us back outward to reality again; they illustrate, rather than ask, imitation.

Interviewer: You mentioned Kerouac a moment ago. How do you feel about his work?

Updike: Somebody like Kerouac who writes on teletype paper as rapidly as he can once slightly alarmed me. Now I can look upon this more kindly. There may be some reason to question the whole idea of fineness and care in writing. Maybe something can get into sloppy writing that would elude careful writing. I'm not terribly careful myself, actually. I write fairly rapidly if I get going, and don't change much, and have never been one for making outlines or taking out whole paragraphs or agonizing much. If a thing goes, it goes for me, and if it doesn't go, I eventually stop and get off.

Interviewer: What is it that you think gets into sloppy writing that eludes more careful prose?

Updike: It comes down to, "What is language?" Up to now, until this age of mass literacy, language has been something spoken. In utterance there's a minimum of slowness. In trying to treat words as chisel strokes, you run the risk of losing the quality of utterance, the rhythm of utterance, the happiness. A phrase out of Mark Twain—he describes a raft hitting a bridge and says that it "went all to smash and scatteration like a box of matches struck by lightning." The beauty of "scatteration" could only have occurred to a talkative man, a man who had been brought up among people who were talking and who loved to talk himself. I'm aware myself of a certain dryness of this reservoir, this backlog of spoken talk. A Rumanian once said to me that Americans are always telling stories. I'm not sure this is as true as it once was. Where we once used to spin yarns, now we sit in front of the TV and receive pictures. I'm not sure the younger generation even knows how to gossip. But, as for a writer, if he has something to tell, he should perhaps type it almost as fast as he could talk it. We must look to the organic world, not the inorganic world, for metaphors; and just as the organic world has periods of repose and periods of great speed and exercise, so I think the writer's process should be organically varied. But there's a kind of tautness that you should feel within yourself no matter how slow or fast you're spinning out the reel.

Interviewer: In "The Sea's Green Sameness" you deny that characterization and psychology are primary goals of fiction. What do you think is more important?

Updike: I wrote "The Sea's Green Sameness" years ago and meant, I believe, that narratives should not be *primarily* packages for psychological insights, though they can contain them, like raisins in buns. But the substance is the dough, which feeds the storytelling appetite, the appetite for motion, for suspense, for resolution. The author's deepest pride, as I have experienced it, is not in his incidental wisdom but in his ability to keep an organized mass of images moving forward, to feel life engendering itself under his hands. But no doubt, fiction is also a mode of spying; we read it as we look in windows or

listen to gossip, to learn what other people *do*. Insights of all kinds are
welcome; but no wisdom will substitute for an instinct for action and
pattern, and a perhaps savage wish to hold, through your voice, another soul in thrall.

Interviewer: In view of this and your delight in the "noncommittal
luminosity of fact," do you think you're much like the "nouvelle
vague" novelists?

Updike: I used to. I wrote *The Poorhouse Fair* as an anti-novel,
and have found Nathalie Sarraute's description of the modern novelistic predicament a helpful guide. I am attracted to the cool surface of
some contemporary French novels, and, like them, do want to give in-
animate or vegetable presences some kind of vote in the democracy of
narrative. Basically, though, I describe things not because their mute-
ness mocks our subjectivity but because they seem to be masks for
God. And I should add that there is, in fiction, an image-making function, above image-retailing. To create a coarse universal figure like
Tarzan is in some way more of an accomplishment than the novels of
Henry James.

Interviewer: As a technician, how unconventional would you say
you were?

Updike: As unconventional as I need to be. An absolute freedom
exists on the blank page, so let's use it. I have from the start been
wary of the fake, the automatic. I tried not to force my sense of life as
many-layered and ambiguous, while keeping in mind some sense of
transaction, of a bargain struck, between me and the ideal reader. Domestic fierceness within the middle class, sex and death as riddles for
the thinking animal, social existence as sacrifice, unexpected pleasures
and rewards, corruption as a kind of evolution—these are some of the
themes. I have tried to achieve objectivity in the form of narrative. My
work is meditation, not pontification, so that interviews like this one
feel like a forcing of the growth, a posing. I think of my books not as
sermons or directives in a war of ideas but as objects, with different
shapes and textures and the mysteriousness of anything that exists. My
first thought about art, as a child, was that the artist brings something
into the world that didn't exist before, and that he does it without de-
stroying something else. A kind of refutation of the conservation of
matter. That still seems to me its central magic, its core of joy.

John Updike Talks about the Shapes and Subjects of His Fiction

Eric Rhode/1969

From *The Listener* 81 (19 June 1969), 862–864. Reprinted by permission of BBC Magazines, London, England. Conducted on the *Third Programme.*

There is a concern, especially on the Continent, with formal problems of the art of fiction. I don't think you can really be very theoretical about it, especially if you're an American, but I do somehow look towards Europe for tools with which to say what I have to say.

When you talk of formal problems you're thinking of French writers like Robbe-Grillet?

Exactly. It's just a question of finding out what is dead in the novel and what really is alive. I don't think Robbe-Grillet has done anything very solid or helpful. Nevertheless, he and Nathalie Sarraute are at least posing the problems in a way that anybody trying to earn his living at the art should be aware of. I'm not aware of the English being very interested in formal theory. On the other hand, it seems to me that you do have here a kind of tradition, or—I hate to say it—craft, or mastery, perhaps. Somebody like Iris Murdoch—whether or not you are totally persuaded by each book or whether or not her total philosophy seems, well, slightly hysterical—is somehow a master in that. She keeps inventing, keeps presenting new patterns, and keeps producing a book a year—which is a pretty hectic rate, but it's a healthy rate. As opposed to this, there is the awful sense in America of the writer being a kind of priest, and a constipated priest at that.

I don't see any affiliation in your work to the French idea of experiment, or indeed to the kinds of experiment that go on in the States. It seems to me that you are much closer to the English novel; there is a very strong sense of the domestic in your work—of the world as it is.

I'm just trying to think of the word 'domestic.' I suppose this is true. It may be less a matter of conscious choice than of the fact that I seem to be a domestic creature. My first novel, *The Poorhouse Fair*, was, at least in my mind, something of a *nouvelle vague* book, particularily in the endings: that is, I tried to create a pattern of tension and then, instead of resolving it, dissolved it. It ended with a kind of brainless fair: people come to a fair and you hear their voices and it all dissolves. In my mind it was a somewhat experimental book and my publishers then, Harper, seemed to think it was, because the ending puzzled them so much that I took it away from them and went to Knopf, where I've been happy ever since. In each of the books there has been, in my mind, at least, a different experiment, an adventure: in *Rabbit, Run* the present tense may seem a mild adventure. It's more and more used now, but at the time it wasn't.

Coming back to The Poorhouse Fair, *the most striking thing there, I think, is the fact that you have so clearly kept yourself out of the book, that you have created these very old men and women. This is an act entirely of the imagination, or so it feels. In fact, Mary McCarthy said that she finds it a rather spooky accomplishment—like those boy actors who play old men—that you have created these characters so credibly. How far was it based on actuality?*

Not very. There was indeed a poorhouse a couple of blocks from where I grew up, but I very rarely went into it, and there was a fair that must have impressed me as a child. I had written prior to this, while living in New York City, a 600-page novel, called, I think, *Home*, and more or less about myself and my family up to the age of 16 or so. It had been a good exercise to write it and I later used some of the material in short stories, but it really felt like a very heavy bundle of yellow paper, and I realized that this was not going to be my first novel—it had too many traits of a first novel. I did not publish it, but I thought it was time for me to write a novel. I was—what?—25, 26. Getting to be an old man, as writers go in America. They were tearing the poorhouse down at Shillington and I went up and looked at the shell. My grandfather, who is somewhat like John Hook in that book, was recently dead, and so the idea of some kind of memorial gesture, embodying what seems to have been on my part a very strong sense of national decay, crystallized in this novel. I wrote it in three months and then rewrote it in three months. It was my first real venture into what you might call novelistic space and it was very exciting. I haven't read it since the last set of proofs, but I'd like to think that

there was some love, and hence some life and blood, in these old
people.

*I think it's a perfect, completely enclosed book and when I read it I
thought: this is a masterpiece, how can he go on from here? I always
have the feeling in your work that the short story, the novella, comes
fairly easily to you. You've probably had enormous problems with the
longer stretch. I would say this because I think your kind of writing,
where you start from within the center of a character, from the character's observations and impressions of the world, and then move on
to a sense of the family, doesn't lead naturally to the discovery of a
form. I feel, for instance, in your second novel,* Rabbit, Run *which is
more ambitious, and where you have a strong plot, that the central situation is the man who is under strain, but then you do move into
melodrama later in the book. This must have been difficult for you.*

I'm afraid melodrama comes quite easily to me. I'm in two minds
about the events in novels. One has this sense that the old-fashioned
novel, and indeed films and television plays, are falsifying life terribly
by making events happen, by creating tensions and then resolving
them, by setting up trials and then handing down the verdicts—for in
fact verdicts don't usually get handed down. All my books end on a
kind of hesitant or ambiguous note. On the other hand, there is a delight in making things happen, in falling through or leaping through
this fictional space. As for the accusation of being melodramatic which
was leveled at the last book, or not melodramatic, perhaps, so much as
Gothic or unreal or coarsely plotted: if there could be a defense it is
my sensation that events, when they happen, do happen rather
lurchingly and suddenly.

*Do you improvise or do you plot things out very carefully before-
hand?*

I really begin with some kind of solid, coherent image, some notion
of the shape of the book and even of its texture. *The Poorhouse Fair*
was meant to have this sort of Y shape of the two things and then the
disappearance, or the resolution. *Rabbit, Run* was a kind of zig-zag.
The Centaur was sort of a sandwich. I can't begin until I know the beginning and the end and have some sense of what's going to happen
between. There are some hinges, but really a novel, even quite a bulky
one—you think of Henry James's 800 pages—has only a few hinges.

I don't make an outline or anything. I figure that I can hold the events
in my head then hope that things will happen which will surprise me,
that the characters will take on life and talk. I keep a kind of loose
rein on the book. I would not begin a book—I would not advise people to begin a book—without knowing where it's going because one of
the aesthetic delights one hopes for is a sense of resolution, of having
heard that phrase before, an echo and a kind of click at the end.

*This image of the book that you have in mind is in fact a rather
geometric image. It's not, say, a visual image, an image of events in
the book which you're leading up to.*

It's sort of an abstract sensation, but of course you have to have a
lot of other things to begin a book. You have to have at least some of
the people and have to be in some ways stirred by the central people.
The main motive force behind *The Centaur* would be some wish to
make a record of my father. There was the whole sense of having for
15 years watched a normal, good-doing Protestant man suffering in a
kind of comic but real way. What led me to write it and what keeps
it going and what gives it its life now, at least in myself, is this thing
of making a solid object and making a pattern. Also there is a certain
element of having a message and wanting to get it across. My message
has not been the kind that is especially congenial to my time. In a time
concerned with urban and political issues, I've dealt with suburban, or
rural, unpolitical man.

*Where I think you are unusual is that you're not a metaphysical
writer in the sense that you might say Melville is a metaphysical writer: you deal with the actual world, with sensations and things. And
yet, religion, in an institutional sense, does appear in all your books.
Often it's something you look at rather wryly, rather diffidently, as
though it's a kind of electric force which your characters are a bit
frightened of. I would think this is both part of the sense that you have
of a tradition of the past, of the world existing as it is, and also of
some anxiety, an inability to relate this to any sense of community.*

The ministers tend increasingly to become figures of fun, or rather,
I'd say, more of a disappointment on the author's part. I seem to have
some expectations of the ministry which it doesn't fulfill. The short
story "Pigeon Feathers," which is about a boy's questions being answered, he thinks very badly, by his clergyman, is the central minister

story. The church continues to exist in the modern world, and it seems
to me to be something rather gallant.

You are religious yourself?

I'd say, yes, I try to be. I think I do tend to see the world as lay-
ered, and as there being something up there; certainly in *Couples* it
would seem to be God, who in a certain sense destroys that inoffen-
sive Congregationalist church. Moreover, and again it's worked out
geometrically, I seem to see all my books in terms of children's drawings, they are all meant to be moral debates with the reader, and if
they seem pointless—I'm speaking hopefully—it's because the reader
has not been engaged in the debate. The question is usually, "What is
a good man?" or "What is goodness?" and in all my books an act is
inspected. Take Harry Angstrom in *Rabbit, Run*: There is a case to be
made for running away from your wife. In the late fifties beatniks
were preaching transcontinental travelling as the answer to man's dis-
quiet. And I was just trying to say: "Yes, there is certainly that, but
then there are all these other people who seem to get hurt." That distinction is meant to be a moral dilemma.

You see the institution of marriage, the institution of the Church, as
something that carries you back to the past, which I think again is
very important in your books. For instance, in The Poorhouse Fair, *the*
one moment that I felt that you emerged as a person was close to the
end when you say something about how we go backwards, how we be-
come our father's opinions, and eventually our grandfather's.

True enough, there is this interest in the past, but in a way the past
is all we have. The present is very thin, it's less than a second wide,
and the future doesn't exist. I think that *Of the Farm* is about moral
readjustment, and the readjustment is somehow in terms of harsh deeds
done in the past; the mother and boy need, in a way, to excuse each
other, or somehow to give a blessing. It's a little hard for me to see
my work from the outside, as it were, but I do notice a recurrence of
the concept of a blessing, of approval, or forgiveness, or somehow
even encouragement in order to go on. I wonder if twentieth-century
man's problem isn't one of encouragement, because of the failure of
nerve, the lassitude and despair, the sense that we've gone to the end
of the corridor and found it blank. So the characters beneath the surface are exhorting each other to action. In *Couples*, Piet is quite a

modern man in that he really can't act for himself because he's overwhelmed by the moral implications of any act—leaving his wife, staying with her. . . . The women in that book are less sensitive perhaps
to the oppressive quality of cosmic blackness, and it is the women
who do almost all the acting. I don't want to say that being passive,
being inactive, being paralyzed, is wrong in an era when so much action is crass and murderous. I do feel that in the generations that I've
had a glimpse of—I can see my grandfather at one end, and I can see
my boys coming up—there has been a perceptible loss of the sense of
righteousness. But many evils are done in the name of righteousness,
so perhaps one doesn't want it back. Nevertheless, I suspect that the
vitality of women now, the way many of us lean on them, is not an
eternal phenomenon but a historical one, and fairly recent.

I wonder, in the case of The Centaur, *why you related the immediate
experience of the schoolmaster to myth.*
   It seemed to me that there was something mythical about the events.
It's an experiment very unlike that of *Ulysses*, where the myth lurks
beneath the surface of the natural events. In a way the natural events
in my book are meant to be a kind of mask for the myth. The genesis
of it was reading in an old book of my wife's this variant to the Hercules legend. It is part of the comedy of the man's plight that he is living in a town full of gods, and he's not quite a god himself, hence this
failure of communication all the time. In fact, my father, who came
from New Jersey, did have this feeling about Pennsylvania, that he
wasn't quite clued in about what was going on. Secondly, there is a
way in which to a child everything is myth-size: people are enormous
and ominous and have great backlogs of mysterious information and of
a life lived that you lack. I don't think that without the myth you'd
have a book. It seemed to me to fit a kind of experience that I'd had:
my father's immersion in the world of Christian morality, in trying to
do the right thing and constantly sacrificing himself, always going off
to church meetings, and yet complaining about it all the time. There
was an ambivalence that seemed to make him very centaur-like. I think
that initially art was tied in with theology and has to do with an ideal
world: the artist is in some way a middleman between the ideal world
and this, even though our sense of the ideal—and I'm speaking really
of our gut sense, regardless of what we think we believe—is at present

fairly dim. It may not always be so. And I find I cannot imagine being a writer without wanting somehow to play, to take these patterns, to insert these secrets into my books, and to spin out this music that has its formal side.

Well, there are ideal worlds and ideal worlds. There's the ideal world of Plato, there's the world of the Music of the Spheres, and there's also the Titian world, the world of the sensuous. This other side to you has really found a fulfillment in Couples, *which, I now see with hindsight, was something you had to write. The whole interest in sensation, in the body, finds its fulfillment here. Were you conscious of this inevitability in writing* Couples?
Well no, it's just my usual simple-minded attempt to portray something. Nothing annoys me more than books ostensibly about sex that don't really describe it.

We're talking about Couples *as a book about sex. It's something quite different, isn't it? And I think it's certainly not sensationalist. What astonishes me is that these descriptions are written with extraordinary delicacy and tact. You must have found them very hard to write.*
They were no harder than landscapes and a little more interesting. It's wonderful the way people in bed talk, the sense of voices and the sense of warmth, so that as a writer you become kind of warm also. The book is, of course, not about sex really: it's about sex as the emergent religion, as the only thing left. I don't present the people in the book as a set of villains; I see them as people caught in a historical moment—a moment now past, by the way.

That world no longer exists?
It was pretty unthinkable in 1964 that there would be openly expressed this constant desire to tear everything down that you hear now from every Western city. It was basically still a world of acceptance, where the abiding institutions were assumed to be substantial, though they received no real homage. The people in the book exist within a society, but have no wish to restructure it; rather, within its interstices they are seeking through each other's bodies, and really through each other's voices too—there's an awful lot of talk in that book—to console themselves.

What's unusual about them is their particular promiscuity, isn't it?

I don't think they are especially notable in that regard. These are the descendants of the Puritans, people who have inherited a work ethic and who find themselves really working no harder than they must. In part, the book is about affluence, which, in releasing at least this class of people from pressing financial anxiety, creates new anxieties.

Not only is there much greater control of all these characters and a much larger canvas, but there is this kind of space in the book which I don't feel exists in the early work.

At least you have a map of the town in your mind's eye and you sort of sail from one house to the other. I think a writer should perpetually be giving himself tough assignments in an attempt to see what he can do. It took courage initially to be able to write frankly about my own boyhood, which, funnily enough, was a very innocuous boyhood. Nevertheless, it seemed to be a step forward to write some of the short stories that have been collected here and there. Then I thought: okay, enough of that, get out of this and write about adults making the usual sort of adult mess. In that sense, the book was a change. But I see backwards through my books a certain continuity: in a way this book is describing a divorce and *Of the Farm* was about the consequences of a divorce. And certainly I've not, I don't think, been shy about erotic detail in the other books.

It's only here that suddenly it has come right into the center of the canvas. You probably won't want to write a book like this again.

I wonder where I'm going to go now. I think it's very bad luck to talk about things you're doing.

Well, talk in a rather magical and mysterious way about it.

It's a rather magical or mysterious book. The proud State of Pennsylvania from which I come only produced one president, a man called James Buchanan, who preceded Lincoln and who has always been dismissed as one of the weakest of a succession of weak presidents between Jackson and Lincoln. I'm attached to him because he's a Pennsylvanian: he was a bachelor too, and he was very old, the oldest president till Eisenhower. I've read now maybe eight books about the 1850's, a period rather like the 1960's, a period of harsh debates, increasingly irrevocable rifts, a period of astounding invective. I was sort of shocked in my prim way by the kind of abuse that Johnson had to put up with, but that kind of abuse was American coin. I see Buchanan as a center of some kind of investigation of what political power feels like. To what extent is it illusory? It certainly was very illusory in his case, because he really didn't have much power—the country was paying no attention to him. And also I'm interested in taking a long, eventful life and shuffling it.

Bech Meets Me

John Updike/1971

From *Picked-Up Pieces*. New York: Alfred A. Knopf, 1975, 10–13.
First published in *The New York Times Book Review* 14 November
1971, sec. 3, 3 under the title "Henry Bech Redux." Reprinted by
permission of Alfred A. Knopf. First of the author's three self-
interviews, via the persona of his own character, Henry Bech.

Updike's office is concealed in a kind of false-bottomed drawer in the
heart of downtown Ipswich (Mass.), but the drowsy locals, for a mere
30 pieces of silver, can be conned into betraying its location. A stuck-
looking door is pulled open: an endless flight of stairs, lit by a team of
dusty fireflies, is climbed. Within the sanctum, squalor reigns un-
challenged. A lugubrious army-green metal desk rests in the center of
a threadbare Oriental rug reticulate with mouse-paths; the walls are
camouflaged in the kind of cardboard walnut panelling used in newly
graduated lawyers' offices or in those Los Angeles motels favored by
the hand-held cameramen and quick-tongued *directeurs* of blue movies. On these sad walls hang pictures, mostly souvenirs of his childhood, artistic or otherwise. On the bookshelves, evidently stained by a
leopard in the process of shedding his spots, rest repellent books—
garish schoolboy anthologies secreting some decaying Updikean mor-
sel, seven feet of James Buchanan's bound works adumbrating the next
opus, some daffodil-yellow building-trade manuals penumbrating *Couples*; and, most repellent of all, a jacketless row of the total *oeuvre*,
spines naked as the chorus of *Hair*, revealing what only the more morbid have hitherto suspected, that since 1959 (*The Poorhouse Fair*,
surely his masterpiece) Updike with Alfred A. Knopf's connivance has
been perpetrating a uniform edition of himself. Beclouding all, the
stink of nickel cigarillos, which the shifty, tremulous, asthmatic author
puffs to sting the muse's eyes into watering ever since, at the Surgeon
General's behest, he excised cigarettes from his armory of crutches.

Updike, at first sight, seems bigger than he is, perhaps because the
dainty stitchwork of his prose style readies one for an apparition of
elfin dimensions. An instant layer of cordial humorousness veneers a
tough thickness of total opacity, which may in turn coat a center of

heartfelt semi-liquid. Shamefacely I confessed my errand—to fabricate an "interview" for one of those desperate publications that seek to make weekly "news" of remorselessly accumulating Gutenbergian silt. Shamefacedly, Updike submitted. Yet, throughout the interview that limped in the van of this consent, as the pumpkin-orange New England sun lowered above the chimney pots of a dry-cleaning establishment seen darkly through an unwashed window, Updike gave the impression of (and who wouldn't?) wanting to be elsewhere. He kept interjecting his desire to go "home" and "shingle" his "barn"; it occurred to this interviewer (the Interviewer, as Mailer would say), that the uniform books, varied in tint and size as subtly as cedar shakes, were themselves shingles, with the which this shivering poor fellow hopes to keep his own skin dry in the soaking downpour of mortality.

I observed, feinting for an opening, that he has stopped writing about Jews. He replied that the book about me had not so much been about a Jew as about a writer, who was a Jew with the same inevitability that a fictional rug-salesman would be an American. I riposted that *he* was a writer, though a Wasp. With the languid shrug of the chronically pained, he bitterly inveighed against the term Wasp, which implies, he said, wealth where he had been poor, Calvinism where he had been Lutheran, and ethnic consciousness where he had had none. That his entire professional life had been spent among Jews and women, that his paternal grandmother had been partly Irish, that he had disliked James Gould Cozzens' last novel, that false loyalties were the plague of a divided Republic, that racism as an aesthetic category was one thing but as an incitement to massacre another, etc.

With the chinks in his armor gaping before me like marigolds at the height of noon, I lunged deftly as a hummingbird. Didn't I detect, I asked, in his later work, an almost blunt determination to, as it were, sing America? Would he describe himself, I asked, switching the tape recorder up to fortissimo, as (a) pro-American, (b) a conservative? His turtleish green eyes blinked, recognizing that his shell was being tickled, and that there was no way out but forward. He said he was pro-American in the sense that he was married to America and did not wish a divorce. That the American style and landscape and impetus were, by predetermination, his meat; though he had also keenly felt love of fatherland in England, in Russia, in Egypt. That nations were like people, lovable and wonderful in their simple existence. That, in answer to the second prong of my probe, there were some things he thought worth conserving, such as the electoral college and the Great Lakes; but that by registration he was a Democrat and by disposition an apologist for the spirit of anarchy—our animal or divine margin of resistance to the social contract. That, given the need for a contract, he preferred the American Constitution, with its 18th-century bow to the pursuit of individual happiness, to any of the totalisms presently running around rabid. That the decisions of any establishment, though properly suspect and frightfully hedged by self-interest and the myopia power brings, must be understood as choices among imperfect alternatives; power participates in the weight and guilt of the world and shrill impotence never has to cash in its chips.

I inkled that this diatribe was meant to lead up to some discussion of his new novel, with its jacket of red, gray, and blue stripes, but, having neglected to read more than the first pages, which concern a middle-aged ex-athlete enjoying a beer with his elderly father, I was compelled to cast my interrogation in rather general terms. Viz.:

Q: Are you happy?

A: Yes, this is a happy limbo for me, this time. I haven't got the first finished copies yet, and haven't spotted the first typo. I haven't had to read any reviews.

Q: How do you find reviews?

A: Humiliating. It isn't merely that the reviewers are so much cleverer than I, and could write such superior fictions if they deigned to; it's that even the on-cheering ones have read a different book than the one you wrote. All the little congruences and arabesques you prepared with such delicate anticipatory pleasure are gobbled up as if by pigs at a pastry cart. Still, the ideal reader must—by the ontological argument—exist, and his invisibility therefore be a demonic illusion sustained to tempt us to despair.

Q: Do you envision novels as pills, broadcasts, tapestries, explosions of self, cantilevered constructs, or what?

A: For me, they are crystallizations of visceral hopefulness extruded as a slow paste which in the glitter of print regains something of the original, absolute gaiety. I try to do my best and then walk away rapidly, so as not to be incriminated. Right now, I am going over old short stories, arranging them in little wreaths, trimming away a strikingly infelicitous sentence here, adding a paper ribbon there. Describing it like this makes me sound more Nabokovian than I feel. Chiefly, I feel fatigued by my previous vitality.

Q: I'd like to talk about the new book, but the truth is I can't hold bound galley pages, my thumbs keep going to sleep, so I didn't get too far into this, what? *Rabbit Rerun?*

A (*eagerly, pluggingly*): *Redux*. Latin for led back. You know Latin: *Apologia Pro Vita Sua*. The next installment, ten years from now, I expect to call *Rural Rabbit*—you'll notice at the end of this book Janice talks about them getting a farm. The fourth and last, to come out in 1991 if we all live, is tentatively titled *Rabbit Is Rich*. Nice, huh?

Q (*turning tape recorder down to pianissimo*): Not bad. *Pas mal.* Not bad.

A (*gratefully, his shingling hand itching*): Thanks. Thanks a lot.

Updike Redux

Michael Sragow/1971

From *The Harvard Crimson*, 2 February 1972, 3–4, 6. Reprinted by permission of *The Harvard Crimson* and Michael Sragow. Conducted in December 1971.

John H. Updike ('54) hopped back to Cambridge one cold day in December from his Ipswich home. With long legs and arms that flopped around with nonchalant grace, he scaled the *Crimson* steps looking like a suburban squire should: work-booted, wearing nondescript dungarees and a good sweater gone bad. With eyes looking out from a face somewhere between a hawk's and a gnome's, he glanced at the fading pictures of fading editors on our tack-marked cork bulletin board, and asked the photographer "How did you get those black borders on them?" Mechanical details and competence in mastering them impressed him—part of the reason he wrote *Rabbit Redux* was his vision of Rabbit as a linotyper.

It was one month after we'd met at an Allegheny terminal in Philadelphia, when, taken by surprise, he had agreed to come to Cambridge to talk about *Rabbit Redux*, and whatever else struck him to speak of. It was one week after he'd been hailed by the *Times* as one of the great contemporary American authors . . . right up there with Roth, Bellow, Malamud and Mailer. (No longer would he be the fall *goy* for all of New York's literary establishment.)

Neither the fortuitous accident which brought him in touch with his *Crimson* reviewer, nor his recent entrance into the literary pantheon, seemed to discomfit him much. After remarking that the *Lampoon* headquarters where he had once held sway were much plusher than the *Crimson's* game rooms, he spoke freely of future plans, in a light-timbred voice which unexpectedly erupted in husky laughter.

His next book will, hopefully, be the historical novel which was to have taken the place of *Redux* as his main output for '69-70. Based on the life of James Buchanan—interestingly enough, the only president to have been born and raised in Pennsylvania—the novel is meant to explore the tensions of a man of personal integrity thrust into a position of national power at a time when his actual strength was

59

limited—and threatened by the cataclysms of pre-Civil War
America. Buchanan had successfully risen above personal
traumas in his love-life, and in a tawdry Pennsylvania political arena; he got caught in the mire of an unfinished capital
and unsophisticated state system once he got to the White
House.

The tape recorder came, and Updike related why that novel has not yet been written:

The trouble is, once you get down into the stream you begin to read
around and you realize how little you know. The problem becomes
how to keep it from becoming just an historical novel. Once, I thought
if I forgot a lot, then I could really begin it. But I've talked enough
about it, it's been in my mind long enough, that I must really do it in
a carefree and rapid way and get it out of my system.

I'm glad, in a way, that I did write *Redux* instead of pulling ahead
with it. This, again, was a bit of a leap of the imagination—I haven't
lived in Pennsylvania for a long time now and this Brewer is a rather
different Brewer from the one in *Rabbit, Run*—which was based on
scenes in my childhood where I knew every wrinkle in the pavement. I
still felt on solid ground in this book in a way . . . the next book will
have to be a jump into the dark.

*The book has been hailed for its portrait of 'Middle America.' Did
the necessity to get that close to a man who is inarticulate and guided
by mass culture to as great a degree as Rabbit require a similar leap?*

Intellectually, I'm not essentially advanced over Harry Angstrom. I
went to Harvard, it's true, and wasn't much good at basketball . . .
other than that we're rather similar. I quite understand both his anger
and passivity, and feeling of the whole Vietnam involvement as a puzzle, that something strange has gone wrong . . . but it's no great leap
of the imagination to do *that*.

I, after all, have moved from one small town in my childhood to another in my adulthood. There may be something also in the novelist's
trade which shades you towards conservatism (I am a registered Democrat, I should say, and on the town Democratic committee). Your sense
of things exists because they evolved to that condition; they cannot be
lightly or easily altered. It is my general sense of human institutions
that they are outcroppings of human nature, that human nature is

slow to change, that in general when you destroy one set of institutions you get . . . something worse. That's a silly thing to say, I'm joking of course.

At one point in Redux, *Rabbit looks over the books that Skeeter, the black radical, carries—Marx, Fanon—and they disgust him, remind him of plumbing. Is that more or less your feeling also?*

Well, I think to some degree yes, not just me but a lot of people have gone along under a number of assumptions based in part on the movies of the '30s, and all these investigations of our origins and terrible flaws, the built-in problems of the way things work in America is a little like scouring the plumbing in your own home. . . . It's hard for some of us to get down in the cellar. That doesn't mean it shouldn't be done. That's a very real thing, the way that book sort of smells; it's the plumbing under the homes, I remember, this stink arising from under the house itself. Throughout the book he smells bad things.

You've written that "an easy Humanism" pervades the land's writing. Given the fact that you deal on a very personal basis with human stress, how do you distinguish your . . .

Difficult humanism? I feel that, as a writer, I put into practice a set of democratic assumptions. Just as in a democracy anybody can be president, so anyone can be a character in a novel, at least in one by me. Every human being who is more than a moron is in the arena of certain violent tensions that are involved in being human. . . . In fact, there is an easy humanism that insists that man is an animal which feeds and sleeps and defecates and makes love and isn't that nice and natural and let's all have more of that.

But this is omitting intrinsic stresses in the human condition—you foresee things, for example, you foresee your own death. You have already been locked out of the animal paradise of unthinking natural reflex.

You are born into one political contract or another, whose terms, though they sit very lightly at first, in the form of the draft, or taxes, eventually begin to make very real demands on you. The general social contract—living with other people, driving cars on highways—all this is difficult, it's painful. It's a kind of agony really—the agony vents itself in ulcers internally, rage externally. . . .

In short, all of our institutions, of marriage, the family, your driver's license, everything is kind of precarious, and maintained at a cost of tension.

Easy humanism, then, lies in the belief that these individual problems can be ignored for the sake of larger panaceas. . . .
Or who even take humanity as some kind of moral index, who say that to be human is to be good and our problems all arise from not being human enough. I think I take a rather darker view. We must of necessity lose our humanity all the time.

When asked about what my philosophy was, I tried to write it down in *Midpoint* in handy couplets and discovered that of all my books it is the least read, and it was hardly reviewed at all. I concluded that nobody really cared what my philosophy was. I think that's right—the novelist is of interest only for what he does through empathy and image-producing, image-arranging; the more consciously a theorist he is the more apt he is to become impotent or cranky or both. Like Harry. I try to remain kind of open. Revolt, rebellion, violence, disgust are themselves there for a reason; they too are organically evolved out of a distinct reality, and must be considered respectfully. . . . I try to love both the redneck and the anarchist bomb-thrower. I think they're both anarchists.

People are basically very anarchistic. Harry's search for infinite freedom—well, he's been kind of ground down, he's never really been answered.

At the end of Rabbit Redux, *Rabbit talks of going back to a farm. Are you thinking of bringing him back again?*
I kind of left the book open, I even mounted a few threads that could be picked up. Janice talks about how he never should have had that awful indoor job. I have a title—*Rural Rabbit*—that's going to be their next stage. I couldn't write that book now. Maybe in 1979 enough will have happened to both him and me that I can, but if it doesn't, that's all right. Maybe I should stop while I'm ahead—at least as far as *The New York Times* goes.

These two complement each other well enough. Anybody who really cared could get some interesting formal things out of the two books together. You never know how this works out in terms of flesh and blood. But certainly Janice bringing Stavros back to life is some kind of counterweight to the baby's death in the first book. She too had to make a passage—go through something to return—to get back into bed with him. All that's there. I'm not sure that a third book could do it again—it would have to be a different kind of a book, a short book, a pastoral book, an eclogue.

There seems to be great nostalgia for the farm running through your books. Is the bucolic life an ideal one for you?

No, I think for Rabbit it is—remember, he is an animal . . . in the first book he was happy brainlessly working in Mrs. Smith's garden. Yes, he does pine after an animal existence.

A lot of men like him really do—I'm constantly surprised at the amount of men who get up at four in the morning in the hunting season and go out with a gun in the miserable weather and try to kill some harmless bird. What is this but some very deep need to get one with nature somehow, something that's remotely denied all of us?

I have few illusions of farm life. It's a good life, but I think it has much of the drudgery of industrial existence without some of the compensations. It's a brutal life. I lived on a farm, but am really not myself a rural creature. I really love New York City. At any rate, I'm not sure that rural life or a big commune is an answer. The earth and agriculture are an index of something we need and are rapidly losing; the human animal is geared to interlock with all kinds of raw natural environments. The coming civilization—that doesn't mean just here, but worldwide—must accommodate people; it's a commonplace, I guess, ecology.

My mother was an ecologist before her time, and bred in me this feeling about land being precious, in some way the ground of our physical being.

Do you find it difficult to keep writing in a cultural context where— as you said once—"Homegrown cabbages" like Mailer and Jones are mistaken for roses? Do you still stand by that sentence, and is there any tradition you do feel a part of?

Since I wrote that sentence Jones' stock has gone down whereas Mailer's has risen. I think that considering Mailer's position at the time it is an apt enough remark. I think Mailer's subsequent career as far as I've kept up with it is a kind of self-resurrection to be admired. I do admire—not without reservation—*Armies of the Night*; there's a

shrillness, and a willingness to accept your personal experience as an
adequate metaphor for national experience.

That little bothers me in a sense—all writers do that to some extent.
Harry Angstrom is supposed to be some kind of an American. But at
least there's tact when you do it as a novel, whereas Mailer's is the
sublime conviction that whatever happens to him happens to Them—
it's like what's good for General Motors is good for the nation. Still,
Armies of the Night was made wonderful by the richness, the ironic
complexity of Mailer's view. He does have a very complicated mind at
times. I quite like *Prisoner of Sex*, which I've just read. It's a mistake
to dismiss the book as a male chauvinist oink—it winds up as just
that, I suppose, yet it's such a lovingly reasoned and felt-out explana-
tion of how he does feel.

Do I feel part of a tradition? I think any writer to some extent inher-
its the mid-nineteenth century New Englanders—we all benefit from
Emerson's marvelous sense of what an American is, from Melville's
superb thunder, from Thoreau's jackal and all that.

But I'm not too aware of tradition. The present cultural scene is so
swiftly changing that to try to orient yourself very distinctly is just to
make yourself sad and miserable. You get into a professional situation
where you are a writer; you do it out of habit; you must write a certain
number of words a day; the older you get the more old-fashioned you
become.

A new kind of mind was produced by raising children on television. I was raised on movies, a different kind of experience entirely.
You had to leave the house, you went to a kind of communal place,
you saw a rather finished product. And movies of that era were incul-
cating a kind of Americanism, not of the official sort exactly, but it
certainly was a sense. . . . You know, when you saw Bogie stoically
shrugging his shoulders, there was a whole world there of what it was
to be an American: what was right and what was wrong. On television, you get this incessant fuzzy melange of little segments of
things, and I think it must breed in you a different set of expectations, of notions of what people should be doing.

I see nothing wrong with trying to sit in a room and turn out stuff
that will repay rereading. It makes something kind of solid, or at least
in its own terms hard to improve. I'm not sure I do it, but that's the
effort.

I can well imagine that from some standpoints it's a silly thing to do. Print is dying. Who, after all, has the time to read novels? A few people seem to. I don't have time, it isn't what I do.

Are there any things you feel so deeply for that you would abandon your novelist's stance for a Maileresque pose?

I'm sure there are—I don't think you quite know until you resist. Mailer himself is not much of a revolutionary. I somehow feel once you introduce the word, you find yourself backtreading or apologizing or something. The threats that have struck me, that have aroused some kind of gut feeling in me, have not been from the right but from the left—I don't know quite why this is, possibly I'm so remote from the right that I don't take them seriously at all. I do take people who run the *New York Review of Books* seriously. I find that their contempt for the democratic system is so pervasive and profound as to be death-dealing and menacing, really.

It expresses this everywhere, from the drawings up to the feelings that anybody who has power, who actually tries to make decisions involving the whole society, is *ergo* corrupt or insane. You get a kind of Calvinist sense of damnation connected with running the machinery. The machinery is going to be there, in any case—you can't revolutionize social machinery. It's a kind of wariness, a kind of unpleasability; a hopeless miasma arises from those pages.

It may be that intellectuals, the kind that get in there, are themselves power-seekers, narrow, angry about not having a kind of power. Certainly, a Cambridge party is political to a fault. It could be that the academic world is a microcosm that breathes into it a certain bias, which, when applied to the national scene, amounts to a negation of the way it's more or less worked for 190 years.

Certainly the *New York Review of Books* seems to me to have rather little time to give to fiction—it regards fiction both in the space it gives it and the kind of reviews it gets as a pretty silly branch of the written word. I think, of course, fiction *can* say more things—it can contain ambiguity and it can show issues mixed in with the flesh and blood.

I think novels should become a little more informational. We have less time to read them—they must dehydrate a little, they must draw a little closer to the textures of things like television, newspapers, magazines, so full of facts.

It's very important that all of us understand what's happening to us—what history is doing to us, in a way, very rapidly. We're not even accepting its being done. How should the novel respond to the changes in human nature and the kinds of things that happen? I think that in some funny way the novel traditionally has an ending: things end badly or happily; events have significance. Somehow we don't live like that now—our sense of irony is so complicated, so the very kinds of stories we tell have to be different. The kind of stories that Salinger wrote in the '50s are different than those written in the '30s.

Updikes Visit Black Africa: Strangers in a Strange Land?

Robert Waite/1973

From the *The Ipswich Chronicle*, 9 March 1973. Reprinted by permission of Robert Waite and North Shore Weeklies.

John Updike, suburban wordsmith, chronicler of upper middle class mores and the Piper Cub set, in Black Africa? It seems as unlikely as Eldridge Cleaver visiting mercantile Danvers.

Yet, with all the world to choose from under the terms of a fellowship grant, the 40-year-old Ipswich author and his wife, Mary, opted for such alien turf recently.

Freshly returned from the four-week journey, John and Mary Updike related their experiences with the kind of enthusiasm all travelers exude. But while most mortals rely on colored slides or home movies to prod the memory and convey impressions, Mr. Updike weaves his conversation into a tapestry of descriptive prose that makes such aid superfluous.

The decision to go to Black Africa was made for a number of reasons, according to the novelist.

"I had never been there—I've recently reviewed some African novels—I thought of it as a part of the world that had a different angle on things," said Mr. Updike, adding, "I am interested in the Black American and the relationship he has to Black Africa, and I was particularly interested in seeing an underdeveloped area that is not overpopulated."

The National Book Award winner was one of four Americans chosen by the Fulbright Board of Foreign Scholarships to occupy Lincoln Lectureship positions for the current year.

The other three men chosen to celebrate this, the 25th anniversary of the international scholarship program, were John Hope Franklin, historian from the University of Chicago, Economist Paul A. Samuelson of M.I.T., and Nobel Prize winning physics professor Charles H. Townes of the University of California at Berkley.

Each Lincoln lecturer was left free to structure his own program. They could travel, lecture, or reside wherever they wished during the current year under the terms of the lectureship.

John Updike chose Ghana, Nigeria, Tanzania, Kenya, and Ethiopia for his lecture series. This choice of nations may seem unusual for the couple—Mary freely admits they are considered "such WASPS"—but the Ipswich author had some firm reasons for going to these particular places.

"I wanted to go to Black Africa, to countries with English-speaking traditions. I got to view America from the Third World and obtained a tactile look at countries that had been just names," said Mr. Updike.

The writer was also interested in the contrasts to be found within Africa: "I found that each country had a unique character that set it apart from the rest."

He was fascinated by what he called "People born into the Stone Age trying to make it in the electronic age." He described meetings with writers "still decorated with the marks of tribal ritual, yet men of great intelligence and sophistication. The experience slightly enlarged my sense of human possibilities."

Mr. Updike conducted seminars and lectures in each of the countries. He told Black writers he believes Africa is finding "some answers to the art of living and that exciting things are happening in African literature."

At the University of Nairobi seminar in Kenya, for instance, Mr. Updike praised African artists for their "instinctive humanism." He added, however, that he had expected "more Africanness. A writer must reflect the temper of change's increasing tempo," he asserted, "or draw himself into oblivion."

In talking with aspiring African writers, Mr. Updike cautioned them to "begin small."

"I think many young writers are stifled by the height of their own ambition. To begin with the idea of writing a masterpiece is to intimidate oneself." Mr. Updike suggested to the assembled writers: "You should begin small and let the masterpiece happen to you."

Both Mary and John Updike commented that the trip was very structured. They also said public relations activities were an integral part of their function as visiting dignitaries.

Said Mary, "For the Foreign Service we were an excuse to throw a party, or an opportunity to get in the papers. When you are traveling as we were, you're a tool used by them and the U.S.I.S. (United States Information Service)."

Despite the official duties (the worst of which, if John Updike's tone of voice is any indication, was meeting with the wives of American Foreign Service officers), the writer was able to engage in discussions with a good number of African authors and university students.

Mr. Updike said the students were typical in some ways of students everywhere: "Students in all countries are turned on to the same kinds of radical revision of things. The Africans were no different," he remarked.

On a number of occasions the Updikes were warned they could expect hostility from at least some of the students at the universities, but what little hostility there was was directed in the form of questions to the Americans.

"Africans were very interested to find out what I believed was the purpose or the role of a writer in my society. They take a much more political view than we have traditionally," he said.

At one of the early lectures Mr. Updike had to field a hostile remark, charging that he was ignoring the black American writer in his talk. Mr. Updike told the man that although there is a difference in black and white writing in America, he also felt "we are all, in a sense, 10 percent Black in my country simply because that proportion of the population *is* Black and provides a shared experience." The answer didn't fully satisfy the questioner.

"You abandoned your set lecture after that," said Mary Updike to her husband in a light vein. He nodded in recognition of the fact.

As to the question of security in Black Africa, the Updikes related they had maintained a feeling of calm throughout the journey.

"The only time I was really concerned was when we were staying in Nairobi," recalled Mr. Updike. "We got into the hotel and on the walls in the room was a long list of warnings about dangers awaiting without. I must admit that did concern me for a time."

As it turned out, the Updikes found Ghana, the first nation they visited, to be the friendliest, and the people of Ghana to be "warm and winning." They are still "haunted by Nkrumah and saddled with his debts," according to Mr. Updike.

In Nigeria, the next stop on the lecture trail, Mr. Updike's visit provided the context for an historic meeting. The country is still attempting to heal the bitter wounds caused by the civil war of the 1960s—a civil war that made Biafra a household word synonymous with starvation for those living in Western nations. Writers from the two previously warring tribes, the Ibos and the Yorubas, gathered together for the first time since the civil war to hear Mr. Updike lecture on literature.

There was some concern about this, but things went well.

"The members of the two tribal groups chatted together, and often one would ask the other 'Where were you during the war?' and there seemed to be no problems," said Mr. Updike.

He described Nigeria as "probably very corruption-ridden and inefficient, but a bustling place now that the trauma of civil war is behind."

East Africa, on the other hand, was faced with some different problems, according to the writer.

"There is an immense Indian mercantile class and the Black governments are trying to deal with them," and "dealing with them," he explained, meant wholesale deportation in most cases.

Writers in Black Africa, whether from the East or West, face a profound literary crisis in their choice of language, according to Mr. Updike. With the exception of Ethiopia, all were colonized by the British, and English is the language used in their literature despite the fact it was the tongue of the white imperialists.

"Oftentimes English is the second language learned by African writers. At some point these artists have to decide whether or not to write in English. What they really must decide is whether or not they want to reach a Pan-African audience, which they can do through the use of English, or a very local audience. It's a problem that tears at the African writer," said Mr. Updike. He compared the situation with that in Ireland at the end of the 19th century.

"There was a movement to return to the native language, Gaelic, in Ireland, but look what people like Joyce and others were able to produce in English!" he said.

"Blacks in Africa have to ask themselves the question, 'Who are my literary ancestors, Joyce or tribal?' It is not an easy question. One Nigerian writer, Wole Soyinka, ended up leaving Africa and went to England because he felt more comfortable in doing so," said Mr. Updike.

Not all of the time the Updikes spent in Africa was spent in literary pursuits. At one point they were able to break away from the lecture circuit to go on safari in Kenya.

"It seemed a shame not to go on one after coming all that way," said Mr. Updike. The safari was strictly to take photographs, and the American couple saw some of East Africa's beautiful game reserves.

"The trip was good because it was a relief from speaking. The reserves have become very civilized, however. The lions seem to yawn in your face—I guess the carbon monoxide keeps them pretty groggy," said Mr. Updike with a chuckle.

They had few other opportunities to get out of the cities, and the journey into the hinterlands gave them one of the few glimpses of the stereotyped Africa conjured up in the minds of most Westerners.

For instance, the Updikes actually ran across people who believed that a camera picture steals their souls. The couple said they were careful to respect this belief.

Near Lagos they were given another taste of local customs when a friendly driver warned, "Don't stop if you hit someone with your automobile, for you will be in great danger of being stoned to death. It's tribal justice." Fortunately the Updikes did not have to appear before that particular tribunal.

Mary Updike, who somehow is reminiscent of the colonial woman painted with dark-hues and sharp angles by Puritan artists, but with none of the severity, spoke of the role of women in the African nations she and her husband had visited.

"I was impressed that an interest in women's rights was evident, to some extent, everywhere. In Ghana I was especially impressed with the strength of women in the marketplace and in the affairs of the nation. I couldn't see any need for women's lib in that country—women are already fulfilling their ambitions. They are a strong economic force. In East Africa there are more problems."

Her husband expanded on some of the "problems," and showed how they have become political and literary at the same time—a phenomenon repeated often in Africa.

"In one influential Kenyan novel, the author dealt with the subject
of clitorectomy, a common form of mutilation inflicted on females.
Clearly this kind of female castration indicates male chauvinism, and
the author was attempting to point out the horrors of such actions."
Mr. Updike said he, too, noticed the people were anxious to talk about
women's rights everywhere, but he also noted a sharp difference in the
various countries in the proportion of women writers.

Again, Ghana led the way, with East Africa lagging behind.

Mr. Updike found that he is not widely read in Black Africa—a fact
which he says neither surprises nor bothers him.

"I don't think they read much American fiction," he said, adding,
"Actually, I don't think of myself as being that read anyway," in Africa or America.

His last major travel experience, to Eastern Europe and the Soviet
Union, produced a work entitled *Bech: A Book*. Will this trip produce
something along the lines of "Bech Visits Africa"?

"I was thinking about the trip from a literary standpoint, but nothing really comes up—not like the Bech-Russian experience. Things
were just too structured. I had to worry about the lectures, about
American wives asking, 'What did you mean in *Couples*?' It was too
official a visit."

Did bringing his wife along on the African trip limit the literary
possibilities? Did Bech, who had traveled sans-mate in Eastern Europe, find a wife's presence constricting?

John Updike laughed and muttered something that sounded like no,
and Mary responded with a laugh genuine enough to keep the reporter
from becoming suicidal after realizing exactly how carried away with
the interview he had become.

The African trip is in many ways another chapter in John Updike's
traveling education, and he admits travel is important to his art.

"I do travel a good deal. It's a professional exercise for me in a
way," he said reflectively.

He rejected the notion that a writer in Essex County, in a small town
like Ipswich, is provincial.

"The media has made the whole provincial thing less valid. New
York, for instance, is much more insular than we are here," he said.

And so, back in the warmth of their Labor-in-Vain, Ipswich home, the writer and his wife return to the Route 128, town meeting, Liberty Tree Mall life we all hold in common. But, for two hours as they sat like bookends on their livingroom sofa, they were able to relate to their neighbors—through the media—some experiences that are now in some measure our own.

Interview with John Updike

Elinor Stout/1975

From "Interview with John Updike." *Sunday Pantechnicon*, WGBH-FM (Boston). Broadcast on 4 May 1975. Reprinted by permission of the WGBH Educational Foundation.

Q: Certainly your reviewers and critics are very adamant one way or another about John Updike's works—calling John Updike a fantastic American author, the great novelist of the century, and then there's one reviewer I read over the weekend who said that "John Updike's work is like a striptease. In each book he shows you some part of his talent. As you open one after another, you wonder: will he go all the way this time?" Do you feel you've gone all the way with your present book, *A Month of Sundays*?

A: I went all the way with that book. I wrote it as best I could, and it was a little different in its mode. I wrote it fairly rapidly and as a kind of exercise or dare to myself, and I thought it came out pretty well, considering. It's a book that gives me pleasure to contemplate in backwards vision. I hope I don't become known only as the author of *Rabbit, Run*, but it's an American fate to be known for one's early works. And the awful thing is that medical science keeps us all alive so long, so that I have many more books in me. I hope some of them would be as good and as happy as *Rabbit, Run* was.

Q: How do you know, John, when you have finished working sufficiently with characters? How do you know when to stop? You could keep on trimming and trimming, and introducing more and more characters. How do you decide?

A: Well, you begin with some sort of a shape in your head. The book isn't just characters only, it's also a kind of an action or a design or a plot, or whatever Aristotle and others want to call it. But somehow the book itself is a thing. It's an action that has a beginning and an end, and the characters are really secondary to that. In this case, I began with the title, so the book had to have 30 or 31 chapters, and I knew when I'd reached the end because I could count up to 31. The stream of the book is not so much a set of characters interplaying, but kind of a dream or an act of therapy in a man's mind as he writes. In a way, the characters come and go—this has been complained about— but to me the characters are as solid as the man's soliloquy will let them be.

Q: Do you decide on what kind of a statement you want to make in developing ideas for a novel, and then fit the characters in?

A: Hopefully you're not such a tyrant that the characters don't have some space in which to be themselves and to be slightly surprising, even to you. You do have, not so much perhaps a statement in mind, as some kind of dramatization of an issue. Everything has at least two sides. My books attempt to show the several sides of something, and leave the reader with the awareness of a difficulty, rather than with the grasping of a slogan or a motto to live by. In this particular book, one can question, Is it right for this minister to seduce his parishioners? Is his brand of Christianity the only kind left? I think, in my mind— speaking of statement—it really was written as a kind of critique of Barthian theology. I was raised as a Lutheran, and in my early twenties I read a lot of theology because I needed to. I was kind of despairing, or at least felt very hollow. Barth spoke to me as Tillich and Bultmann and the various liberals did not. This man [Marshfield] is a Barthian grown old. He has faith, but not much in the way of works. His works indeed add a curious, morally neutral quality to him. He's almost a witness of his life. I think many Americans are like that, though. We're witnesses of our lives, and surprised witnesses at that. I wanted to make the book kind of offensive and abrasive, and to show a life in a human being whose profession demands that he stand up at least on Sunday and try to give other people reason to keep on living.

Q: Your character at one point mentioned that when he was a child he was very stimulated by church, but the problem with religion was that it did not quench his thirst. Do you feel that way?

A: He, suffered, I think, an not untypical minister's child's syndrome of being put off by church and knowing it too well. I remember my own father, who was not a minister but was a very faithful deacon, regarded the church as a place where he was at home—so he'd chew gum and shuffle his shoes and wear pants that didn't match his coat and talk during the sermon and behave, in general, I thought, much too much at home. In even that exposure to church, you see the back-side of the pulpit and see that it has water glasses and electrical wiring and so forth.

Q: You mention the water in the book.

A: Yeah, I do. I was rather pleased with that bit. You begin a book not quite knowing what you know or what you don't know, and I was pleased to see myself evoke some sense of the church as, in part, a stage set, and it's perhaps all too contrived. Even the cathedrals some-times seem a little stagey to me, and his particular life had exposed Reverend Marshfield overmuch to the back of the stage set of the church. He found his religious faith, really, elsewhere in objects: in carpentry, in lovemaking, and in golf—a rather unusual syndrome or combination, but they all have a certain element of craftsmanship, and they all have a direct relationship with the material world. In each case, maybe, you're trying to make something fly or fit. Maybe it's the fittingness that spoke to him. A kind of pantheism, I suppose, is the germ of his belief.

Q: Religion certainly has been a common thread in your novels. Do you feel this playing more and more of a part in your own life, in your own thinking?

A: A touch less, I fear, and this particular book is, in some ways, anti-religious. Certainly his sermons verge upon, if not slop over into, blasphemy. I continue to be a professing Christian. I went to church on Easter—I hadn't been for a while—and I remembered suddenly what I liked about it. What I like about church is that the sermon gives me time to think about something else. I used to plan my whole week's work in church. *Couples* was written a week at a time, and these little inspirations would always come. I mean, in some way my mind was open to receive a certain creative energy. Marshfield's trouble, in a way, is that he *is* a believer, and to believe exposes us to all kinds of hopefulness. Hopefulness breeds energy, energy breeds mischief, mis-chief breeds, in his case, being sent away to a desert retreat to cool off.

Q: How did you happen to choose a desert retreat?

A: Well, of course, Christianity was nurtured in the desert. The Old Testament is very full of the desert, and you have a strong sense in the Bible, indeed, of the circumambient desert. In the first couple centuries of the Christian faith, monks were all in a hurry to get into the desert.

Being an easterner—born and always living in the American East—I took my four children at just the age before they would really resist such a "square" family expedition, and we packed into a rented car and drove from Albuquerque and visited a canyon a day. I really loved the West, and I think the book, in part, is an attempt to use some of those scenic impressions in a nice way. I love *A Month of Sundays* being in the desert. I don't know how authentic or keen the sense of its being in the desert is, but for Marshfield, as for me, it was kind of a revelation.

Q: I find it amazing how authors use recall without realizing that they are resorting to it. I was thinking about that when you mentioned behind the pulpit, the wires—is that something you saw as a child?

A: You know, I may never have seen it. I feel as though I've seen it now, because I've written about it, and when you write about something it does rather displace your own memories. One of the writer's many problems is that writing eats up his past almost faster than he's able to live a past. I think I must have, at some point, been aesthetically or morally offended by the fact that they had to put in wires for the sermon, because it seemed to me that if God were really on the job, he wouldn't make this kind of acoustical boost necessary. There's even something offensive, as Voltaire pointed out, about churches that fall down. If God is really behind these buildings, then at least he could ensure that during an earthquake they wouldn't collapse on the faithful.

Q: Another thread that runs through your novels is your evaluation of the American value system. One critic mentioned that you seem to reminisce a great deal, that you look back to the early 1900s and perhaps are disputing what the present-day value system is all about. Let's take marriage, for example. How would you look upon that now, in relation to how you saw it at the turn of the century?

A: I, of course, wasn't alive at the turn of the century, and have only storybook impressions of what life was really like. It does occur to me that my father's life witnessed more drastic changes than mine has; he really did see the era of the horse yield to the era of the gasoline engine, and what a shock and a transformation that was. Am I really nostalgic? For some reason, at the age of 20 I was keenly aware of having actually lived long enough to have a kind of past, so I wrote a great deal about my past as though maybe it was more significant than it was. Just as an observer of the American truth, I can perceive that this country has never been really at home with urban or urbane ideals. Its notions of virtue are all countryside notions. The country was founded in a kind of false pastoral mood. We, in our suburbs, each try to construct a little piece of outdoors for ourselves, with the barbecue pit and the quarter-acre of land. Land is terribly important to Americans, and there are things that go with the great European cities—manners, ease, and a variety of social intercourse—all that comes rather hard to Americans. So I just think it's a fact (my nostalgia aside) that we feel lost. Our cities are uglier than they need to be, our lives are harsher than they need to be, and we all, to some extent, are a kind of captive to an America that never was—the Indian being the chief symbol.

In my own life and observation, I did not really feel as pessimistic as you might think from my nostalgia. I think all this is true, that we're always venturing from a radiant past into a dark future, but I'm rather happy to be alive in the '70s. I think we do have an edge or two on our forebears—medical, for one. And something quite nice has happened to the American spirit in the last traumatic 10 or 12 years. It has been a time of trial. It began with Kennedy being shot, and one bubble after another has broken, but there's something very resilient and, to me, dear about the American temperament. I feel we'll do alright.

Q: I understand the feminists are after you, however, because of your portrayal of women in your books. Is that true?

A: Well, I have heard some such rumors, and if so, I'm deeply sorry. I can't think of any male American writer who takes women more seriously or has attempted more earnestly to show them as heroines. *Couples* was dominated by its women, afterall. If there were a male equivalent of the feminist movement, I would think I'd be more vulnerable to attack by them. Whatever I don't know about women I apologize for, and find, right now, actually, that I can only write fiction from the standpoint of women. I'm trying to do a long piece of a novel from a woman's point of view.

Q: That must be interesting.

A: I've done it before. I've written short stories from the female point of view. One does it a little gingerly, but I don't believe a writer should be scared off, by this and that political movement, from encom-

passing as much of humanity as he can. I think that women writers
have, with various success—sometimes amazing success—crossed over
into male minds. After all, both sexes are two-legged, mortal, fallible
creatures with, I think, much more in common than not.

Q: You mentioned *Couples*, and I remember a reviewer talking
about how he thought that *Couples* related to life and death. But *Time*
magazine felt that what you had said in *Couples* was so relevant that
they wrote a cover story on American morality. Was *Couples* about
morality?

A: It was certainly an attempt, maybe an all too deliberate and ambitious attempt, to show how estranged the slightly-above middle class
was in the '60s from all the institutions that had traditionally served as
some kind of inspiration. Politics to these couples is unreal. They can't
even stop having a party to honor the fact that their president was just
shot. Church is either a formal observance or nothing. Work has become a kind of boring toy for the men, so that they don't really have
anything except each other, except the games people play. The cover
story—I think *Time*, having blocked out that cover for me, then was
slightly embarrassed and had to run it. For one thing, the cover picture
showed my lower teeth as if they were my upper teeth, so I had a kind
of Draculan look that has haunted me ever since.

Q: Poor John. You have no control over that, do you?

A: I would have thought they could have gotten the right teeth as-
signed, but it might have been the way I was holding my mouth. I also
think that, although it was a big book physically, they thought "big
book, Updike, a funny name . . . might as well." And then they *read*
the book and discovered, I think, that, the higher up it went in the
Time hierarchy, the less they liked it. So the whole treatment of that
article was kind of a mess. I didn't think they said much about American morality or, indeed, the book. My observation about American
morality was that the introduction of the pill, and now whatever other
handy contraceptive device there is, has had an effect on sexual morality, and that the fading of the work ethic and of Protestant belief has
certainly changed our way of looking at things. These couples are a
little too late for any revolutionary or counterculture bandwagon. They
are just stuck with a kind of emptiness and with a lot of children who
they're raising more or less well-intentionedly, but sort of neglectfully.

Q: How much does criticism affect your attitudes toward your writing? I would think you'd have to develop a fairly hard shell after a while. Do you find that it still bothers you?

A: One would rather read a kindly review than an unkind one, and some things stick in the mind—especially those which confirm your own worst fears about yourself as a writer. On the other hand, with the creative act, once you're engaged at it, you can feel morose and resentful away from the typewriter, but when you get in front of the machine, the need to perpetrate an illusion, the need to conjure up characters, and the need to find the right word somehow restore you to yourself. And in the end, you can only be yourself. It's just like having your personality criticized at length. What, really, can you do about it? Not an awful lot, except try to become somebody you're not. A lot of the critics seem to me to be saying that they would have written a different book. Well, why don't they, and not ask me to write it? I'm trying to work out of my own baggage and my own slant, so by and large I've tried not to be too hurt. I have received a lot of unkind reviews, and I was interested in the unkind reviews of *A Month of Sundays*, of which there were a fair number—though I can't on the whole complain—how many of them now hark back to books that, at the time, weren't very well reviewed either? *The Poorhouse Fair*, my very first, seems to be emerging as the standard whereby all the others are judged deficient. And at the time it was thought a very quirky little book. So I guess it all kind of averages out. In the end, you're stuck with the fact that this is what you do for a living, and what else can you do? Robert Lowell, in one of the poems in *The Dolphin*, talks about a critic who was sent by God to chastize him, but he and I go on typing for the same reason: to go on living.

Q: Is Bech your author-hero?

A: Bech is my author-hero. His experiences tend to be somewhat mine—at least he goes to the same places I do—but he himself is pretty different. He is nine years older than I, he is Jewish instead of being Protestant, he is unmarried and childless, whereas I am the father of four children, husband of one wife. And so I tried to set up a lot of differences so I could get some distance. I think it's important to distance your characters, especially the novel-length ones. They must be enough unlike you so that it's kind of fun to pretend to be them. And it *was* fun for me to pretend to be Henry Bech. By now the device has worn a little thin. I've tried some post-*Bech: A Book* stories, and he is so tired, he's even more tired than I am. Tired of travel, tired of being Henry Bech. But those first stories did open, somehow, a door in me that hadn't opened before, and I find the prose—if I must say so—quite charming and lively and on the mark.

Q: You talk about his distaste for literary fame, in a way, because his life is no longer private—and how he retreats into silence and privacy. You also have a reputation for maintaining a low profile.

A: Low*ish*, and getting higher every minute we're on the air. I think that the American educational system is now set up so there's a tremendous interest in writers and writing. Creative writing is taught as a course in many a college, and so if you get any kind of a name going, you become an object of interest, like something in the Mardi Gras parade, a sort of float that can be dragged in front of the kids, and you sort of wave your arms and roll your glass eyes and things come out of your mouth. And it seems quite possible to get bewitched by this, so that you lose all sense of the privacy and the *urgency* of writing. The terrible importance of trying to do it well is something that shouldn't be ruined through overexposure. It's one thing to sit here and say that, but it's another thing to live it, really. Hemingway was a writer who was truly, to some extent, destroyed by his own persona and his own huge name, as well as by his own private lust for alcoholic fun.

Q: Are you a disciplined writer? Do you make yourself sit down and write a certain amount of hours per day?

A: I try to do it more by pages than hours. In other words, if I can have a quick day, then I can give myself a treat. But I work every morning and try to produce three or so pages of something. I also seem to be a reviewer in my dotage, and so I can read books to review at night. Really, there's never an idle moment. It's an odd truth that my life is terribly busy while seeming rather languid.

Q: How long did you work for *The New Yorker*?

A: I was in the offices only about two years, as a "Talk of the Town" reporter, and inhabited those halls which Brendan Gill has now made famous in his book on *The New Yorker*. I did a lot of "Talk" stories and did enjoy doing them, but after a while it seemed to me I'd done enough, and I tried moving up to New England to write only fiction and poetry. And if I couldn't make it, then I'd go back to New York.

Q: Is it hard to get feedback when you're so far removed? Do you find isolation bothersome sometimes?

A: A touch, but also a touch encouraging. The trouble with New York is that it gives you too much feedback. I mean, you have men trying to take you out to lunch all the time to talk about some deal, and it's all kind of fun and fascinating and it's nice to eat in a decent restaurant free, but it doesn't help you advance your own artistic cause an inch. Indeed, it's counterproductive. I wouldn't say that life in Ipswich has been totally isolated. I think life in New York, where you're sort of apartment-bound, and bound into a clique of like-minded fellow workers, is perhaps more confining.

You *do* like feedback, or I find *I* need quite a lot of feedback. I admire someone like Pynchon who's able to devote years to one book. It's fun to have short stories and things appear, to deal with the proofs, to get a check in the mail and all that. I try to mix it up, so that a long project is followed by a number of shorter things.

Q: Was *Rabbit, Run* a novel that you particularly enjoyed working on? You certainly got marvelous reviews on that.

A: In retrospect, I get great reviews, yes. Like *The Poorhouse Fair*, it seems to get better all the time. At the time, I got the usual mixed reception. I did like it. I won a Guggenheim, I was fairly young, and it was a bit of a venture for me to block off that much time to a non-profitmaking job. I wrote it roughly in a year, maybe a little less. I enjoyed writing it, feeling it grow. It was my first full-length book.

Q: How about more plays? You've written *Buchanan Dying*.

A: So I did.

Q: You're sort of wincing. You're not happy with that?

A: Well, it is indeed in play form, and I felt that it was the only way that I could deliver that particular material which I had accumulated. I'm not dissatisfied with it as a book; as a play, it certainly is twice as long as it should be, and perhaps impossibly pedantic and static. A Lancaster group is trying to put it on now. I've always steered clear of the cooperative arts as being time-wasting and bewitching and, in general, distracting. I don't have much romantic feeling for the stage. The few times I've seen my words spoken have somehow made them seem worse than they looked on paper. My favorite theater is the lap of a good reader. It's a kind of cowardice on my part. I may try another play sometime, but I don't have any plans at the moment.

Q: How often do you work on poetry, John?

A: Not often enough to suit me. It's something you do at odd mo-

ments. Writing in airplanes is a great poetry-writing time. I haven't
done much lately, would like to do more. I write about a poem a
month, I'd say.

Q: Do you? I mean, you send a lot of them to *The New Yorker*.

A: And they send a lot of them back, too. But yeah, I do try to
keep that side of myself alive.

Q: In *Midpoint*, it was mentioned that you had considered this the
beginning of the second part of your career. And I was really curious
about that.

A: I think I just meant that I'd reached 35, which is half of our al-
lotted Biblical span, and rather presumptuously wrote the story of my
life in a variety of poetic forms. I hope it was somewhat earlier than
the middle of my career, since my career began at 20 . . . but no, I
thought it was a good moment, maybe, to look around and take the
holiday of writing this long poem.

Q: Did you start writing when you were at Harvard?

A: More or less. I was writing before. My mother was a would-be
writer. We had a typewriter in the house and I could perceive her
struggling. I did a lot of work for my high-school newspaper and was
a cartoonist and wrote for the Harvard *Lampoon*. I just slowly got to
writing prose. I took a couple of writing courses and tried to figure out
how to write short stories, and was fortunate enough to have *The New
Yorker*, rather early after I had gotten out of college, take a story or
two. But I still feel a little puzzled by fiction—that is, what it should
be doing, and what it is indeed, which may make all of my books a
little different from each other. Every one is something of an experiment.

Q: Do you feel you've explored all dimensions now?

A: Far from it. I feel that the gap between reality, on the one hand,
and the novel, on the other, is still excitingly large and waiting to be
closed. And it's not a gap that will be closed permanently by anybody,
because the quality of life keeps changing and the way we look at
things keeps changing. Formally, my interest in the novel is quite
keen, and I'm excited at the idea of making another book. My people
tend, a touch, to be doing the same things, and I've had so many
he/she conversations already that I'm not sure I've too many more in
me to write. You have to bring a kind of excitement to any artistic endeavor for the excitement to get out.

Interview with John Updike

Jeff Campbell/1976

From an appendix to *Updike's Novels: Thorns Spell a Word.*
Wichita Falls, Texas: Midwestern State Univ. Press, 1987, 277–
304. Conducted at Georgetown (Mass.) on 9 August 1976.

Campbell: How important do you see the epigraphs as suggesting the meanings or the shapes of the novels?

Updike: Quite important, really, and I've read very few reviews or critical articles that seem to me to take the clues that the epigraphs meant to offer. I tend to discover the epigraphs at some point in the work in progress. I don't think a book has to have an epigraph. In fact, maybe it's a little fussy for a book to have an epigraph—*War and Peace* doesn't have one, and so on—a book should be its own. On the other hand, I've enjoyed other people's epigraphs, and if I find a quote that seems to me to hit it, as a sort of mystical offering given to me, I use it. *The Poorhouse Fair* uses the rather specially worded quote from Luke. [*If they do this when the wood is green, what will happen when the wood is dry?*—Luke 23:31, E.V. Rieu trans.] I meant, if they do this when the wood is green—that is, now—what will happen when the wood is dry— that is, in the future? And there's a good deal of wood imagery, carpentry imagery, in the book, and a sense of dryness—of the old people being dried up. I guess that's a fairly straightforward epigraph, really. . . .

Campbell: Since those words were spoken by Jesus as he was going to the crucifixion, I wondered if there was any indication here that maybe Conner was some sort of Christ-figure or false Christ.

Updike: Certainly the book is a very consciously Christian one. I was twenty-five and very intellectually concerned. I wouldn't have been reading this modern translation of the New Testament if I weren't. I didn't know, in fact, until you said so, that the words were spoken by Jesus on the way to being crucified. I saw Conner as some kind of pseudomartyr—a martyr of a new religion, really a materialist or social-humanist martyr, not so much as a Christ-figure. Throughout, I was consciously dealing with a period analagous to the early Christian period, that is, a time when the established religion was crumbling and something new was trying to be born and meeting resistance. The book was written by a young man who saw the time he was living in—the Eisenhower years—as a dry period, certainly a dry period for the established church.

And the next epigraph [for *Rabbit, Run*] was from Pascal, as I remember it. [*The motions of Grace; the hardness of heart; external circumstances*—Pascal, Pensée 507] I took the quote as I found it, and it's just, of course, a jotting. Obviously Pascal meant to elaborate it if he ever wrote the full work that the *Pensées* were meant to be. I think what struck me was that those three things describe, in a way, our lives. The external circumstances are everywhere, in this case the pregnancy and family responsibilities and financial necessities. The motions of grace represent that within us which seeks the good, our non-material, non-external side. And the hardness of heart? Clearly Rabbit shows hardness of heart, and there's a way in which hardness of heart and the motions of grace are intertwined. I was struck as a child, and continue to be struck, by the hardness of heart that Jesus shows now and then in the New Testament, advising people to leave their families, driving the money-lenders out of the temple in quite a fierce way. And I think there seems to be an extent to which hardness of heart is tied in with being alive at all. But, in a way, the epigraph in its darting, fragmentary, zigzaggy form fits the book, which also has a kind of zigzaggy shape, settles on no fixed point. . .

Campbell: You said when you found the other one in Luke you were reading the Bible. Does this indicate that you were also reading Pascal? Do you find yourself in harmony with his basically Jansenist position?

Updike: I first read Pascal in my twenties and was attracted to his particular line of Christian thought, which I take roughly to be the Augustine-Pascal-Kierkegaard-whatever line. This is the one that seems to me to address my plight more than the Thomist—although I did read some St. Tom, too! Yes, I think I clearly am attracted to Pascal, but I confess I never have read him through; I just sort of dart around in it. I happened upon this, and this particular quote seems very apropos.

Campbell: In *The Centaur* the epigraph is from Barth, a rather typical quotation. [*Heaven is the creation inconceivable to man, earth the*

creation conceivable to him. He himself is the creature on the bound-
ary between heaven and earth—Karl Barth]

Updike: Again, I think I came upon the quote while working on the
book and was unable to resist it because it did say so tersely and definitely that we're all on a boundary and all are centaurs. It made the
book typographically a little unclean since I already in a sense had a
long epigraph, the actual Greek story. But, unlike the others, it was
tucked in with the title page, and I think it looks quite well there. The
book's texture is sort of lumpy, anyway, so it could take one more little bubble on it.

Campbell: The epigraph of *Of the Farm* is Sartrean. [*Consequently,
when, in all honesty, I've recognized that man is a being in whom existence precedes essence, that he is a free being who, in various circumstances, can want only his freedom, I have at the same time
recognized that I can want only the freedom of others.*—Sartre] Is it
possible that the epigraphs might sometimes be ironic? It seems to me
that freedom is exactly what Joey and his mother and Peggy, all three,
don't want—either for themselves or for each other.

Updike: As you know, a critic is entitled to his own reading, and in
a way a book is mysterious to the writer. My conscious intention was
to say that if you love someone you want them to have what they
want. Joey and his mother forgive each other and there's some kind of
double blessing bestowed at the end. The book may not really work
that way; sometimes the pattern you think you've created doesn't connect. It's true that none of the four people are utterly free.

Campbell: It seems to me that Joey does not want to be totally free
of his mother; she does not want to be free of him, nor does she want
him to be free of her. They each want a kind of community.

Updike: You're right, and the book is, in a way, about community—
about social interaction.

Campbell: In *Couples* the first epigraph is from Tillich. [*There is a
tendency in the average citizen, even if he has a high standing in his
profession, to consider the decisions relating to the life of the society
to which he belongs as a matter of fate on which he has no influence—like the Roman subjects all over the world in the period of the
Roman empire, a mood favorable for the resurgence of religion but
unfavorable for the preservation of a living democracy.*—Paul Tillich,
The Future of Religions] The parallel decay of our own time and the

Roman empire seems obvious, but I wonder if there may not also be
an ironic putdown of Tillich. This was a mood, he says, favorable to
the resurgence of religion. But what kind of religion is favored for resurgence in *Couples*? It doesn't seem to be primitive Christianity. . . .

Updike: No, again it's as in *The Poorhouse Fair*. It's the idea of an
unchristian religion emerging, a religion of human interplay including
sexual interplay. To some extent, in the years since I've written *Couples*, that has happened. There are more formalized ways now of getting together, of touching—T-groups, and so on—and all this is
foreshadowed in the book. The generation after mine seems to be attempting to find religious values in each other, rather than in looking
toward any supernatural or transcendental entity. These epigraphs were
meant to be in themselves interesting—I thought Tillich's remark was
quite interesting. It's linked with a little Blok quatrain—Alexander
Blok. [*We love the flesh: its taste, its tones,/Its charnel odor, breathed
through Death's jaws. . . ./Are we to blame if your fragile bones/
Should crack beneath our heavy, gentle paws?*—Alexander Blok, "The
Scythians"] This, I think, is the first set of epigraphs that appears on a
dedication page. It was to my then wife Mary, whose father was a
Unitarian minister and a great Tillichite. We had just come back from
Russia, and quoting a Russian poet was meant to be a sort of personal touch. I guess, though, the main thing was the sense of sex as
something brutal, crushing, barbaric even. It's sort of hardness of
heart again, isn't it?

Campbell: In *Rabbit Redux* there are four epigraphs, one at the beginning of each section. The first is from a Russian cosmonaut, the
next one from an American astronaut. Then the next one's Russian,
and the last one's American. Does this suggest that the problems dealt
with, which in one sense seem intimate and domestic and personal
and noncosmic, are, in fact, the same sorts of issues that affect international relations and world affairs?

Updike: Sure, there's some attempt in these epigraphs to remind
the reader that these domestic events are occurring simultaneously
with this unparalleled venture into space and that it wasn't just Americans that did it. I think the first quote, which I've forgotten, was the
crucial one—the one that I'd intended to use alone.

Campbell: "It took me quite a while to find you, but now I've got
you."

Updike: Yes. But as I went through the literature of what the first cosmonauts and astonauts said, I found a couple of others that seemed too good to leave out, and then I especially love Armstrong saying that it's kind of different out here but pretty. This seemed to be a much more natural remark than the first words he had prepared—much less stilted.

Rabbit's adventures in this book are a kind of launching free of the very terrestrial world of Pop and Mom and Janice to a kind of no man's land. In some way I felt the little ranch house to be a space capsule spinning in space, and the reunion with Janice—even their bodily jockeyings were meant to be a kind of jockeying in space, like these linkups. I guess that's obvious, although not everybody seemed to know it—to notice it. So in some way the whole thing, the whole fantasy of the book—and the book is a touch fantastic—is related to the true fantasy of our space invasion.

The men, of course, are very much just men, aren't they? Even though they're way out there. The things they said were so mundane; I kind of like that—like that quality. The Russians as much as the Americans, actually, were very informal. Of course, they're all pilots, and I suppose that being a pilot in some ways trains you to tame the unusual.

Campbell: In *A Month of Sundays* the first epigraph is from the Forty-fifth Psalm—"my tongue is the pen of a ready writer." The second is from Tillich: "The principle of soul, universally and individually, is the principle of ambiguity."

How important, if important at all, is the balance of the Forty-fifth Psalm? Are you conscious of the rest of that psalm?

Updike: I doubt if I am, although I'm sure I read the whole psalm through when I picked the quote. What is the psalm about?

Campbell: Well, it's a marriage celebration. The poet opens with the affirmation that his tongue is like the pen of a ready writer or scribe, and then he goes on to sing the glories of his king and his new bride, and there's at least some fairly logical evidence that maybe this psalm was composed for the marriage of Ahab and Jezebel.

Updike: Really?

Campbell: Another possiblity would be Solomon and Pharaoh's daughter, or it could have been post-exilic. Certainly it was left in the Psalms because it was allegorized to be the Messiah and Israel, and of

course later Jesus and the Church. It is also very fitting—the totality
of the psalm to what happens in the book.

Updike: It's not bad, not bad, but I'm not sure if I can claim much
credit for it. I was aware of the psalm being one of praise and celebration—indeed, almost all the psalms are—and to that extent I liked it.

These two quotes appear on the same page as the dedication to
Judith Jones, who is my editor at Knopf. The first is a little joke on
me: I've often been accused of being much too ready a writer, and
Marshfield is himself, of course, in the book a very ready writer. I
think the book is somewhat ambiguous, even more than the others, and
maybe to some extent Tillich's remark made sense of the ambiguity; I
think I came upon it later and couldn't resist appending it in the hope
that it would somehow be helpful. I like the idea of the principle of
soul being ambiguity; it's a very neo-Platonic, I suppose, notion.

Campbell: You've said several times that as you begin a novel you
frequently have some certain shape in mind. *The Poorhouse Fair* is
variously a gladiola or fireworks that shoot up and spread out, *Rabbit,
Run* is zigzags or Z's, *The Centaur* is a sandwich, *Of the Farm* an X.
How about *Couples*?

Updike: I think I'm maybe running out of shapes! I've forgotten in
what interview I produced all those images. It is true that with every
book I do begin with some image. Herbert Reed coined or used the
word "haptic," trying to differentiate the pleasure that sculpture
gives—some sense of its *seizability*, of its mass. I have to have that
even before I begin a book. But now you've asked about *Couples*—
what was the shape of *Couples*? The shape is the turn that occurs between the first and last paragraphs, even the first and last sentences,
where the Hanemas become a different pair of people. In other words, a
couple changes—one couple replaces another. Other than that I'm not
sure that I can offer a shape.

When I think back over the shape of the book, what I remember is
the second chapter, "Applesmiths and Other Games," in which I was
trying to show the ground—the kind of social terrain—that these
events were occurring in. Although it seemed to some to be a long and
unnecessary flashback, to me it was necessary. It was important also
that this is a coupling that occurs within the social network and does
not harm it. It may harm the people in it, but the couples—the group—
remain intact. Then in Piet and Foxy I meant to show that one couple

does in fact break out. And they are socially unacceptable. Piet is snubbed at the end in a way he never was in his previous phase. It's no accident that the book is in five chapters, as seems to be a distinctive thing for me. I saw each one as steps, in a way. The turn, the revolution, that turns Piet and Angela into Piet and Foxy was the shape.

Campbell: Did you have a specific shape in mind for *Rabbit Redux*?

Updike: I doubt it. I think I've somewhere committed myself to writing four books about this man. *Rabbit Redux* paired up, deliberately, but also happily, with *Rabbit, Run* so nicely that in a way they look at each other—they seem to me to make almost a set. I do think he's learned something. I think that he shows—especially in the second book—the American quality of openness; he is, in a sense, unprejudiced. He is willing to entertain these outlanders in his house. I'd like then to write a sequel showing that he did learn something.

Campbell: One of the recurrent criticisms of your work is that you avoid violence.

Updike: I am aware of this complaint and I detect in myself a wish not to have *false* violence. It's terribly easy when you're sitting at a typewriter, of course, to kill and maim and produce explosions. I think that Mailer's an example of a good writer who nevertheless has much too easy access to violence, so that the violence becomes hysterical, impersonal. I've led a rather quiet life—I think most men would prefer to lead quiet lives if they can. I really haven't witnessed much violence. The incident of the house burning down was based on something that actually happened in the particular section of Pennsylvania that I come from, and it impressed me as a piece of authentic social violence. A black and white couple were living in a house and the neighbors burnt the house down—somebody burnt the house down. This piece of violence did fall within my ken, and I tried to use it.

There is a way in which the television set invades the guy's life. That is, these are sort of headline figures who come upon him, and I think it was true of a lot of us in the late sixties that all the things we preferred not to think about became unavoidable. So in a way he is the middle-class man whose living room becomes the scene of atrocities and teach-ins and all those things. I wrote the book rather rapidly. I was trying to work on the long Buchanan thing at the time, and I've kind of forgotten the composition of *Rabbit Redux* except that as I was witnessing these events as they unfolded, they seemed real enough to me. I was trying to let out my own anxieties and doubts, puzzlement over the issues that are raised.

Campbell: Let's go on to *A Month of Sundays*. I was struck here with the possibility of a circle, particularly since we start off with a motel in omega shape and of course he stays a month, which is, in a sense, a circle—the circle of the moon. But I'm not satisfied with a circle because I don't think he returns the same as he left, and here I will just have to put in a little Barth, who insists that history is real— there's not a meaningless cycle, but a purposeful movement. So I don't know—I think circle and then I say no it can't be a circle—maybe a spiral.

Updike: I guess I agree with Barth, if I understand you right, in that nothing is ever the same twice, and that the stream—what does Heraclitus say? We never put our foot in the same stream twice. Marshfield goes to the motel; it is a kind of end point. He is pretty thoroughly disgraced and out of it and yet still obstinately alive, kind of the way Beckett characters are. They are reduced to nothing yet keep talking and refuse to be crushed or dismissed. Of course it is true the motel is a self-enclosed bubble and Marshfield does return and possibly to much the same. . . . Well, I doubt it; I don't think he will repeat those exact same adventures. I meant to show a pattern of ab-sence. That is, when one is violently taken out of one's milieu, it slowly fades. I meant the month to show that the surroundings in the end eclipse the memories of what he's left, so that at about chapter twenty Frankie and Alicia and all those other people fade, and he tries to look at the people around him. I'm not sure it worked, but that was the idea, that Ms. Prynne and his fellow guests come forward and oc-cupy his mind and in some sense refresh him. It's sort of a vacation that's being described. He brings to the desert this mass of emotion and memory and humiliation and so on, and it finally runs dry and the sun keeps coming up on a different kind of terrain.

Campbell: What relationship do you see between painting and fic-tion? Have you consciously attempted to apply any principles or theo-ries of visual art to your writing?

Updike: In some sense I, of course, do see a book as having a tone before you set out and a certain shape and texture. In *Rabbit, Run* the present tense and so on is very different from the kind of very cali-brated prose of *The Poorhouse Fair*. I am a sort of frustrated painter, or rather I have painted a bit and was told I have a very good sense of composition. So maybe I see the book as a canvas with things disposed in it. Of course, as you write it turns out that things that you thought would take twenty pages somehow dismiss themselves in one and other things blossom, so it's not quite as spatial as that. I came to writing a little sideways. My initial talents and ambitions were all in the pictorial/graphic way. My mother took a writing course from a man called Thomas H. Uzzell, who operated out of Texas, I think, somewhere. He would analyze various classics in terms of plots so that you saw the plot as a set of directions, and I don't scorn this; I think that when all is said and done some impetus, some direction, some tension or conflict, must be set up. In other words, some movement along a linear path happens, and to some extent a plot can be broken down into this kind of diagram. Detail is bearable only if you feel it's strung or bestowed on some kind of general seizable form; otherwise it becomes suffocating and you're lost in it. I really feel I can only add detail when I know where I'm going and feel the reader is with me—I mean when he cares and has a sense of being taken somewhere.

Campbell: Do you keep up pretty generally with what seem to be at least relatively serious attempts to evaluate or interpret your work?

Updike: It's hard to get a book about yourself that you can ignore entirely. Of course one is interested. In general, that kind of scrutiny is a little painful and a touch unreal for some reason, so I don't think I've really read any of the books through. I've looked at all of them and I'm glad that some man or woman has thought enough of me to want to devote the year or more, or whatever it takes, but I've not read them thoroughly because I just don't think that you can steer your own ship by those stars.

Campbell: Have you found any that you looked at that you find most acceptable or congenial; and have you found any that you think are serious misreadings?

Updike: I do think that the Hamiltons, who I think were almost the first into the field, are wonderfully careful readers, and they're always dredging up puns I didn't know I made, and connections that I wasn't conscious of. Also, they take me seriously as a sort of theological or at least religious thinker. And it's true there's a kind of germ of philosophical or moral or even supernatural inquiry in my stuff. On the other hand, they tend to enlist me in their own Sunday school a little too quickly and efficiently, so that in some cases where I meant to raise a question they take it that I provided an answer. I remember reading Joyce Markle's book feeling that she was more with it than some others. Alfred Kazin has some pages on me in his sort of survey of the contemporary novel that seem to me to be nice and—nice means what? He likes you? I think I mean that he seems to be able to read the books.

Campbell: How would you respond to David Galloway's concept that your protagonists are examples of the absurd man as saint, particularly George Caldwell and Rabbit?

Updike: I do see them as absurd in the sense that they live in a world with no unavoidable values. In other words, they are adrift and they have to make up their own. Rabbit I would not call a saint. I meant him to be a kind of you and me, or a sort of Everyman. George Caldwell I do see as exceptional in his altruism, but in a way I'm questioning him as a saint, also. In some ways he's an unbearable man: embarrassing to his son, annoying to his wife, and there's an antic mischievous something. But yes, he'd be my candidate for saint-hood—if I had one.

The question of sainthood is an interesting one. We *are* interested in saints, and I notice that in the novels my heroes are all males and they all seem to be in some quandary. They're all uncomfortable in this world to a degree, which then suggests that there's another world where they'd be more comfortable; but they're a far cry from saints. The God that they speak of and the God that they search for has some of the hardheartedness that is in the Pascal. He's God of the earth-quake, of the volcano, as much as of the flowers.

Campbell: Robert Detweiler has a phrase he uses over and over again. He calls your style and approach "secular baroque."

Updike: Secular baroque? I think I *am* a secular man in the end. And the baroque, yes, I suppose. Classicism, I suppose, suggests a certitude of the kind that I don't seem, as a writer, to have—clear meanings, definite presumptions; I seem to write always in the hope of turning up the truth around the corner somehow, of finding a secret truth, hitherto hidden, that just needed greater and more intense groping.

Campbell: Michael Novak suggests that your sensibility is specifically Christian, an alert, open, human, sensual Calvinism, almost wholly Platonic, with a radical dualism that makes myth and symbolism necessary tools. He says it is difficult for the Jewish sensibility or the hard pragmatic secular sensibility of our critical establishment to understand this world-view. Do you see your sensibility as specifically Christian?

Updike: I think so. I think Christianity is the only world-frame that I've been exposed to that I can actually look through.

Campbell: Novak suggests that one has to accept this world-view in order to understand what's going on in your work. He says Calvinism, but from my point of view I see you as much more Lutheran than Calvinist. Does that distinction make any sense to you?

Updike: It makes a lot of sense to me and I agree with you. I was raised as a Lutheran. Now to an extent all Protestant churches would look alike to a Catholic like Novak. I can't claim to have had a Lutheran upbringing in the rigorous way that Ingmar Bergman, maybe, did. In the county I was from, the Lutheran and Reformed churches existed on the same block, but they were distinctly different churches. The Calvinist church just gives off a different vibe. I do think that in some way the personalities and fundamental emphases of the two great founders show through still. Lutheranism is comparatively world-accepting; it's a little closer to Catholicism than Calvinism. I don't feel much affinity with the New England Puritan ethos insofar as it still persists. No, I would call myself a Lutheran by upbringing, and my work contains some of the ambiguities of the Lutheran position, which would have a certain radical otherworldly emphasis and yet an odd retention of a lot of Catholic forms and a rather rich ambivalence toward the world itself. That is, Luther's feelings about the devil and the world are quite interesting to me. He seems to greatly admire, to adore, the devil.

Campbell: I was struck with Marshfield's one great religious experience, which seems to me very Lutheran—certainly you must have had Luther in mind. When Marshfield calls himself a cheerful sinner, I see Luther's "sin boldly" and Luther's "freedom in Christ" much more than what I associate with Calvinism.

Updike: Quite so. And very few of my critics have been by their own conditioning equipped to make the references you just have, to look to some of Luther's memorable sayings which do add up in the books, especially in this one.

Campbell: All right, if there is a valid distinction between Lutheran and Calvinist, what would be some of the distinctions between a Catholic sensibility and a Protestant sensibility?

Updike: Trying to think with you on this, certainly there is a very clear difference. What strikes me when I think about Flannery O'Connor and Graham Greene is how far they are willing to go in presenting a suffering, apparently Godless world. That is, the very scorchingness with which God is *not* there is something that I don't feel in my own work. It amazes me. In other words, there's something kind of Jansenist—I was going to say Calvinist—in both of these writers. I think there may be a Protestant emphasis on the individual conscience and on attempting to locate a consecrated or a graceful inner state of mind that perhaps is not necessary for these Catholic writers. My heroes, at least, are all struggling for some kind of inner certitude, illumination, or something.

Campbell: Are there any contemporary writers that you think do express the Protestant sensibility?

Updike: Living . . . my own generation has been dominated so much by Jewish writers. . . . I'm trying to think. . . . There were sections of *Nat Turner* in which Styron, it seemed to me, was convincingly evangelical. I was moved by some of Nat Turner's earlier meditations on God, but. . . . You do feel something in Faulkner, certainly, that's Protestant. . . No, I can't think of too many, off hand. Most Protestants who come to writing have pretty thoroughly put it behind them, I guess.

Campbell: Would you accept Novak's dictum that you are Platonic and dualistic, or one of them if not both?

Updike: Yes, if I understand the words, I would. I don't *mean* to be dualistic, but there is a way in which I see things as mind or spirit on the one hand and body on the other. It's more a gut way of looking at things than any sort of intellectualized position. I think Novak, by the way, is one of the better people who have written about me. I'm grateful for the seriousness with which he takes me, and he seems to be able to deal with the Christian matter of the early stuff, the early stories, very well.

Campbell: In reading *The Poorhouse Fair*, I couldn't help thinking what Flannery O'Connor might have done with the mock stoning scene. Why do you seem to deliberately avoid the dramatic moments that are typical of her work?

Updike: I guess my experience fits *The Poorhouse Fair* that I wrote. That is, most pebbles don't brain us and most troubles are non-drastic.

Campbell: Novak cites the centrality of myth and symbol in your work. Certainly your concern with myth and symbol is obvious in the first three novels, and quite overt in *The Centaur*. Would you comment on the importance of myth in *The Centaur*?

Updike: I guess the mythological references mean to show that everybody, the existence of any person, any thing, is in some way magical and highly charged, and rather strange—and gaudy. There's a gaudiness about life that means you almost have to produce an extra effect, you have to bring up fiction to the gaudiness of actuality. Something *extra* has to happen. It might be the verbal play, or these myths. From the standpoint of an adolescent boy who hasn't been anywhere else, all of these ordinary or less than ordinary people are very large and significant. That is, you live the rest of your life with the categories that you build up in these early years.

I think what attracted me to the Chiron legend is the notion, rather rare in Greek mythology, of the centaur sacrificing himself for somebody else. It is true that his life had become unbearable to him in a way that the life of Christ or any Christian martyr had not. In other words, it became a convenient thing to do—it's almost a thrifty thing to do, to give up a life that's become sheer pain and at the same time bail somebody else out. I'm no ancient Greek, and I'm not even a student of these stories. I still would not have written the book without the myths. They are important to me and I think give the book its proper tone of eccentricity, or surprisingness—the sense that everybody comes to us in guises. I think I've used myth less since. There was something in *Couples* almost centaurlike in the texture, without the allusions being so specific.

Campbell: Barth doesn't have much use for myth. He says myth deals with the timeless reality, while the Christian creation story cannot be a myth because it affirms the objective reality of life.

Updike: I think I know what he's saying, and I think there is a limitation. He's saying that the concrete historical reality of Jesus is better

than any myth. Myth is part of the cyclical, Asiatic religiosity, and has
nothing to do with the real thing. Barth is very absolute, very tough
on this point, as I guess logically he must be. In a way it's a little like
what evangelists in this country talk about, about the concrete experience of Jesus—again it's something definite, you know, like a hic-
cough or a shoelace. I mean it's something very real: it's not other
things disguised as—it's not a flavor of other things—it is a *thing*.
Lacking, I think, this kind of concrete experience, I'm not so willing
to dismiss myth as Barth is. But basically I'm with him, not so much
religiously as for a way of viewing reality: you have to take a thing seriously as itself.

Campbell: Could I say, then, that the point of *The Centaur* is not
that George Caldwell is Chiron all over again, but that there is a kind
of universality or unity, a continuingness about life. . .

Updike: And in fathers—fathers and sons. In a way, every father
lays down his life—well, not every, but many—for the son. Or the
child. Parents and children. The Greek mythology is probably appropriate to this particular "schoolish" novel, because really Greek myths
are things we learn in school. They're not imbibed, not even in a landscape; they're just something we learn.

Campbell: You have stressed the "yes—but" quality of your work,
and ambiguity does seem to be a recurrent emphasis. How would you
compare "yes—but" as you see it to the Kierkegaardian "either/or"
imperative?

Updike: Both the "yes—but" and the "either/or" imply there are
two sides to things, don't they? So to that extent it is Kierkegaardian,
and no sooner do you look at one side than you see the other
again. . .

Campbell: And this also would fit with Barth's "God says yes and
God says no." And perhaps not fit quite so comfortably with Tillich's
"both/and."

Updike: Not so comfortably. Even though I recognize Tillich as a
kind of wonderful spirit, and he does have these flashes, I find his
overall attempt to have it several ways basically impossible. It occurs
to me that Kierkegaard and I might be tedious in the same way, too, in
that this constant turning it over and seeing the opposite side and ex-
pounding it is what makes him able to write almost endlessly, and enables me to write a fair amount because, yes, there is a lot to be said

on both sides. A book like *Rabbit, Run* was a deliberate attempt to present both the escapist, have-it-my-way will to live versus the social restraints, the social voices in the book, the ministers', and other people's too. . .

Campbell: Also Kierkegaardian would be the individualism, and here we're back to something we mentioned a while ago as something maybe basically Protestant. I wonder if there have been some elements of existentialism that you found particularly viable or attractive. One thing, for instance, specifically: I find in Sartre affirmation of man's radical discontinuity with nature and his radical aloneness. Would you share these affirmations or not?

Updike: We are obviously very much in nature and have to be well aware of it. All our various kinds of health depend upon some recognition that we are natural beings. On the other hand, there is a radical jump between one's individual sense of me—I—and any other kind of reality. These exterior forms exist in a realm quite other than my ego, my inner voice. I am impressed by that—or was—and still am, really, because I haven't as much altered my philosophical-theological views as let them sit, and fade, I guess, a little bit. And Kierkegaard—what the existentialists picked up was his insistence on the importance of the individual. He almost says that God is there because I so much want him to be there, doesn't he? There's a building upon terror. The first thing you lay down is the fact that you're terrified. I find, from the standpoint of someone trying to present human experience, existential philosophy more useful in a way than the more social views of humanity, which somehow don't come over into fiction terribly well, do they? I don't know why that is. Saying that, I wonder if it's true or not. I do think that somebody like Bellow . . . his fiction is much enriched by his innate sense of society. Not only all the talking his characters do, and all the theories, but his very real sense of the family and the city. That is good, and I guess I can't claim that as my own.

Campbell: In Sartre's radical aloneness I don't find the I-Thou bit that you get out of Buber, and I feel this possibility at least in your work. I even wonder if Ms. Prynne becomes a Thou at the end of *A Month of Sundays*.

Updike: I was just going to say that there is a touch of the I-Thou in that last ending, the saluting and the—sure. ["What is it, this hu-

man contact, this blank-browed thing we do for one another? There
was a moment . . . when your eyes were all for another, looking up
into mine, with an expression without a name, of entry and alarm, and
of salutation. I pray my own face, a stranger to me, saluted in turn."—
A Month of Sundays 228] She is Thou, and also in some way she is
meant to be the ideal reader. I mean the I-Thou is also the writer-
reader I-Thou. She is his reader.

Campbell: Do you think there's some possibility your work might
develop into some sort of saga?

Updike: I don't mind the interconnections when they come upon
me. You know it becomes increasingly hard to work with things you've
already established. Often it becomes necessary just to give the thing
spring somehow. Obviously I have written interlinked short stories,
and revived characters. I've written a sequel to one of my novels.
There's a way in which *Of the Farm* is a sequel to *The Centaur*, and
so on. I'd like my *oeuvre* to have some blend, continuous without being a formal shelf's worth the way in which some of the French writers
attempted—Balzac and so on. I think just by moving out of Pennsylvania and living in another region, I have created the discontinuity in
my own life that, say, Faulkner did not have.

Campbell: Can we bounce some ideas about *Midpoint* around for
just a while? You say in Canto V: "Atomically all writers must begin,
the truth arises as if by telegraph,/ One dot, two dots, a silence, then a
laugh,/ The rules inhere and will not be imposed/ *Ab alto* as most li-
brals have supposed." Is this ironic or not? One dot, two dots—
silence. There aren't going to be any more dots? Because the rules inhere and therefore our dots aren't ever going to get anywhere? Or the
rules inhere and therefore what we think are random dots turn out to
be illustrations of something that comes from beyond?

Updike: I think the latter. The image that I must have had in mind,
at least that comes to mind now that I hear it, is scientific inquiry into
matter. Instead of beginning with some broad suppositions and trying
to make them apply to little phenomena, you look at the little phenomena and try to extract the rules that inhere from them. And so in writing, I try to adhere to the testable, the verifiable, the undeniable little
thing. Somehow, I hope the pattern in the art will emerge, and I guess
I must have some such hope cosmically.

Campbell: Again in Canto V, after all the hero's praise of pointill-
ism, calculus and all and so on, you say "all wrong, all wrong." Now
I couldn't exactly see what was all wrong.

Updike: Of course, I've been saying all along since the second line
of Canto I that there's something wrong. The author of middle age,
the man at midpoint, has the sensation, no matter what he's saying,
that something is all wrong. Things are not quite right; there's an unease pervading the poem. He sort of doubts and mocks what he's just
asserted. Certainly as the writer of dogmatic couplets I felt uneasy.
You *could* say original sin. I mean, original sin says it's all wrong,
doesn't it?

Campbell: But when you say "nothing has had to be," I think immediately that Pope wouldn't agree with that—"whatever is, is . . . "

Updike: I think one of my independent philosophical obsessions
was that there is a certain gratuitousness in existence at all. That is,
however riddles are unraveled, why the void itself was breached remains permanently mysterious, and, in its own way, permanently hope-
ful-making.

Campbell: Here also you say that the author gives intelligent he-
donistic advice; I would never have known it.

Updike: I think there are two kinds of advice, as I remember, giv-
en. One is, you might say, ecologically sound. That, I think, is somewhat distrusted by the author of these lines as being true, but somehow
something's wrong with it. The other is—which I frequently find myself saying—to be grateful, be grateful for existence; that is, "nothing
had to be." And that advice, I think, is religious advice.

Campbell: You also say here in your "argument" that he appears to
accept reluctantly his own advice. I think he very plainly does not—

Updike: Does not accept his own advice?

Campbell: —accept this advice, and when he says here at the end,
"Henceforth, if I can, I must impersonate a serious man," I think the
first, third, fourth, and the beginning of the fifth sections all clearly
indicate the irony there. What he's really doing is impersonating a
clown. That's what he's been doing all along, when in reality he is a
very serious man all the way through. So I don't think at all he is accepting this advice. I think he's rejecting all this well-meaning advice.

Updike: And he's going to keep clowning, you think? . . . I can't
help it.

Campbell: But at a deadly serious level.

Updike: I'm glad you're looking at *Midpoint*, by the way. Just in the way you talk I realize that *Midpoint* and *A Month of Sundays* are in a way among my franker books. Because Marshfield to some extent is speaking for me. Just the sensation—trying to talk about experiences as it, you know, first arrived—dot, dot. Marshfield's passage about fixing the window sash and how it speaks to him and the sense of . . . ["I had never taken apart a window before. What an interlocked, multi-deviced yet logical artifact one is! And how exciting, all the screws unscrewed and stop strips removed, to pull forth from decades of darkness the rusted sashweight, such a solid little prisoner, and fit him with a glossy new noose and feel him, safe once again in his vertical closet, tug like life upon the effortlessly ascendant sash!"— *A Month of Sundays* 115]

Campbell: Yes, he finds in the furniture his Ground of Being.

Updike: Right, right . . .

Campbell: Let's go on to *A Month of Sundays*.

Updike: You might be interested to know that my original plan was to have chapter thirty-one blank. The trouble is, being the end chapter, it didn't look blank. That is, it just looked like the book had ended. But then I wrote it as you read it. In this blankness some kind of merger of I-Thou. . . . I might say of the sermons that I meant them not only to pick up the events of six days just past and in a way cap them, but also to show a normalization. The first is meant to be the most blasphemous; it's really a sort of assault on the Bible. The second is somewhat . . . well, the second is also pretty defiant. But by the third sermon you wind up with a fairly orthodox message. And as she [Ms. Prynne] says, the fourth is a sermon that really could be preached. So there is some kind of lessening of anger and whatever, and he is, in fact, despite himself, being returned to usefulness.

Campbell: Well, it strikes me that evidence emerges here in an overt way, or in a more overt way, of concerns that you have had all along.

Updike: It's overt, all right, it really is. It may be also a trying to say goodbye to some of these concerns, to move to something else.

Campbell: Let's talk about Barth a little more. Obviously, you do acknowledge your debt to Barth, saying that at one point in your life his theology seemed to be your whole support. Could you say something about what elements of this Barthian position particularly attracted you?

Updike: I think it was the frank supernaturalism and the particularity of his position, so unlike that of Tillich and the entire group of liberal theologians—and you scratch most ministers, at least in the East, and you find a liberal—whose view of these events is not so different from that of an agnostic. But Barth was with resounding definiteness and learning saying what I needed to hear, which was that it really *was* so, that there was something within us that would not die, and that we live by faith alone—more or less; he doesn't just say that, but what he does say joined with my Lutheran heritage and enabled me to go on.

Campbell: This statement that I referred to was made ten years ago and even then it was referring to a time in the past. Does the past-tense nature of that reference suggest that your enthusiasm has cooled for Barth or that you've found other things in addition to Barth, or does it mean anything?

Updike: I certainly have not renounced Barth, nor have I read him much lately. The great period of my reading Barth— I'm trying to fix the time—I think it was about 1960 or 1961, so I would have been in my late twenties. Either I have become as a middle-aged person kind of too numb to care, or, what I would suggest instead, I am able, having assimilated Barth and somehow being permanently reassured, to appreciate Tillich, say. . . . After one has conquered this sort of existential terror with Barth's help, then one is able to open to the world again. *He* certainly was very open to the world. Wonderfully alive and relaxed, as a man.

Campbell: As I read Barth, I find that he heavily stresses three particular things. First of all is the very centrality of Christology. This is the touchstone—belief in Christ. Then the importance of the church, and then the Christian as new creature in Christ, sign of the resurrection. Now as I read your novels particularly, I find Christ-references relatively rare. And in the second place, I find the church, when it gets in there, is usually portrayed in its bland decadence and seems pointless and useless. And then the new-creature, resurrection images seem distinctly absent in the novels until we get to Marshfield, where it is very clear at the end. Now my question is, simply, have I missed something obvious, or are these in fact parts of Barth's enthusiasm that you are not concerned to try to illustrate?

Updike: No, I'm afraid you're right, and to that extent I'm a very poor Barthian. As I've said before, my religious sensibility operates primarily as a sense of God the Creator, which is fairly real to me, and secondly as a sense of the mystery and irreducibility of one's own identity, mixed in with fear of the identity being an illusion or being squelched. I'm not a good Barthian—I'm not a good Christian, really, when you come right down to it. I don't find that these emphases on Barth's part get in the way, though, somehow. I'm willing to believe that Christ was real, to him. Barth's own images now and then of the church in action are more scathing than anything I've presented. I do remain fascinated by the church. I'm grateful that there are churches. I find going to church generally comforting and pleasant, and I admire ministers for trying, as it were, to maintain the impossible in the midst of the all too possible.

Campbell: Barth's view of creation, history, and God's participating in it implies the importance of eschatology, yet I see your work under-cutting any apocalypticism. Things do not come to some great end.

Updike: It's true I do see the world as something that, as far as my horizon goes, will plug along. Even the holocaustal disasters turn out to be survivable by humanity in general. And in our own lives we sur-vive all of our disasters but the last one. Yes, I do see the world much more in terms of persistence. I feel that it's going to limp along.

Campbell: I see I've got a red herring in my question, anyway, be-cause Barth's eschatology is not apocalyptic. He, too, in *Dogmatics in Outline*, right after the Second World War, mentions that we made it through all this. People are still people, and he even supplies his own answer to my question: in the Eschaton, he says, light falls from above into our lives, the dailyness . . .

Updike: Barth is not always easy to pin down because he has a way of subjectifying these terms that to Paul's generation were clearly his-torical events. To this extent, he, too, is a liberal theologian. . . . He , too, is a bit of a "yes, but" and a master of having it both ways. I first read him in the collection of sermons and speeches, *The Word of God and the Word of Man*. In one of those, after having presented a devastating picture of our society and of the church's condition, he says do not ask me, then, "What shall I do?" Just go on doing what you are doing—but doing it differently. As far as concrete action, he seemed to think it was all more or less hopeless in the sense, at least, of producing any absolute result. [See "The Christian's Place in Society," in *The Word of God and the Word of Man* (New York: Harper & Brothers, 1957), 272–327.] I don't know. I think obviously one could find in the vast corpus of Barth's pronouncements a number of shades of opinion on this and that.

Campbell: I have but one other comment. Barth at one point says that "Christian art" is well intentioned but ultimately impotent. A real Christian, he says, wants no imagery. Your work, of course, is full of all sorts of marvelous imagery.

Updike: But I've never really offered it as Christian art. My art is Christian only in that my faith urges me to tell the truth, however painful and inconvenient, and holds out the hope that the truth—reality—is good. Good or no, only the truth is useful.

John Updike: 20 Books and Still Counting

Lorrie Dispenza/1977

From *The Blue Print*, Georgetown Middle Senior High School, March 1977, 8–10. Reprinted by permission of Georgetown Middle Senior High School.

Clad in his tennis whites, John Updike arrived at this brown and gold colonial house promptly for the interview granted. He was warm and friendly, making his guests feel at ease from the outset.

Munching on his lunch—a bologna, cheese, and lettuce sandwich with a side order of milk—John Updike, definitely not the archetypal stuffed-shirt author, spoke in carefully chosen, even tones.

Updike, born in the small Pennsylvania town of Shillington, explained that he likes Georgetown and other small towns because he spent part of his youth on a farm.

"People here in New England say what they mean and mind their own business. I think people respect each other and I've been allowed to write with very little comment from my neighbors," said Updike, who has resided at the former Elmer Liebsch residence on Main Street for just under a year after living in Ipswich for 17 years.

A Harvard graduate, Updike started trying to write at the age of 15, but notes, "Even as a child I enjoyed playing with pencils and paper. When I was a child, I drew a lot and wanted from quite young to do something in the creative line."

This creative bent led him to some formal artistic study. Updike thinks his writing is better because of this artistic training.

"I've never done anything harder than try to paint things the way they are. The amount of concentration it takes to try to mix a color and put it in the right spot was really a very good lesson for me as far as accuracy in all things artistic.

"Words should also make pictures to give the reader something he can visualize. I try to do that. I try to make them move because that's the difference between writing and 'reading' things on the wall: you have all day to look at (a painting), but as a writer, you have to have something moving, something musical," said Updike.

"Actually, a lot of 19th century writers did have some artistic training. They could draw, more or less, the way people can now take a
picture. Everybody can operate a camera now, but I think that ability—that sort of sketchy colorfulness—went out of writing."

In high school, Updike wrote for his school newspaper and yearbook. "I guess I wanted to be a writer even then," he said, going on
to add, "I just thought it would be fun to have words made into books,
and to work your own hours and things like that.

"If I'd known exactly what I was getting myself into, I might have
had second thoughts. But there's no profession that's easy, that doesn't
require a bit of foolhardiness," he said.

His interest in art has also kept Updike interested in the mechanics
of bookmaking and type. "I've remained interested in that. My books
are pretty much designed by me. I take a hand in the jackets and even
the color of cover cloth," said Updike.

When asked how he ended up in New England, Updike replied,
"It's very simple. I came to college in New England and attended
Harvard for four years, did live abroad for a year, and in New York for
two years. When the time came to do my own thing artistically, I remembered New England."

Updike lit a thin cigar, sat back, taking short puffs, and continued.

The characters Updike writes of are fictional, but are based upon his
"experiences of humanity." He explained that during his first ten years
in New England, until about 1965, he was basically writing from his
Pennsylvania memories.

"I wrote a great deal about, I suppose, my boyhood and about the
society that my father's being a school teacher exposed me to." After
1965, Updike wrote from his New England experiences, "but I'm certainly not a New England regional writer in the sense that Frost was,
or Ralph Waldo Emerson was," he admitted.

Updike's books, to some degree, are based on actual experiences,
"but they all try to take off from the experience and make more of it
than there really is."

Rabbit, Run he said, was sort of what might have been for Updike,
if he had been a good basketball player and stayed in Pennsylvania.
He, in fact, was not a good basketball player, though he said he would
have liked to have been.

The most autobiographical of Updike's works, "and one that remains a favorite," is *The Centaur*, a book about his father. "I had to dress it up in the mythology and compress a lot of boyhood memories into just three days. So there is always some distortion," explained Updike.

One of Updike's more recent novels, *Couples*, is set in a small New England town, which is "a more fantastical one and really the behavior was based as much on what I read in the newspapers as what I saw out of my windows," he said.

His book, *A Month of Sundays*, isn't even set in New England—it's theoretically set in the Midwest. "I would like to avail myself of the geographical freedom which you have in this country now that the sections are so similar. We all watch the same television shows and almost speak with the same accents. The regional accents are another thing that's dying out," said Updike.

Before going on, Updike leaned back in his chair, collecting his thoughts. He then looked out the window and commented how beautiful it was outside.

All of Updike's characters are drawn out of a few people who have made a deep impression on him. "In the course of a life, a dozen people really matter and of those dozen, we maybe gravitate toward the same type," he said.

In *Of the Farm*, Updike said, he is talking about his mother, somewhat. "But it is a somewhat heightened version of her. I had hoped she would become 'a mother' and not just 'my mother,' in the course of the novel."

The setting of this short novel is the farm where Updike spent five years between the ages of 13 and 18, and according to him, the central situation of the novel is untrue. (The story concerns the visit of a divorced male character to his mother's farm, accompanied by his new wife and stepson.)

"The book is imagined. The action is imagined. But I drew on real landscape and to some extent on real people."

Stylistically, Updike's intention in writing *Of the Farm* was to create a novella—"I mean it wasn't a novel. There are just four voices in it, so it was meant to be sort of musical. The four people are like the four instruments of a string quartet: they talk to each other in their duets and trios within the quartet, but no other voice is heard," said Updike.

In this book, there was some intent on Updike's part to show the characters as isolated, or interacting as in a kind of pocket society. This is true also of the four people in *Marry Me*, Updike's most recent novel "in that you get very little sense of other people interlocking with these individual destinies. The relationships are different, but again there is the sense of isolation," said Updike.

The characters in *Couples* and *The Centaur* were not meant to be isolated, according to Updike, but, "to open outward: that is, to show nobody is an island. There are no islands, so that strangers are momentary characters—they all come into play and are engaged and disengaged. Those two books, I guess, are more social commentary about our society."

Updike disagreed with a suggestion that the women in his novels are stereotypical—either sexy broads or motherly rocks. "I didn't really mean them to be stereotypical. To me, they (the women) seemed different, one from another. But it may be that my palette is more limited than I know."

Although Updike admits some of his women characters are similar, he finds women to be, in general, kind, witty, and dissatisfied.

"Maybe that's why my women tend to be like this (stereotypical).

"You get away from this in novels like *Bech* which treats of a different scene—New York intelligentsia. I think the women are somewhat different. There are some quite sharp women in there. I haven't shown a great many career women, mainly because most of the women that I've known have been domestic, essentially. But I would hope maybe as I get wiser, I'll relieve this sense of stereotypes. I don't want to be a stereotyper."

Updike went on to say he tries to look at each woman the way he does each man: as a separate case and not really with sexist expectations. "Actually, my professional career has been spent, to a great extent, being tutored by women," he said. He added that he credits his mother with stimulating his initial interest in writing.

Updike said he respects women for their brains and personality. His present editor at Knopf is a woman and several of his most important editors at *The New Yorker* have been women.

Updike also disagrees with a suggestion that his characters' indecisiveness is a bad characteristic.

"I'm not sure that decisiveness is itself an admirable quality—

Hitler was very decisive, for example. But the world is full of people who are willing to make decisions for us, men who are all too decisive. This kind (indecisive) of man interests me more because he holds within himself all the possibilities and some of the contradictions. In a sense ambivalent, torn, he kind of dithers in a situation, without being able to control or channel it," he said. Updike believes to some extent that indecisiveness and impotence are human conditions. He also thinks the ability to make meaningful decisions is rather limited.

Updike expressed some concern about the direction of American literature. "Just looking at the paperbacks on racks now I'm struck by the number of Gothic horror things there are and also by the number of romances. There is a surprising amount of escapist fiction; I say surprising because there has always been a lot, but you'd think these people who are escaping this way would escape by watching television, which is a lot easier than picking up a book and deciphering it," he said.

Updike did however express confidence in the time-honored tradition of American realism.

Updike feels it is difficult, but not impossible for a writer to survive solely on book royalties. "A number do. Two or three of my own novels have, in fact, done quite well.

"Some books don't sell very well; most books don't sell at all. But surely it can be done. These are not easy times for writers—there are more people who want to write than want to read. There are so many competing claims to our time that I would advise people to go into it only if they are prepared to live modestly and gamble a bit," he said.

"I've never trusted solely to book royalties," Updike added. "I really began as a magazine writer for *The New Yorker*." He said he loves appearing in the magazine and thinks it is a good way of getting in touch with his readers in a more immediate way.

Updike has been writing professionally for 23 years. It was the same month he got out of college that he sold his first short story.

"I wish for any young person that kind of happiness I felt when I had my first sale," he said.

His first book was a collection of poems at the age of 25. His first novel, *The Poorhouse Fair*, was written when he was 25.

In the beginning of his career, Updike said he promised himself a book a year.

"But I find I write less easily now and sell less easily; but there's always new things to say it seems. You have to avoid a certain intellectual stiffness. If you've written over a million published words, for me it's more like two million, your own words begin to haunt you. You tend to say things the same way," explained Updike.

He thinks this staleness shows more in writing because people can sense when they are getting a copy. "Twenty-three years is a very long time to be producing this product," he said.

Updike likes Georgetown and expressed a wish that it not change too much. Contrary to popular belief, Updike's next book will not be about Georgetown. The setting is in Africa, "which is about as far away from Georgetown as you can get," according to Updike.

Updike did not know when this novel would be finished. A collection of poems entitled *Tossing and Turning* will be out this spring.

"It is the twentieth book [with a major publisher, not counting children's books] and I feel now that I should take a little rest."

John Updike on Poetry

Helen Vendler/1977

From *The New York Times Book Review*, 10 April 1977, 3, 28.
Reprinted by permission of *The New York Times Book Review* and
Helen Vendler.

On the occasion, next month, of the publication of John
Updike's new collection of verse, *Tossing and Turning*,
Helen Vendler asked Mr. Updike some questions about
poetry.

Q: You imply in a story, as I recall, that your mother wanted you to be
a poet. Did her wish influence your writing, or did her taste guide
yours?

A: There was little, come to think of it, mention of poetry in my
house while I was growing up. My mother remembered *not* remember-
ing a poem she was reciting at about the age of 12. She felt permanently disgraced. The first poem I recall reciting in school was that
passage from Sir Walter Scott that begins, "Breathes there the man
with soul so dead. . . ." I got through it, and maybe that made the difference. The first poets I recall enjoying reading for myself were Phyllis McGinley, Arthur Guiterman, Robert Service and, somewhat later,
Ogden Nash and Morris Bishop. I wonder how many 16-year-olds now
have heard of any of these fine and funny writers.

Q: Were these poets the chief models for your exquisite light verse?

A: In the early fifties, when I did verse for the Harvard *Lampoon*,
we looked toward *Punch* and toward the consoling notion, demon-
strated in *Punch* week after week, that sheer metric neatness was halfway enough for a good light poem. That all seems long ago. Light
verse died when it no longer seemed even the littlest bit wonderful to
make two words rhyme. At about the same time, dancers in movies
stopped going up and down stairs in white tie and tails. We had
switched our allegiance from agility to energy. Auden was the last poet,
I think, to make the one seem the other.

Q: In your giddy self-interview, "Bech Meets Me," your gifted interviewer asks: "Do you envision novels as pills, broadcasts, tapes-

tries, explosions of self, cantilevered constructs, or what?" The equally inventive interviewee answers that "they are crystallizations of visceral hopefulness extruded as a slow paste which in the glitter of print
regains something of the original, absolute gaiety." Would you like to
say what you think lyrics are?

A: I think you could say the same of lyrics, except that the paste is
faster, or the tube at least is smaller. Since I have never been taken
very seriously as a poet and since I write less and less of what there
seems no demand for, I am a poor one to theorize. As I recall, the
poem comes with a perception—a breakthrough into nature, which en-
circles our numbness day and night. And married to the irruption of
nature must be something live that surfaces out of language; the language, even when rhyme and meter and syntax and punctuation are
brushed aside, brings a formal element without which nothing happens, nothing is *made*. One of the charms of concrete poetry was that
this element, after generations of *vers libre*, was re-emphasized, from
an unexpected direction. A lot of poetry I read now just washes
through me, nothing has crystallized to ignite crystallization in me.

Q: In "Why Write?" you say that as a child you used to draw on a
single sheet of paper "an assortment of objects—flowers, animals,
stars, toasters, chairs, comic-strip creatures, ghosts, noses—" and then
connect them with lines "so that they all became the fruit of a single
impossible tree," and you added that the pleasure this gave you returns
whenever you work "several disparate incidents or impressions into the
shape of a single story." Does this apply to your poetry too?

A: I have tried more than once to give this "collecting" impulse
some place in esthetic theory. Rhyming words are in a sense a "set"—
in a form like the ballade, a big set. Some of my light verse strings
some similar things—French inventors, semi-extinct animals, new developments in particle physics—in a kind of necklace of stanzas, and
steps back pleased. A kindred human urge, I suppose, is toward the
exhaustive. We like a feeling of mopping up, of complete fullness. A
jingle through the alphabet does also. We are *dismissed* by the work of
art. I am talking as if art still pandered to our hopes or inklings of order. I'm not sure it does, except in this mysterious sense of fullness.
In the days when I wrote poems habitually, I would know I had one,
the idea of it, when my scalp crawled. When the skin on my head felt
tight. My hand would shake and I couldn't write fast enough.

Q: Recent lyric poetry (Ginsberg, Berryman, Lowell) has incorpo-
rated a lot of the detail hitherto reserved for fiction—family tales, social scenery, public affairs. Do you like this sort of thing, or is it
better done in prose?

A: Done better perhaps in the best prose. Prose, that is, can make
tableaux move, cinematically, whereas in poetry the same material becomes a set of slides. Yes, I like some of Lowell's scenes and character sketches very much. In his poetry, human nature becomes quite
tropical, stifling. I also like the late Ed Sissman's framed moments of
his own history, and the palpable "others" in Anne Sexton, or Merrill,
or Dickey. There is a limit, after all, to what can be done with daffo-
dils and sunsets. Nor is this material novel; Chaucer, Shakespeare and
Milton are all dramatic poets, and Romanticism unleased a new passion for the psychological. Wordsworth turned it inward and Browning
outward, but between them surely they covered all the anecdotal and
confessional possibilities open to us now. Except, perhaps, that of sexual detail.

Q: You've decided, in your new collection of verse, to prescind
from "taste" altogether, in some of the poems about sex. Have you
any sense that this has been done successfully by others? Is it possible
to avoid the ridiculous in such enterprises?

A: Well, why avoid the ridiculous? The poem in this collection that
you must have in mind is meant to be, among other things funny, and
indeed is based, like many of my light verse poems, on something that
came in the mail. I think "taste" is a social concept and not an artistic
one. I'm willing to show good taste, if I can, in somebody else's living room, but our reading life is too short for a writer to be in any
way polite. Since his words enter into another's brain in silence and
intimacy, he should be as honest and explicit as we are with ourselves.
I find some of Donne's poems, and Whitman's, quite unridiculously
sexual. Odd, that no modern celebrant comes to mind. Lawrence's
poems seem to be mostly about animals.

Q: Do you have any regrets that you turned out to be essentially a
novelist rather than a poet?

A: No. And yet I feel more at sea writing a novel than a poem, and
often reread my poetry and almost never look at my old novels. Also,
poetry, especially since we have purged it of all that is comfortingly
mechanical, is a sporadic activity. Lightning can't strike every day. It

is always at the back of my mind to be a poet. Lately I had occasion to get out the collected poems of my fellow Pennsylvanian Wallace Stevens. He didn't publish his first collection until he was almost my present age and didn't publish another for 12 years more. Yet the total production, in the end, weighs like a Bible, a beautiful book as published by Knopf, with big print on big white pages, all this verbal fun and glory and serene love—what a good use of a life, to leave behind one beautiful book!

Q: Would you like to do more reviewing of poetry?

A: I try to deal with the poetry when it comes up in connection with a poet's biography, but no, I wouldn't presume to review it head on, and book upon book. I don't know how you do it, all these poets operating at what they think of as the height of intensity, exquisiteness, mystery. For me it would be like candling golden eggs. Did you notice, the Brancusi head on the jacket of *Tossing and Turning* is shaped like an egg? And my first book, a book of poems, was called *The Carpentered Hen*. That was my first book, this is my 20th, and none in between has seemed more worth—how shall I say?—crowing about.

A Visit to Mr. Updike

Iwao Iwamoto/1978

From "A Visit to Mr. Updike." *Nami* (Japan), August 1978, 21–23. The introduction supplemented with additional material from the audiotape that was a source for the interview. Translated and reprinted by permission of Iwao Iwamoto. Conducted in Georgetown (Mass.) on 22 June 1978.

We may have no words for the flaming colors of New England in the fall, but its scenery clad in fresh summer green is no less appallingly beautiful. To get to Georgetown, Mass., a small town 20 miles north of Boston, I took I–495, which runs in a huge circle around Boston, This way I could avoid going into the busy traffic of the city, and also enjoy the country drive. Getting off I–495, and after passing Andover, another small New England town, I drove by a lake which had a funny Indian name, and down a rolling country road flanked by tall trees to Georgetown. As I drove along the road which seemed to me like a long tunnel of elms and maples, I felt the presence of New England there. It gave me a kind of soothing satisfaction which I could not hope to get from driving on the expressway, where I had to drive all the time only to compete with distance.

Georgetown was a really small town. In the center of the town there was a crossroads and there a gas station, a drugstore, a restaurant, and several other stores stood clustered together. About 10 miles away from the beach, it had no bustle which you would find in some of the resort towns in New England. And four or five houses away from this peaceful center, there is one old frame house covered with reddish-brown clapboards, where Mr. Updike lives. Although the front of the house looked small, it had a long back, and there was an added part jutting out of that long back. Its shape was unique among the colonial houses around there. After I tapped the knocker twice, Mr. Updike came to the door, tall and smiling.

When I, as a translator, meet the original author, I always feel some awkwardness—something like embarrassment. For more than half a year I had been involved in his novel, day by day putting his words into my own words. In the first few months I began to feel as if I were stealing something very precious from him, and then, when the translation was almost done, I felt as if it were my own from the first. But now, in front of me, the original owner was standing, implicitly claiming that it was his own. I had a strange feeling that I must confess my crime and hand back to him what I had stolen.

However, Mr. Updike, now a middle-aged amiable man, handsome and generous, effaced my awkward feelings with his beaming smiles. He was very different from that image of an extremely sensitive young genius which I had created from his pictures and works. He led me to his office, a big-boarded room built in the added part, and he busied himself bringing me a chair, making room on the desk for my tape-recorder, and all the time talking to me, asking about the details of my trip out from the Midwest. He was frank and kind, not showing any pretension that he is one of the best writers of the day.

Q: The publisher just sent me the second galley proof of my translation [of *Marry Me*].

A: And look, you've made changes. What's happening?

Q: I changed Chinese characters into Japanese characters.

A: You have to have very good eyes, I think, to read Japanese. I'm always amazed by my Japanese translations, they're very beautifully done, you know. They're lovely little books.

Q: Do you remember Mr. Kenzaburo Ohe, who talked with you? He wrote *The Personal Matter*. He is very famous also. He is going to review your new book.

A: Is he really? Well, he might not like it. I like it. But I'm glad that he's still alive and well. I remember we sat opposite each other and talked about Okinawa.

Q: Yes, he's very political. You know, *The Personal Matter* is very similar to your *Rabbit, Run*.

A: It has a character with some other animal name.

Q: Bird. And he wants to get away from Japan to Africa. He always dreams of Africa.

A: Yes, I've read the book in translation—I have it—because it was, in some ways, very similar to *Rabbit, Run*. It's nice. That's the only book I know where I did have any influence. I mean, as far as I know.

Q: He was very much influenced by Mr. Mailer, and also by you. One thing that I'd like to ask about: *Couples* and *Marry Me* are very much alike but also very different in some ways. The time of *Marry Me* is around 1961, I think, and *Couples* takes place in 1963.

A: The relationship between *Couples* and *Marry Me* . . . actually, some of *Marry Me* was written a long time ago. There was a short story from it—the second chapter came out in *The New Yorker* in 1968, I think—and *Couples* is really, in a sense, later an inspiration that treats somewhat the same material in a more sociological, more removed way. Trying to get above it somewhat in the manner of Count Tolstoy. Years went by, and this manuscript, uncompleted, sat around. And there came a point in my life when I really couldn't think of much else to write, so I got out the manuscript and revised that, liked part of it quite well, published it, and now you're translating it. And so it goes. What I liked about the book was the dialogue and the little family scenes. There's a kind of painful truthfulness that I thought was worth getting into print, although it is a little too close to *Couples*, and maybe some other writer would have suppressed the whole thing. But there was something about the book that I wanted to get rid of, to make permanent—so it's published. But it really is a slightly older book and is somewhat different, perhaps, in texture from my recent novels, such as *A Month of Sundays* and a new book that's coming out this fall called *The Coup*. It takes place in Africa, a continent I've been to a little bit. But it's basically about a made-up country. Here you see my African library. I'm a subscriber to a magazine in Africa, so I've had to flesh out my intuitions with a lot of research. It took a long time. I think the book was begun a year and a half ago, more or less, and I was thinking about it before then. I've just been told that it's the choice of the Book-of-the-Month Club, which is good for the publisher, at least. It was an attempt to get away from the domestic, marital subject matter of *Marry Me*. But there are many things I like about *Marry Me*. I don't know how the ending struck you, but I liked that, and I meant it to be fairly clear what really happens.

Q: In Milwaukee, I talked about the ending of *Marry Me* with several professors, and one professor said that Jerry is apparently out of his mind. I think that Jerry is choosing a place where he can be very free and say what he really wants to say, imaginatively or actually.

A: My idea was, the first part, Wyoming . . .

Q: Wyoming was a dream.

A: Yeah, a dream, it's something that did not happen. In some way it happened, because this is a very romantic book. I mean, it's called "A Romance" in English. But they talk throughout the book about getting to Wyoming. It's become a place they're going to go, and so I wanted to show them there and show that they're much like anybody else—the same irritations, the same children crying, and so on. But then the next two I meant to be real, that they really did go to France and really did go to St. Croix. You felt that?

Q: Yeah.

A: I thought it was very obvious, but the editors were curious, and so I tried to make it even more obvious.

Q: You like to end a novel, like in *Rabbit, Run*, just as it is—leave something to the reader.

A: In the air, yes. Well, that is how I do think of endings. That's how life is, and that's how a book should be. It's a little like music, in that you arrive at a note where you seem to quit. Everything is resolved, in a way, even though there's still life that goes on beyond this, at some point. My endings are not accidents. I think always of the ending. I know the ending I'm going to, but people said about *Rabbit, Run* that . . .

Q: Mr. Mailer said, quite a long time ago, that . . .

A: My style smelled like garlic, he said. He wrote an article for *Esquire* early in the 1960s in which he discussed ten of his contemporaries, and he more or less took us all to task. But in a way, he was not totally unkind to me. He said my style was terrible and I was surrounded by *The New Yorker* magazine somehow, but also he rather liked the sense of doom in the book. So I didn't come off too badly.

Q: You have a very beautiful style. When I first read *Rabbit, Run* in 1962, it took me away, the writing itself. It's very fascinating.

A: It was a bit of an experiment for me. I don't know how it is in Japanese, but in English it's written in the present tense, which was sort of unusual at the time. But I find writing in that tense is very quick, and you can quickly pick things up, like in reality. I've not written much else in the present tense. The sequel, *Rabbit Redux*, I wrote in the present tense. It's an exciting way to write. It's very vivid. You can pick up things in the corners of your eyes a little, and the thoughts that just come and go so quickly. I think it can be very true-to-life, the present tense. I suppose I'm going to have to write another Rabbit book someday. I didn't mean to write the second one. But now that I've written the second one, I think I should write four, perhaps. In some ways, Rabbit is an American of his time, but it's not easy for me to know what is happening to him, because he and I live rather different lives now. When I wrote *Rabbit, Run*, I was just out of my boyhood and all those scenes and that kind of life was very familiar to me. But the older you get the more narrow you become, in a way.

Q: You become very stagnant, yeah.

A: You become stagnant, and you sit in Georgetown and you don't really know what goes on in Pennsylvania.

Q: Well, I was in the United States in 1954–55 at Columbia University, and I came to Middletown in 1966–67, and then in 1972 and this time at the University of Wisconsin-Milwaukee. Just like *Rabbit, Run* and *Rabbit Redux* . . .

A: You've tasted every decade.

Q: Yes, and so I can see that you're very good at presenting the American scene. The late fifties were very different.

A: It's hard, if you live here, to see those changes. If you come back every five years, I'm sure you see more. I get that in England. I lived in England in the middle fifties, and went back in the late sixties, and we've briefly been back in the seventies. And certainly there's been a lot of change. So how do you find America this trip?

Q: This time I feel everything is becoming very backward.

A: As opposed to the rest of the world, it's backward?

Q: Yeah.

A: I think the Vietnam episode and the oil dependency are two things that constitute a pulling in, a kind of a shrinking, a making sure of what you have and not being too ambitious—internationally, at least. It's, in a way, a pleasanter country to live in than it was ten years ago. I mean, there's much less stress. That was a very difficult time, the late sixties here, as in *Rabbit Redux*. Everybody had to re-think where they were and what things meant. I don't wish to return to that.

Q: You usually use places you are very familiar with, like *Rabbit, Run* and the place you were born, or *Couples* and Ipswich.

Q: Yes, there's some resemblance.

Q: But this time, *Westchester*?

A: Connecticut. It's a very vague Connecticut. I have of course, some knowledge of Connecticut. I moved it there, in part, to get away from New England. I think New England carries with it a whole set of associations. I mean, you're in Hawthorne's territory, and Thoreau's and Emerson's. *Couples* was, in a way, about New England and the Puritan faith. It was sort of that—the church burning and everything—from which I'm trying to get away. These are Middle Atlantic people. I'm a Middle Atlantic person, basically. Everything between Baltimore and New Haven is sort of a middle region, with New York as the capitol. I'm from Pennsylvania, so I'm not really a New Englander. I tend to write here still as an outsider. It's very beautiful and the people are kind of nice, but there's something a little distant. I don't feel quite at home here. I go south to Connecticut and I feel more at home, though I've never lived there. Basically, the Northeast coast is all one region. But if I were to set a book in California, that would take as much imagination as to set a book in Africa, for me. I would really have to think, at every step, what would they do? What does that look that? But if you stay in the Northeast, I think it's good to try to stretch your scenery a little bit.

Q: I read recently Mr. Gardner's *On Moral Fiction* . . .

A: I didn't read it. My wife picked it up in a bookstore and read the pages about me, but didn't think I should read them. So I didn't. I think he's down on a lot of people in that book. From the reviews, it didn't sound as though it made an awful lot of sense, really. It's all kind of vague and angry. It's more a plea for himself than for any "moral fiction," indeed. We've all disappointed him in some way. But I think that the first item of morality for a writer is to try to be accurate, to tell the truth as you know it, and not to get onto a preacher's platform.

Q: He's very conscious that he sometimes preaches.

A: I haven't read all of his books, but he began as really a very interesting writer. Is he known in Japan?

Q: Yeah. He came to Japan maybe three years ago. I interviewed him for a Japanese magazine. Your book, *Rabbit, Run*, is very popular now in Japan, one of the best-sellers in modern fiction, I think.

A: Wonderful. I find it very mysterious to be published in Japan, and I'm well published. Shinchosha does everything. They do the

short stories, too. Do you want to ask to any questions about writing
in general?

Q: Would you talk to me about how you will write in the future? I
am studying under Professor Ihab Hassan, who is very avant-garde. I
did quite a lot with William Gass, John Barth and [Thomas] Pynchon.
But I have been writing a book on Bernard Malamud, and I'm going
to see him on the 26th of June. He's just back from England. I like his
book. I like him and I like you. I like the realistic novel and I also like
the experimental one.

A: And, of course, it's not a hard or fast distinction. In Malamud,
for example, there's much fantasy, isn't there? Wasn't his first novel
[*The Natural*] surreal and experimental? His style is electric and brief.
It's not as if there are realists, on the one hand, defending their territory with slogans and rocks. I enjoy John Barth very much and I see
what he is trying to do. I wouldn't try to do anything quite like what
Barth has done. I think it's almost too much . . . I mean, he's playing
games with the paper. But I've done some of that myself, and I think
that I'm aware, as I write now, that it is no longer enough just to put
realistic things one after the other. Somehow it once seemed, in the
fifties, enough to capture accurately a room or an exchange between
people, but my new novel is somewhat experimental, as was *A Month
of Sundays*—though always with some base, I hope, in American
truth. I mean, there *are* people like this.

The Coup is kind of an attempt to have a Nabokovian unreality, a
made-up country and other things, to have layers as in *The Centaur*, in
a way, bubbling up and merging. But I think my overall theory, if I
have one, is that the life of a piece of fictional prose comes from its
relationship to reality, to truth, to what actually happens—and that a
book without any reference to that is apt to be boring and not to really
be alive.

Since words and reality are very different, there are many ways to
relate them one to another. I enjoy a lot of experimental writing, but
some avant-garde writing seems to me to be almost unreadable. I
would cite the recent books by William Burroughs, not *The Naked
Lunch*, but the ones since then. I find them very hard to read. There's
a kind of feedback from the world in general that I need to feel. To
that extent, I suppose that I'm a conservative realist writer.

Q: Shall we go back to *Marry Me*? Do you realize that we Japanese people are very different, thousands of miles away from the United States, and still we feel just as Jerry Conant feels?

A: You do?

Q: Yes, and your *Rabbit, Run, Couples,* and *Marry Me* have the same kind of theme as our Japanese fiction.

A: I don't know what your society is like. I expect it is a bourgeois society with a great emphasis upon the family. The breakup of family is strenuous, it's hard work, it's a terrible thing to do. There are certain Christian ghosts hanging over these people, but perhaps they don't have to be Christian. Perhaps you'd feel guilty anyway, and torn. It's interesting to me that my people—certainly Harry Angstrom and Jerry Conant—are very romantic. That is, they really do believe there's a better world out there, as in the movies—someplace to get to. Do you feel that in Japan, too?

Q: Yes, we always believe in some very gleamy place called Nirvana. Especially men—just like Rabbit Angstom and Jerry Conant—want to get away from actual society, actual reality.

A: With its compromises and its unsatisfactory qualities. I had thought that the Japanese man was better adjusted than our poor Western fellows.

Q: No, I don't think so.

A: Well, we picture Japan as a very efficient and orderly place, with everything in its place and very industrious. And any industrious people have repressed a great deal in terms of pleasure-seeking, or feeling, even. One of the phenomena that I've noticed in my lifetime has been a loss of the sense of the urgency to work. My father felt it was very important that he work, otherwise he would starve and his children would starve, and so work had a kind of sacred importance. It was bread. And now I'm not sure that my sons have that sensation. They are much less earnest than even I was to find work and to do it. They are less scared. I was sort of in the middle. I wasn't as scared as my father, but I was scared enough to put steady work at the center of my life and to have it be important. My heroes tend not to. Not being writers, they don't take their work very seriously. I think this creates a kind of a vacuum which has to be filled with other things—with romance, or sex, or even games.

Q: I like George Caldwell very much.

A: He's a worker. It's bad to live in that kind of pressure, but it also dignifies a lot of your daily routines. It gives a purpose to your life. Survival becomes kind of sacred.

Q: Peter is always watching his father, but he ends up a very mediocre painter.

A: I guess he's mediocre. Does he say that?

Q: No, he doesn't say that. But I could guess . . .

A: It's possible. It's hard to succeed as a painter. You know, very few reviews that I've read of *The Centaur* ever take very seriously the fact that Peter is telling the story, and that I've given him a life, too. He is living in Greenwich Village, he has done something very different than what his father did, and so on.

Q: But Peter ends up a mediocre painter. That means, in George Caldwell's life, he was twice dead.

A: But that's true of almost all fathers and sons. All fathers give up their lives, in a way, for children who aren't worth it, in some sense, since few children turn out to be great.

Q: I read that book when I was very young. It was very interesting.

A: I'm interested to hear you say that. One never knows what will make sense outside of one's own country, I suppose.

Q: It made sense. I had been writing an article on American drama since I was a student, but when I read *Rabbit, Run* and *The Centaur*, I wrote an article on American fiction for the first time, compared with Mr. Kobo Abe . . .

A: I read *Woman on the Dunes*, and it is a very powerful image of life in general. We're all sort of in dunes, in the sense of sand getting in everything.

Q: I compared *The Centaur* [with Abe], where Peter's in a frame. He is framed in George Caldwell's life.

A: There is a frame, and I think it's very important in fiction that it be, at heart, rather simple—no matter how large the book or elaborate it becomes—because if you don't have that in mind, you lose the reader. It can be quite simple. Things often are.

A Conversation with John Updike

Charlie Reilly/1978

From *Canto* 3:3 (1980), 148–178. Reprinted by permission of Charlie Reilly.

Those who have followed John Updike's "Rabbit" through his literary warrens will not be surprised to learn the author's garage is attached to a basketball hoop. Not only that, the vintage condition of the net and generally leafless state of the driveway suggest the author repairs to the court at least occasionally—say, when he senses a Bech-like moment of aridity in the offing.

This conversation took place in Mr. Updike's north-of-Boston home during the summer of 1978. It began inauspiciously: an inert tape recorder, some head-shaking about the state of modern electronics, a shift from Reilly's new-but-useless batteries to Updike's weathered-but-functioning extension cord, and a spilled cup of tea. The scientific method, wonderfully supported by John Updike's patience and sense of humor, prevailed in the long run, however, and we were soon off and chatting about the novels.

Reilly: In one of your interviews you said, "We're not going to get anyone like Hemingway for awhile, someone who so intensely and instinctively cared about the language. Instead you get showmen and professors." Also, at the end of *Midpoint* you said: "Art offers now not cunning and exile, but blank explosions and a hostile smile." What kind of shape do you see contemporary fiction in?

Updike: To see it really well I'd have to read more of it than I do. Although I review some new books, I spend most of my time trying to continue learning how to be a writer myself, and the very nature of my attempt to become an American writer precludes my studying much contemporary American fiction. I do read, however, any new work produced by people like Bellow, Cheever, Malamud and Roth—and if Salinger were to produce one, I think we would all fall upon it avidly. These names are slightly dated, but maybe my own reading in contemporary writing is a little dated. Anyhow, when I hear remarks like that quoted, I find it hard to disentangle myself from the natural sensation we all have that things were somehow better before, regardless of the historical reality. But I think there is no doubt that, since the twenties, cultural fashion has in a sense moved away from fiction writing. It was quite fashionable at the time to flatter and support people trying to become writers, and there seemed to be a much healthier market as well. Not only did fiction have proportionately more of the book market, but there were certainly more magazines printing fiction.

Today if *The New Yorker* sends something back, what do you do with it? You send it to *Playboy*—at least that's what I would do. And if *Playboy* sends it back, you're reduced to the slicks, which you can't quite write for, or to the little magazines, who can't pay. I'm just rereading the letters of one of our fellow Pennsylvanians, John O'Hara, and couldn't help but notice the large number of magazines he was dealing with—and that was just a generation ago. He happened to hop onto *The New Yorker* bandwagon when it was starting to roll, but he also worked with *Scribner's* and the *Post* and *Collier's* and a number of others. I'm making a long answer out of what perhaps should be shorter, but I do cling to my sensation that today it is a little harder to bring to fiction the kind of intensity necessary to produce masterpieces. Also, it may well be that the great achievements of modernism in literature might have been based upon an unproven faith that a writer *could*, as Joyce said, forge the uncreated conscience of his race. What I had in mind in the quotes you cited was that Hemingway was certainly trying, in a very radical way, to refurbish his prose and maintain a, well, continued literary gleam. That gleam is hard to fabricate today.

Reilly: I noticed John Gardner took a look at modern letters recently and more or less groaned. Would you regard modern fiction as being in a bleak state, or are you saying simply that gifted writers like Gardner and Thomas Pynchon are laboring in an uncongenial market?

Updike: Let me take a minute to think of an honest answer; it's important that I qualify this with a recognition of my own ignorance. I have a good deal of trouble reading Pynchon, who I am assured is very wonderful, because I tend to be put off by gag names. Gag names remind me of my own days on a college humor magazine, and I can't persevere with characters who are so much, in a sense, *Lampoon* figures. Perhaps if I had more time, I'm sure I would better appreciate

Pynchon. As for Gardner, I've read some of his work, although I've by no means kept up, and I do recognize something there that's authentic and ambitious. I haven't read the book you referred to, though, and I do understand I am one of the many who is found wanting.

Reilly: I wasn't trying to be combative: I haven't read all of it myself. Gardner popped into my mind because his fiction reminds me of your own.

Updike: I guess that's fair. He cares about the American middle-class and tries to write about a wide variety of people. I admire that. He's more erudite than I, though, and he's very inventive. I'm not sure, however, that after *Grendel* he has ever quite put the screws on himself tightly enough. A lot of words have come out, but are they really as well considered as they might have been? I don't know, of course, but there seems to be an unchecked quality about Gardner's production. I think there is something of the artificial heroic about anyone who sets out to become a Great Writer today. This is just a guess, but writing is an individualized and lonely endeavor, which Pynchon has dramatized by cutting himself off entirely from the media. Perhaps Gardner could be described as a slightly forced flower . . . but all these pessimistic impressions are as nothing when any of us sits down and tries to do his best. Really, these cultural appraisals amount to nothing when compared to the excitement of really getting down to the act of writing. I think it's very hard to chart literary vitality in a culture. Proust came out of a tired age, and yet he somehow made decadence work. And so at any moment, in any age or country, I think good things can be done.

Reilly: You've written in so many forms—novels, poems, stories, essays, at least one play. And one of your poems, "Midpoint," seems to range over a variety of poetic forms, like Whitmanesque verses and heroic couplets. Do you consider yourself primarily a novelist?

Updike: More and more I seem to be reduced to that, although I persist in writing short stories. As a matter of fact, now that I have finally gotten out from under *The Coup*, I am assembling my stories of the last seven years. I hate to be judgmental in this regard—in fact, I don't know—but the short story may be what I do best. I certainly feel quite comfortable with it, whereas with the novel I occasionally feel uncertain, almost lacking. The problem, I think, is when you write a novel you become aware of the enormous amount of "stuff" you ought to know. When I have to compare short story writing to writing novels, I think of what happens with a box when you double the linear dimensions. You wind up with something four times the volume—at least I think you do. What I am getting at is, the bigger the work the more you have to put into it. But that's part of the excitement and charm, isn't it: to see if you can fill the box.

The beauty of writing a novel is that you don't have anyone looking over your shoulder; you're not trying to screen it through a magazine editor. Perhaps I flatter myself, but I think my publisher at this point would print anything I sent them that wasn't the work of a deranged mentality. So I guess I do want to work most on my novels. The poetry is pretty well withered. I began as a poet and loved writing it, loved seeing it in print. I'm sorry I don't write more of it; I even regret I don't compose more verse solely to please myself. The last spate of poetry writing that was successful occurred in Spain. I took my mother, who is a long-time Hispanophile, and my younger daughter to Spain for a week. I suffered a terrible jet-lag and in my lonely hotel room began to write a sonnet a day about each day. They were published in the *New Yorker* about a year later and they seem to be the best thing I've ever done. But who knows what the future will bring? Occasionally, I see myself as an old man writing poetry, having that kind of flowering that John Hall Wheelhock had.

Reilly: You see yourself "inclining," at least, toward the novel?

Updike: Definitely.

Reilly: Now that I think of it, you've said that your play, *Buchanan Dying*, started as a novel, and ultimately you even seemed to measure it against a novel.

Updike: Correct, and it's still in my mind to transform it into a novel. I just found myself at that point overwhelmed by the things I don't know. Henry James discussed just this. He said when you write about the past you're just torturing yourself because you can never really know what people thought—you can barely determine what they wore. So, *The Coup* is set in Africa, and this time I tried to utilize my ignorance, to make it a kind of veil. But it would be fun sometime to return to *Buchanan Dying* and try to do it as I had originally seen it: a novel with a Beckettian tone that concerned a historical figure.

Reilly: I'm very interested in the use of myth in some of your works, a number of them actually. You used Greek mythology in *The*

Centaur and evoked an old Hawthorne tale in *A Month of Sundays*. Also, you said *Rabbit, Run* was keyed in part to the tale of Peter Rabbit. All of this reminded me of Joyce's *Ulysses* and reminded me of a question which I would have liked to ask Joyce: which came first? I wonder in *Centaur*—a book in which you consciously and elaborately adapted an ancient tale—which came first? Did you want to write about the centaur story and then decide to link it to your father? Or, was your first intention to write about your father?

Updike: No, the book had its origins in a little children's book of Greek mythology which my ex-wife had as a girl and which I was just reading around in. Somewhere in it, I came across this variant, this footnote almost, to the Centaur myth.

Reilly: Was that the source of the novel's opening quote?

Updike: Yes. And I thought, well, this is an unusual myth, especially in the sense that so few Greek myths involve the idea of sacrificing or laying down one's life for another. It was just one of those things that appealed to me as needing to be somehow returned to popular attention. So, I began with the myth, and then my own father very naturally attached himself to it because he sort of loomed as a centaur in my own life at that time. The novel really took off with the myth, and for that reason the myth is really in the foreground of the novel, not in the background as in *Ulysses*. In *The Centaur*, the real events are meant to be some kind of shadow of the myth. I don't know whether it works. The book got a lot of resistance when it came out; some people felt it was forced, and so on. But to me even the jangliness and jumpiness of it were somehow part of what I was trying to say.

Reilly: There was much to admire in it. After I finished it, I recall I did some digging into the myth and, after I had read the entirety of the story you quote in Greek at the end—after I had read Apollodorus, in other words—I was really impressed with how sensitively you used the material. Your handling of Chiron in terms of George Caldwell was brilliant, especially in the way you combined his flawed, struggling nature with his role of teacher and father.

Updike: There was something attractive about a good man who at the same time was uproarious and complaining—sort of a noisy altruist. This kind of moral ambivalence, I guess, does interest me and makes my heroes somewhat unattractive to a lot of people. But it's the kind of hero I come up with again and again: a person who combines good and the absence of it in an interesting, sometimes comical, way.

Reilly: That's fair. I rarely find myself relaxing and enjoying any of your heroes. Rather, I generally wind up being jolted by something they do or say and find myself re-examining them.

Updike: I suppose the hope is to make us all think about what goodness is and what the good life really is. I read Kierkegaard at one point and received a sensation of human life being intrinsically difficult and intrinsically flawed, a sensation that there are more problems in life than solutions. But it's also an exciting and beautiful world. To go back to your question, I suppose there's nothing in my work quite like *The Centaur* insofar as a formal working-out of a double-layered myth is concerned. But there surely is something similar in *A Month of Sundays*. That book is, of course, a re-telling of *The Scarlet Letter* in some way, and Hawthorne was very much on my mind when I wrote it. I re-read Hawthorne before beginning and there are a couple of passages where some of Hawthorne's words are simply inserted into the text. But it's more than just a re-hash of *The Scarlet Letter*. I think that even though there may be greater American books—let's say, for the sake of argument, *Moby-Dick* and *Huckleberry Finn*—*The Scarlet Letter* somehow sticks in my mind as the first American masterpiece. Among other things, it masterfully considers the problems of religion, the plight of woman in general, the problems of a fascinating woman in particular. It's amazingly well written, too. The more I read it, the more I'm struck by how "right" everything is.

Reilly: It's almost eerie to hear you say that, because Hawthorne reminds me very much of you. You both seem concerned with similar experiences; you both have earned reputations for stylistic excellence.

Updike: Well, one would love even to aspire to be as good as Hawthorne, and, living in New England as I do, I find myself thrown almost by accident into Hawthorne territory. To return to the question, I suppose I always have some sort of mythological referent in mind when I write. Peter Rabbit figures, if dimly, in *Rabbit, Run*. The idea of a rabbit as a character is there, for example. I was somewhat traumatized as a child by my first readings of the tale, especially in the sense of someone's being trapped. My "rabbit" is trapped, of course, and I work in the brick-colored city of the tale.

Reilly: And with *A Month of Sundays*, you did have *The Scarlet Letter* in mind?

Updike: Very much so. The issue of an adulterous minister dominates the book, although this is a modern minister in a society where adultery has become less dramatic an issue. Also, there's a kind of self-flaying in the novel, which is consistent with Hawthorne.

Reilly: Now that you mention it, I suppose the novel is a re-telling of the tale from Arthur Dimmesdale's point of view. But I guess there is a difference in that your minister is hardly reforming.

Updike: Perhaps I didn't fully convey the moral notion I had in mind. If you'll look closely, perhaps you'll see that at first my Reverend Marshfield writes entirely about the suburban and sexual confusion he left behind. But the longer he stays the more he becomes interested in the people around him, and also the more orthodox his sermons become. So ultimately, he is somewhat ready to go back and try to become a minister again. He is quite concerned at the end with his fellow ministers, and I suppose you could even regard Ms. Prynne's gift of herself as a kind of benediction. I don't know. I guess this is a difficult world to be a good minister in. Perhaps you're right that he isn't as repentant as he might be, but, surely, he's as repentant as he's going to get. . . . There were other considerations in the book besides doing something with Hawthorne. For one thing, the book is about a vacation, anyone's vacation: that strange experience of going away somewhere, entering a new environment and having it dawn upon you that the new environment becomes a reality to you and, to a degree, replaces the place you've left.

Reilly: And as Ms. Prynne said, he did finally come up with a sermon which she felt was acceptable.

Updike: Yes, she did.

Reilly: And I suppose she came up with one of her own?

Updike: Yes. Also, there was a parody of the entire reader-writer relationship in the book. In other words, he was a writer trying to seduce his reader—his only reader, in this case—and her name could be taken as "Miss Print" or "Misprint" as well as "Ms. Prynne." There was a certain "papery" quality to the whole business.

Reilly: Now that I think of it, there were those footnotes too, footnotes that typically emphasized drafts and revisions and puns.

Updike: I wrote and worked on the novel with a machine that I was

unused to, and I did make an annoying number of typos in the drafts.
Finally, I decided I should work some of them into the text. They were
all genuine, by the way; I didn't trump any up. It was an interesting
book to write, really. I was trying to duplicate a diary, and I wanted to
write a novel quickly because I had invested an enormous amount of
time on *Buchanan Dying*—which had come effectively to nothing except a fairly pretty book that had made no sort of splash. I felt I owed
Knopf a novel, and I wanted to produce one as efficiently as possible.
I decided the most efficient strategy would be to work with a man
writing whatever popped into his head each day. Of course, I didn't
pump it out as quickly as Marshfield did: writing is a long and careful
enterprise. But I did more or less imitate his "See what happens" attack. It was fun really, typos and all.

Reilly: I'm curious about the way you compose. For example, when
you're working, do you go directly onto a typewriter?

Updike: No, and I don't recommend such a method. As a rule, I do
a lot of my first writing in longhand. I find I can usually work with
short stories and book reviews on the typewriter, but when dealing
with something the length and scope of a novel, it helps to have that
quiet little operation of a pencil, and an eraser, on paper. The problem
with this method is you find yourself stuck with a manuscript that only
you can type—and typing itself becomes a form of revision that can
add months to the process. So, although I occasionally will switch to
the typewriter for a passage or two, most of my original work is done
by hand.

Reilly: And, as you say, you revise in the process of typing?

Updike: Right, perhaps "tamper" is an appropriate and honorable
word for that stage. At the same time, you have to keep in mind that,
although you're trying to get it right, you don't want to become so
hung up in your search for instant perfection that you disrupt whatever
might develop. Frequently it helps to put the manuscript away for a
time so when you come back to it, you have a fresh eye. Of course,
you never stop fussing. I am working on the proofs to *The Coup* right
now, and that has suffered from I don't know how many readings and
revisions.

Reilly: This is your new work, set in Africa?

Updike: That's correct. *The Coup* is the sort of book that, if it's
going to be right at all, should be, well, exquisite—it should chime.

There's a kind of echoing effect which I attempt in the novel, so I find
myself constantly adjusting valves and fretting over small things, like
repeating adjectives over a space of many pages. It's been a fussy sort
of book.

Reilly: For this interview, I've re-read most of your novels and
found myself, the second time through, being very moved by the two
Rabbit books. What I am particularly shaken by was your use of the
catastrophe: in *Rabbit, Run*, the death of the baby; in *Redux*, the immo-
lation of Jill. First, am I correct in assuming that throughout the writing process of each novel you knew in advance that particular character was going to be destroyed?

Updike: Yes. A writer has at least a dim sense of his plot as he
begins and, unlike Nabokov or Faulkner, I am not very casual about
killing off my characters. Violent death, indeed death of any sort, is a
fairly unusual occurrence in my work, and I am reluctant to insert it
gratuitously. So it takes a lot out of me to kill a character. I recall
when I wrote the scene when the baby drowns, I was in Vermont. I
had dreaded writing that particular episode for some time. Obviously,
there was no real baby involved; only a few sentences and adjectives
on some pieces of paper. But I had babies of my own at the time,
and I found the prospect of writing about the infanticide unsettling. I
wrote the scene virtually at a sitting. Actually it was a very long day
in which I composed, as I recall, seventeen long pages. I never much
changed that section either; I kept it in Janice's mind, I retained almost all of the words. So, yes, writing that scene took a good deal
out of me. And, yes, I knew from the start I wanted a catastrophe
that would be both surprising and shocking.

Reilly: And Jill's death in the fire?

Updike: I'm pleased you associated the two because the death of
Jill was designed as a counterpart of sorts to the baby's death. Janice
inadvertently kills an innocent in the first book, so Rabbit more or
less presides over the destruction of an innocent in the second one.
There's a grisly balancing between the two. Each character strays—
Rabbit in the first, Janice in the second—and their reconciliation is
based at least in some way upon these, if you will, murders. So, I'm
glad you responded positively to them, and I'm glad you sensed a
connection.

Reilly: Even while re-reading the two, I imagined I was in a position similar to a Greek watching an ancient tragedy. The second time through, I knew what was going to happen, I could study the way you anticipated each catastrophe throughout the novel. And yet I was all the more shaken. And I wondered: God, what must the creation of such a carefully anticipated, harrowing event take out of the writer?

Updike: There is a frightful disparity in the narrative arts. The person doing the creating must be in some sense aloof and removed—moving around the machinery, in other words—while the reader gets lost in the tale. I'm sure, for example, the people who make horror movies are by no means as horrified as the people who watch them. But, sure, a writer in this circumstance does try to stir and appall the reader with a guessed-at emotion, and he *does* undergo at least a degree of that emotion.

Reilly: I thought, too, the shift to Janice's viewpoint there was perfect.

Updike: You could almost describe *Rabbit, Run* as an exercise in viewpoint. The entire novel concerns the problem of "Ego" versus "Society," the paradox of being a social creature and still longing to be an individual. The reader naturally sees a good deal of Rabbit's mind and problems, but it's critical that he get a sense of other characters' viewpoints as well. So, Ruth has a monologue, Eccles has an extended scene, and although we don't see a good deal of Janice's mind, we do live with her at this moment of crisis. That's one of the exciting aspects of the novel: the potential of getting out of the hero's head and into someone else's.

Reilly: And, not to belabor what you may have said, in *Rabbit Redux* you weren't brooding over what to do with Jill? You had decided to destroy her from the start?

Updike: Yes, you could say that was a part of the plot right from the start. And not just that, but also the idea of Rabbit and a, let's say, militant black man in some kind of collusion that will result in the death of a "flower child"—that was part of the plan from the beginning. I use the term "flower child" carefully. The book is very much set in the late sixties and is very much informed by the news of that unhappy time.

Reilly: And yet, the reader is always grounded by the perspective of Rabbit. There's always that conventional, at least consistent, point of reference in the face of so many shocking and, I guess, radical events.

Updike: I feel a lot of Americans at the time, probably myself included, must have felt rather invaded, almost pushed out of sight, at
that time. The idea of a black man with his very different, oh, "world
views," moving into a small town suburb, provides, I think, a legiti-
mate context for my story. Those small cities—and not simply the
ones in Pennsylvania but in many places in the country—are almost
like self-contained ghettos. Surely they've enjoyed rather tame and un-
complicated race-relations. The relations tend to operate entirely to the
benefit of the white power-elite, and the blacks do tend to be rather
docile. Just compare the awareness and assertiveness of the inner-city
blacks who tend to take a vigorous role in the administration of their
cities. So, I feel it is natural for Rabbit to have grown up fairly un-
aware of the events that were about to engulf him.

Reilly: I feel one of the services you perform for us readers is your
habit of subtitling your novels. In the case of *Marry Me*, you subtitled
it *A Romance*. Now, when I think of a "romance," I think of idealized
lovers and Virtue Triumphant. And when I read *Marry Me*, I found
myself constantly measuring your work against those ideas. Ultimately
I wondered whether I was indulging in a form of "reader over-kill." I
wondered whether you threw in the subtitle because there were a few
love affairs going on, or whether you were involving that old tradition.
Or whether you were making a comment about the inability of modern
society to nurture romance?

Updike: The book has a curious history. It was a manuscript that I
had, for a long time, put aside for a number of reasons—not all of
them personal. Some *were* personal, but in addition I just didn't think
the book, well, "came off." It lacked the kind of playful, creatorly
"something" that the novels I'm proud of, and the novels by others
that I enjoy, possess. On the other hand, it did seem too good to lie
fallow and the second chapter had appeared in *The New Yorker* some
years earlier. So I did bring it out. At any rate, my unease about the
book's lack of, let's say, sociology led me to give it the subtitle as a
way of cutting it off from the other novels. I suppose you could consider the subtitle a put-down of the book. There were a number of other reasons why I added the subtitle, though. I think people behave
romantically in it—they behave in a manner no one could now—and it
is all about being in love. Also, I had the perhaps idiotic notion that,
since romances are so popular, perhaps the subtitle would help the

book's sales. I don't think it did. People can readily distinguish me from Barbara Cartland, I'm afraid. Then there is the fact that by the time I came to publish the book, the historical moment in which this behavior was typical, or possible, had passed. In that sense, you could say romances themselves recall better "Olden Days," and the vents of the novel happened in those Olden Days under Kennedy when Camelot was still flourishing. So, there are a number of reasons to justify my calling it a Romance. But the quintessential reason was to set it apart from the eight or so novels I've written.

In the same way, I called *Bech* a "book" because it's not a novel. It began as a single story which was quite successful and it almost seemed to call out for the type of "redux" I later gave Rabbit. It was a way of unpacking the kinds of experience that only a writer has, but I unpacked it via an alter ego who wasn't myself. Rather, he was my opposite in many ways, and that made it rather fun. The last couple of stories in *Bech* were written, of course, with a book in mind. They were composed to round out—"fill in" might be a better term—the book as such, but basically *Bech* is a set of short stories, not a novel.

Reilly: Now that you mention it, wasn't the "Journal" at the end of *Bech* adapted from something else?

Updike: Yes it was. The "Journal" was part of a long Russian piece which I had contemplated but which didn't work out. As it turned out, I salvaged the little chapter, "Rich in Russia," and the "Journal." It would appear they were all I had to say about the Soviet Union.

Reilly: I gather in the case of *Marry Me* and *Bech* and *Buchanan* you drew a line and decided a particular work could not appropriately be called a "novel." I'm sure you don't have a list of definitions on hand, but do you recognize criteria that make a novel a novel?

Updike: I suppose anything that is a compilation of book-length fictional prose by a single author qualifies, and sometimes I wonder if that isn't all there is to some novels. But I feel there is more to it. I feel that some of the long prose works that, oh, some of my fellow *New Yorker* writers produce from their short stories are novels in name only. Personally, I'm rather pleased when no one can excerpt from a novel of mine and make it stand alone. It shows the work really is a novel and not simply a cluster of pieces. I didn't mean to denigrate *Bech* when I called it a book; in fact, I think it has a number of admirable qualities. And I thoroughly enjoyed writing about Henry Bech. I

write so often about middle-brow or low-brow people that it was fun
to write about someone—there's no adequate way to phrase this—who
permits me to write without holding back, without compensating for
the character's mind. But the whole texture of the book was that of
short stories, and I couldn't bring myself to call it a novel.

Reilly: Bech has some dismal things to say about the agonies a writer
must endure. Is it really that bleak? Do you find yourself tormented by
bouts of depression, unfavorable reviews, periods of stagnation?

Updike: Alas, poor Bech. I just published another Bech story in
The New Yorker, and someone sought me out to inquire whether it's
all that bad. Actually, it's a happy kind of unhappiness. I'm very happy being a writer and, despite his protests, I think Bech is too. For
one thing, I don't feel that my stories are that depressing—at least the
Bech ones aren't. I suppose some of my domestic tales could be described as depressing, and surely some of the *Rabbit* episodes are
meant to be disturbing. But, no, the *Bech* stories treat a sort of playful
misery and they shouldn't be extended to suggest I'm bewailing the lot
of the writer. I do know some writers who could be described as being
stalled the way Bech is—you don't have to know many writers to meet
such people. But even though they're stalled in a period of aridity, like
Bech they continue to enjoy most of the benefits of being a writer in
our society. They seem to be able to generate that certain charisma
writers are associated with, and they manage to find people to admire
them as artists. It's not so bad. Bech's career, I think, is based to a
degree on Salinger's and I guess there is something of Kerouac in him.
He's a writer who has stopped writing. But keep in mind that Bech's
novels, and the novels of other stalled writers, have not been forgotten.
His problem is that he has to live with the consciousness that, even
though he is famous and making money, he's no longer doing his
thing. I suppose he's kind of a modernist. Perhaps I share his faults
after all. Bech is nine or ten years older than I, he wants his work to
be absolutely right, and he frequently worries that nothing he does is
ever quite good enough.

Reilly: As I recall, you said you wrote *Buchanan Dying* as ''an act
of penance'' for having authored a commercially successful book. I'm
sure you were being whimsical, but that got me thinking. Was the successful one *Couples*?

Updike: That's right.

Reilly: I wonder, do you ever sense in the process of writing that, "Wow, this one is really going to go over well?" For example, with *Couples*, did you have any idea that it would be the success it was?

Updike: I really didn't think I would make a lot of money out of *Couples*, although I did hope it would do all right. Again, it began as one of these "design problems" of trying to write about interwoven people and a community. In my mind it was an honorable attempt to describe a certain current reality. It may have passed my mind that, since it was long, it might sell. But I never dreamed it would enjoy the popularity it did. Ironically, once it proved successful, I was annoyed it wasn't selling even better; that's the terrible thing about writing even a moderately successful book.

I was joking when I spoke about an act of penance, of course, but with the success of *Couples* I did think I could afford to undertake a couple of arcane projects. One was the composition of a long philosophic poem that turned out to be *Midpoint*. The other was a novel on James Buchanan—at least it was conceived as a novel, it wound up a drama. However it turned out, *Buchanan Dying* was quite a project. The research tied me up for over a year, and in the end I didn't have a novel to write anyway. But when you make a lot of money, you are given a certain license, not to try to make more, but to attempt something that's been on your mind.

Reilly: The amount of work in and around *Buchanan* was impressive. As I recall, the "Acknowledgements" indicated you even did quite a bit of field research.

Updike: I tried to find out what could be learned about a single historical figure, but when I began I honestly didn't know that Buchanan had had such a long and documented career. It was far from unpleasant, though. After a little digging, I discovered that what seemed obscure was reasonably available, and it was fun to visit those southern colleges and ramble around in the letters. I became very impressed by a biography written by Phillip Klein, and I suppose in a sense I wound up trying to duplicate Klein's achievement: that of reading a pattern into Buchanan's life. I'm not sure it came out in my work as clearly as I had hoped. But, briefly, it was the pattern of a man who had been stung by experiences early in life, had spent all of his life trying to avoid trouble, and had received a big dose of it at the end. Now that really *is* a Greek plot, if one could do it right. But this cautious, peaceable, evasive, even cowardly, fellow was suddenly saddled with the imminent Civil War.

Reilly: Well, I enjoyed the play very much. You said last month in the *New York Times Book Review* that you were working on "a musical comedy version of *Middlemarch*." Much as I enjoyed your first excursion into drama, I hope that isn't true.

Updike (smiling): No.

Reilly: Thank God. I wasn't prepared to labor through all 800 pages of Eliot for the interview.

Updike: You never know, though. There is no idea so whimsical that it couldn't find its way onto the stage some day. The things they're making musical comedies about almost defy the imagination. Someone just made one about Mrs. Peron's adventures, for instance. But my *Middlemarch* was meant as a joke.

Reilly: I'm sure I'm one of many who would welcome another play by you. I should add I haven't seen your *Buchanan* staged, though.

Updike: Your opportunities were limited. It was produced once in Lancaster, Pennsylvania, with hard scenery and with actors who actually memorized the lines. And it was given a more casual reading in San Diego. Both times it had to be cut, however. The trouble was, I sat down to write it with a novelist's frame of mind, and I ultimately wanted to tell the tale fully, even if in play form. A real playwright would have reduced his material to the ninety or so pages that are feasible. If I ever could locate a producer in whom I had confidence and who was enthusiastic about the project, perhaps I could produce a "cut" version of my own. As I conceived it, the play was going to consist of only two acts. In the first one, we find him in bed, everyone urges him to get up, get out, do something; finally he does get out of bed. In the second act, he's reduced to the same bed by these terrible events. It was supposed to have been a simple play.

Reilly: I suppose then you didn't originally plan to end it the way you did, with that final scene. It reminded me of Conrad's Kurtz with his final recognition of "the horror."

Updike: No, I don't think so. What happened was, I got too much material and then the working out of the historically verifiable events and speeches became unwieldy. So I resorted to a three-act form. But my feeling now is that I did fail with respect to my own design and intentions. *Buchanan Dying* should be a two-act play.

Reilly: It's ironic that, despite such a wealth of historical materials, some enigmas remain. I'm thinking especially about Anne Coleman's death: the question of whether or not she killed herself.

Updike: I think I come down on the side of suicide, don't I? But it's just a guess, maybe a bad guess. I have to confess I was astonished that her sister wound up meeting an almost identical end just six years later.

Reilly: True. Even in the same city.

Updike: Perhaps that's something we should ponder. Philadelphia: Suicide Capital of the Nineteenth Century.

Reilly: So, at least for the moment, you're not contemplating any more plays?

Updike: I don't have any ideas now, and I don't relish the thought of dealing with the people who produce plays. You get involved with so many other egos and, in the end, what you have is only partially your own creation. Actors and directors have such an impact upon it. Now, what *Buchanan* could be productively done as is a television drama. They do, it seems to me, more and more serious two-hour dramas on television, and *Buchanan* would lend itself to the possibilities television close-ups present. What you need in *Buchanan* is a good deal of emphasis upon Buchanan's face, and you also need the ability to fade out and in. On the stage this is always clumsy. I tried to allow for it in my text but I'm not sure I was entirely successful. A filmic medium could do it easily.

Reilly: Did you have any influence upon the Lancaster production?

Updike: To an extent. Lancaster is quite close to where my mother lives and so I was able to combine my trip with a visit home. Ed Brubaker, who is the head of drama at the college there, and I went over his cuts and I felt that, since he was brave enough to undertake the production, I had no business second-guessing him. But I went over the cuts, made a few suggestions, and encouraged my publisher to cooperate with him. My thought was that, although the Lancaster people had very little money, they cared deeply and this would probably be the best production we were going to get. Ironically, they chose to delete quite a few of the local references; their attention seemed focused more upon the national figure than upon the "Lancaster boy." Finally, I attended a dress rehearsal and made a few suggestions and couple of cuts of my own. But that was it. I can't claim I was very much involved.

Reilly: Did you see the actual presentation?

Updike: Oh sure. My editor came down from New York, and we both attended the opening. It's an odd and exciting feeling to see something you've created acted out, and I thought they did very well. A problem of sorts was that both the Lancaster and the San Diego productions were done with largely collegiate casts, and what you need for those politicians are corpulent, authentically old men. Even though their parts aren't major ones, it's critical that they project a sense of contending power and a sense of Buchanan's being pinched by their pressures. So, it would be fun, if possible, to see a full-fledged production.

Reilly: And, ideally, you'd like to see that production on television?

Updike: Yes, I think television would be the best medium. I've been thinking a lot about television of late. A number of my stories dealing with people called "The Maples" are being produced for something scheduled, I think, for early 1979, and it occurred to me that I might use this opportunity to feel out reactions to a *Buchanan* project. But I've seen too many writers become infatuated with the movies or the theater and waste an awful lot of time. The beauty of novel writing is that it's a small enough industry that you can pretty much call your own shots. You don't have to fight over strategies and details. It's your product and, when you sign your name on it, it's entirely your own. Also, I like books physically: they travel easily, you don't have to go to New York to see them, you don't have to tune them in at a precise time. But still there is a bliss to writing plays: not having to move people in and out of rooms, not having to describe the furniture and costumes—just the raw string of words.

Reilly: I guess there is less to worry about in playwriting. You brought out in your "Afterword" to *Buchanan* that it was convenient to have a director to brood about costuming and movements and whatever.

Updike: I did say that, didn't I? I suppose I said a good deal in the "Afterword." I didn't mean it to be quite so long, but I really found myself being drawn into it. I'm referring to the passages where I described the type of novel I wanted to write and that almost eerie sense of being in contact with a dead man. It was fascinating to be probing behind the man's name and reputation to find the reality there. I can imagine why historians get really hooked on their craft; it's remarkable to discover that, well, "Past" that's alive under there somewhere.

Reilly: I think portions of the "Afterword" profit from being the product of a novelist and, if I may, amateur historian. I think the part where you describe going back to Buchanan's home and not being able to get inside was almost metaphoric for the problem you had in attempting to write the novel.

Updike: It very much was. I couldn't get in in a number of ways. You can read and read and write and write, but sometimes you just can't get in. I wonder if I'll ever stop trying. I was down there recently with my wife—I thought she would like to see it—and I found myself still learning. During the hostess' prattle I found myself being startled by things I didn't know and I recall thinking, "Well, God, maybe that's an angle." But a terribly difficult aspect for me is the task of imagining what the daily life of, not just a politician, but a lawyer must have been like. So much of the novel would have to concern him as a lawyer and would have to be about the law as a shaper of political perceptions.

Reilly: In one of the interviews you gave after the book *Buchanan Dying* was published, you made a remarkable statement. You were asked if you were drawing an analogy between Buchanan's aborted Presidency and Richard Nixon's, and you said a better analogy would be between Buchanan's and Lyndon Johnson's Presidencies. Did you have that in mind while you were writing the play?

Updike: Yes. I began the research for the play when Johnson was still President and, yes, the play was much more concerned with Johnson's agony. Like Buchanan he pretty much brought his problems upon himself but, again like Johnson, he inherited a long and building set of historical circumstances that he neither caused nor could be expected to entirely control. Also, Johnson had to live with that sense of being hated—recall that for a long time he could speak only at military bases, while at the same moment an anti-Johnson rally could attract thousands. Buchanan went through some of that as the Civil War developed during his Presidency and, although I don't make much of it in the play, he endured it after the war as well. Now, Richard Nixon's problems came along in a different way. I did mention him in the "Afterword," but Nixon's problem was basically a trivial one involving

petty dishonesty, something that needn't have happened. Whereas
Buchanan and, to an extent, Johnson were obliged to cash a lot of bad
checks, not all of which they wrote.

Reilly: Is *The Centaur* still your favorite book?

Updike: I keep saying that, but it is getting older and older. When I
glance backward, I tend to like those books which have something, oh,
tricky about them. So to *The Centaur* I would add as favorites
Buchanan's Dying—its strange hodge-podgy nature notwithstanding—
and *A Month of Sundays*.

Reilly: I'm glad you said that. I admired *A Month of Sundays* very
much.

Updike: I'm glad *you* said that. I felt it was an earnest book and
was disappointed to find it rather snippily received. To me it was a
kind of breakthrough. The material wasn't unprecedented, but I was
able to grapple with topics like the church and religion, and even now
when I pick it up and read a few pages I'm amused. Maybe that's not
the test of a novel, though; maybe the test involves what a novel does
to you during a long immersion.

Reilly: I think I know what you mean. I enjoyed the way you could
approach issues like religion and adultery, perhaps even "the abyss,"
in a beguiling manner. It's not a whimsical approach but . . .

Updike (smiling): Possibly I've been there too often in the past.

Reilly: I didn't mean that. I meant the book had a fresh perspective
and I found it very effective. Ultimately, I began to take the novel very
seriously: studying the sermons, scowling at Tom, trying to develop a
sense of moral outrage about him. He was a hard character to dislike,
though.

Updike: Well, good.

Reilly: One thing that has always struck me about novels is they
seem so less susceptible to post-publication revision than a poem. I
think of Whitman who revised so frequently in each new edition. Is
there ever a time when you would like to return to a novel and revise it?

Updike: I recently asked for, and was granted, the right to bring out
a revised edition of *The Poorhouse Fair*, which was my first book, but
I changed very little of it. It's curious, but you find that your naïveté
at the time is inextricably bound up with the virtues of the book. So I
think you go back to re-write earlier works, as Henry James did, at
your peril. *Couples* was so deplored I've found myself wondering

whether I shouldn't trim it a bit; but, even there, no. Some books have typos and errors; surely you can find a sentence here and there that could be improved upon. But, no, I don't want to go back and change what I've written. I'd much rather tackle a similar problem in a new way. I may seem a "fast" writer, but I'm not. Nor do I consider myself a careless writer: I feel all my books are carefully considered and written.

Reilly: This isn't an example of revision, but you did re-create many of the characters in *Rabbit, Run* for your *Rabbit Redux*. When you were working on *Redux* did you find yourself fighting to maintain consistency in your depiction of characters like Harry and Janice?

Updike: No, but maybe I wasn't as worried about consistency as I should have been. I have noticed that people do change and that people themselves aren't consistent. But I re-read *Rabbit, Run* before beginning and I know I wanted to show other things about the characters. Ten years had passed, in other words, and they now have almost reversed roles. She is liberal and open, he has become rather stolid and closed. The book is really about his re-education. Personally, I think such a reversal is quite possible in the course of a human life. And the rest is just done with faith: a faith that the characters are sufficiently "in you" so you can treat them with integrity and consistency.

Reilly: You've been asked this before, but not for awhile. You so brilliantly resurrected Rabbit and his warren for *Rabbit Redux* and in an interview you devised for the *New York Times*, "Henry Bech" predicted you would write at least one more *Rabbit* novel. Now that *The Coup* is behind you, are you considering going back to Rabbit?

Updike: I wonder whether I should try it again. You can muddy a good impression with a sequel, I think, and you run a very definite risk with a sequel to a sequel. An attractive possibility would be to create a tetralogy in the end that would have a massive nineteenth-century quality to it. But if I did, it would be crucial that I maintain something of the right level throughout the works. To follow with a weaker book would be unfortunate. I wrote *Rabbit Redux* at a fairly rapid, for me, pace and without too much reflection. And it seemed to take off. I became hypnotized by it, in other words, and I hope the reader became somewhat hypnotized too. But because the novel received a number of kind reviews, and continues to receive them, I'm dubious about having at it again. For example, I should worry about whether I'm too removed from the Pennsylvania *milieu* to really do it right.

Reilly: Well, I know you're not looking for advice, but you did say once that 1979 would be a good year to consider a third encounter with Rabbit. And at one point you did more or less sketch a tetralogy.

Updike: At one point, I did have a rather elaborate quartet of novels in mind. My thought was to write one novel, *The Poorhouse Fair*, set in the future; another, *Rabbit, Run*, in the present; a third, *The Centaur*, in the remembered past; and a fourth, *Buchanan Dying*, in the historical past. But your point is a valid one. I have kind of promised a tetralogy, and I do tend to keep my promises. My next one won't involve Rabbit, though. I know what I want to do next, something you could call a "New England novel." Let's put it this way: if Harry Angstrom and I both live into our sixties, that means I'll have a couple of decades to get back to him.

Reilly: In 1957, you published a poem called "Ex-Basketball Player." Was that the source of *Rabbit, Run*?

Updike: The ultimate source is not particularly literary. Berks County, Pennsylvania, is crammed with ex-basketball players and, because my father was a ticket-taker, I went to a lot of games. My first treatment of the theme was a story I wrote in my senior year in college. It's called "Ace in the Hole" and, if you haven't seen it, it was re-printed in *The Same Door*. It's the oldest piece in there, even older than the title story. I wrote the poem, "Ex-Basketball Player," the first summer I was out of college, although it took about a year for *The New Yorker* to publish it. I have fond memories of the poem: it was one of the very first of my verses which *The New Yorker* published, and it's far and away my most anthologized poem. Indeed, that single poem has probably made more money than all my others put together. So, the theme for *Rabbit, Run* was simply there, and I wouldn't say the novel derived from the story or the poem as such. All of them came out of my interest in the phenomenon of an athlete outliving his time.

Reilly: Perhaps I'm straining for connections now, but is there any link between Reverends Eccles in *Rabbit, Run* and Marshfield in *A Month of Sundays*? Is Marshfield, in effect, Eccles Redux?

Updike: There was no conscious link on my part. Like the ex-basketball player, the minister seems to figure in our society, and certainly each of those characters shared something that attracted my imagina-

tion. Both are "caught." The practicing minister is in a terribly difficult position in our pretty well de-Christianized, inconsolable age. But
they keep going, don't they? I have a number of friends in the clergy,
and I admire them.

Reilly: I guess this is my "Say it ain't so" question. You said at the
end of your remarks on James Buchanan: "This book constitutes, I
trust, my final volume of homage to my native state." And yet I can't
help but sigh fondly over your lines in *Midpoint*:

> The Playground's dust was richer once than loam,
> And green, green as Eden, the slow path home.

What a line! I digress, but that's such an extraordinary poem!

Updike: I'm glad somebody liked it. I worked very hard on it and
wanted it to be good. As I said, I don't feel I'm as successful with poetry as I once was, but I remain pleased with *Midpoint*. It's about the
mystery of being alive—of being *you* as opposed to being somebody
else. Perhaps that's the abiding mystery in my metaphysical universe.
But your question was about Pennsylvania?

Reilly: Yes. You have no wish to sow again in the rich loam?

Updike: Well, I did write *Rabbit Redux* after I wrote those lines,
didn't I? So I am not averse to returning to Pennsylvania if I think I
can. I did have that rather elaborate quartet of books in mind and, as I
said, the novel *Buchanan Dying* was going to have been the last one. It
would certainly please me to finish that project. But a writer can use
up a place. I haven't lived in Pennsylvania for nearly thirty years—can
that be true? yes, I guess it is—and I sometimes wonder if I can return once too often. One thinks of John O'Hara continually coming
back. . . . But I suppose what I would really be returning to is "my"
old Pennsylvania, my boyhood in essence. I've tried to write about
other parts of the country, though, and *The Coup* is set in another
country entirely. But if a Pennsylvania topic presented itself, I wouldn't
turn away from it.

Reilly: For the moment at least, you've "moved" largely to New
England?

Updike: More or less. The Connecticut of *Marry Me* is a bit
sketchy, but a lot of the short stories are firmly placed in New England.
And the New England of *Couples* reflects the complexities of using a
given locale. I had lived in Ipswich, Massachusetts, for a long time
and, because I had young children, became quite involved in the com-

munity. My wife and I worked on civic projects, we enjoyed the varied types of people in town, we learned Ipswich's history. So I felt I knew enough about it and was sufficiently excited about it to locate a novel in a somewhat similar town. It's quite an experience to attempt to re-create that type of dense reality. . . . Yet even as I talk I'm driven to contrast New England with Pennsylvania. The type of reality one feels as a child is provocative. It's a time where, in your helplessness and what-not, you're truly exposed to a place, almost thrown into it. Inevitably, things impress you as being very exciting and immense. The older you get, the more selective you become in your activities, and in a sense the more restricted you become in your social knowledge. Anyway, this novel I have in my head right now seems definitely to be a New England novel.

Reilly: Do you give yourself a break between novels? With *The Coup* in final galleys and the new one still in your head, do you take a long layoff or experience a dry period?

Updike: The break I gave myself this time was to work on some short stories, which I have been trying to get to for a long time, and squeeze in a couple of reviews. But typically I get nervous and unhappy if I don't write something after a little while. I like the sense of putting something on paper. In addition, the day to day business of being a writer provides a constant break from writing itself. Most people don't realize the amount of energy a writer expends reading proofs or doing research or answering letters. As for dry periods, I am not inordinately bothered by those, although I suppose I've had my share. Lately I've had a couple of bouts of "word craziness," though. For a time it seemed that after every sentence I wrote, I sensed I had written it somewhere before. I began to wonder whether my vocabulary wasn't shrinking under me. So right now, I'm not pushing myself. I'm collecting my reviews and collecting my short stories since 1971. And while I'm waiting for the novel to form in my head, I'm writing some short stories as well.

Reilly: Is a short story a fairly spontaneous endeavor when compared to a novel? Does it more or less spring quickly from the head to the pen?

Updike: Yes. What you need in a novel is for several ideas to come somehow together in an interesting way. But with a short story you need only one spark to begin writing. So it is fairly spontaneous, and I

think the better ones I've written have resulted from a fairly direct de-
livery from inspiration to production. Otherwise, you tend to cool on
the idea and forget what excited you.

Reilly: Are poems similar in nature? Are they written directly and
from an occasion?

Updike: Yes, and then you sit down during what you hope is a moment of peace and try to roll it toward a conclusion. Finding the right
conclusion for a poem can be difficult, however. There is always some
unrolling along the way: getting lines going, then finding they don't
take on their own life. I recall that in the early sixties when I was writing poems well—or at least when it seemed to *me* I was writing them
well—it worked that way. I used to write many of them in the eve-
ning, say, when my wife was off singing, and the kids were in bed,
and there was a moment of peace. At any rate, when it works, you almost run into the ending the way a ball hits a wall. You know you've
found the ending. And when you're not doing it right, you can't find
the ending at all. Perhaps it's true of short stories as well, perhaps of
all the verbal arts. If you're not doing it correctly, you can't determine
when you've ended.

Reilly: When you speak of the endings of your works, I have to
think of the final pages of *Marry Me*, where there is a pair of surprising endings. I realize now that the beginning of the last chapter is a
dream of some sort, but the initial effect of Jerry and Sally's settling
happily down in Wyoming was shocking. Within a couple of pages
you made it obvious that their ending was far from idyllic, that Jerry
in fact was losing his job and perhaps even his mind. But had you
planned the "shocker" all along?

Updike: That was the ending I had in mind, although it wound up
annoying a lot of people. But it honestly was part of my conception to
suggest that somehow after all this vacillation, after Richard's finally
forcing the issue, after ensuring that the resolution was clearly drilled
home—I thought it appropriate for the concept of romance to be reas-
serted. I wanted to have Jerry and Sally get to their "Wyoming," even
if only in a unreal way. Of course, even then reality intruded. The
children were still noisy; and, no matter how intense the romance, life
inevitably becomes qualified by the needs and problems encountered
when two human beings live together. The subsequent "ending" was
meant to impress the real reality, although it honored the spirit of

romance too, through the exotic locale and the final lines. But I didn't want the ending to be as confusing as it apparently was, I thought I had made it clear that they hadn't really gone to Wyoming—that, in fact, Wyoming had been established throughout the book as a fanciful paradise which they were never going to get to.

Reilly: I didn't make myself clear. We were speaking about endings and what I meant to say was I recalled the impact the inital revelation of the Wyoming trip had. But I quickly figured out the illusory nature of the trip—and I'm not quick to figure out anything.

Updike (laughing): Well, good, you pierced my clouds. I'm glad you did, because it took a certain amount of stubbornness on my part to get the book through that way. Editors tend to be pretty literal-minded. They were puzzled by what I was up to, and I had some difficulty persuading them that particular portion did reflect what was happening in an ideal—better, a romantic—realm.

Reilly: Do you have any enormous, long-range projects in the back of your mind? I think of Joyce, for instance, who was muttering at the end about an epic on the sea.

Updike: True, but Joyce was wonderful for setting himself an impossible task and then doing it. You know, I sometimes think that when reviewers and critics search for "Great Writers," they tend to look for that type of massive production. "Bigness" as such is not a special problem for me—witness *Couples*, which was long and not terribly difficult to write. If I find the right place to locate, I do seem to have a lot to say. Although this isn't always the case; I've seen well-placed novels evaporate under me. So at this moment, I have no big book in mind. And, as you may remember, my Henry Bech foundered upon something he called *Think Big*.

On the other hand, if I have a future artistically, I do think it's with the novel. I don't think I can write better short stories than some I've already done, and lately I can't seem to write any poems at all. So, it is the novel that I would like to work with, and the prospect of producing a big one is intriguing. but it would have to be one that deserved its bigness. Who knows what will happen? Thomas Mann's *The Magic Mountain* and Joyce's *Ulysses* grew from short stories and, whatever happens, I feel it is important that such a book simply grow of its own accord. Bigness itself can be problematic. I don't know how you find it, but I suspect I'm similar to many readers in that I'm grateful for a book that's less than 300 pages, and I feel many novels can be written within such limits. On the other hand, large works continue to appear. I've just received a copy of Günter Grass's new book, *The Flounder*, and its size is considerable. I haven't gotten into it yet, but I think he's an author who can write a large book and bring it off well.

Reilly: I guess you're saying that, whatever the length, you're committed to interpreting the world around you in general and important topics in particular?

Updike: I'm not sure I've got a satisfactory grip on the way things are now. I think that as late as *Couples* I understood the currents in our society, but I was still fairly young then. It would seem the older you get the less confident you are of what's going on—and therefore you're not quite as sure about the appropriate style and form for a particular topic. *Couples*, for instance, did strike out confidently to say something about the American middle class in the early sixties. But maybe long works on topics of social importance aren't mine to do. It's hard to be certain. One needs only to recall the rather knife-like nature *Candide* assumed to see how superbly a shorter book can address such issues. I have been thinking quite a bit about myself as a writer and about what I should be doing. But I'm not sure I've come to any absolute conclusions. I sometimes wonder if I couldn't be content simply writing book reviews. I imagine myself on occasion writing a book review each month for *The New Yorker* for the rest of my life.

Reilly: I can tell you don't take such projects lightly. I think your review of Joyce's *Giacomo Joyce* was one of the best I've ever read.

Updike: I got excited about that one and I did quite a bit of work on it. I spent a good deal of time in libraries; I studied, for the first time, Joyce's play *Exiles*; and I read up on Svevo [pen name for Ettore Schmitz].

Reilly: I also admired the review you did on Kurt Vonnegut's *Slapstick*. I've spoken to Vonnegut about it and I felt your analyses and the way you placed it in the context of Vonnegut's other works were admirable.

Updike: I put myself to school over that one because I hadn't read enough Vonnegut. I read the later books as they came out, but I wasn't very familiar with his earlier writing. I think that *Sirens of Titan* is a terrific book and, in some funny way, is his most ambitious one. He's a fascinating writer and I'm not sure I said all that should be said about him. In a sense, you could call him a "lacking" writer. There is a lot he doesn't do—in fact, a lot he doesn't attempt to do. You never feel the kind of human interaction in Vonnegut that you do in almost any page of Tolstoy, for example. But on the other hand, there is something terribly honorable about his work. I think he deserves far more thoughtful consideration than the panning he's been getting lately in the popular presses. *Slapstick*, to me, was an ambitious book, especially considering its small size. It had a lot of ideas in it—it was rather dense in that respect—and I felt it was superior to *Breakfast of Champions*, which was well received. *Slapstick* is an angry book; in fact, so many of his books are angry. Yet there are those extraordinary glimpses of sweetness in Vonnegut's anger—and some of them are wonderful. As an example, recall that black man in *Breakfast of Champions* who more or less hangs mindlessly around the Howard Johnsons. He seems inconsequential, but the character is felt so clearly that, somehow, Vonnegut has made him a true and important piece of America. I admire touches like that.

Reilly: I couldn't agree more. He has an uncanny way of somehow conveying a sense of life the way it is.

Updike: It's often occurred to me that the genius of the novel seems always to involve realism in one way or another. The true novelist is in love with reality. He is a mediator between reality and the reader, and not simply someone who operates in a world of printed words. I suspect that once a writer loses that almost childlike wish to celebrate reality, he begins to churn out unnecessary books. I suppose every writer likes to think his books are necessary, but there seem to be so many around that it's hard to feel that way about.

Reilly: I'm reminded of your statement that you regard each book as "a moral debate" between yourself and the reader. I know that's the effect your work has on me. So often I find myself snapping back at a character or measuring my own life against events in our works.

Updike: Well, great. That's certainly the hope, but you never know what the effect will be on a reader. There is so much that is merely neurotic and personal in a novel that you're never sure whether you're delivering the kind of challenging and relevant description you should be. But it's so important that you keep trying.

Is Updike Up to His Literary Tricks?

Heather Thomas/1980

From the *Reading Eagle*, 31 August 1980, 4. Reprinted by permission of the Reading Eagle Company.

Tasseled corn brushes the late summer haze along the road to John Updike's childhood home. The old red sandstone house stands rooted in earth the color of fire.

Inside beyond the screen door, a man laughs with hearty joy. A collie jabbers and in a minute, the author appears, tousled and blue-jeaned, briefly shy before he becomes articulate and twinkling.

John Updike may be up to his old tricks again.

Still producing—serenely, he says—the work that has made him a literary giant in America—Shillington's native son is working on a new novel with some familiar strains.

"Oh," he says, trying to sound casual about the formidable issue of a work in progress, "it's the same old middle-class muddle that continues to charm me and that I continue to investigate as if it was going to reveal the secret of life.

"But I'm especially secretive about this book," Updike cautions, adding he has said too much too soon about previous works.

Updike, who hopes to finish his 11th novel by December, was talkative, though, on other subjects Saturday during an interview at his mother's home near Plowville. He was here this weekend for a family visit and to attend his 30th Shillington High School reunion.

"For one thing, the Class of '50 was big on class loyalty. Some of us went to kindergarten together," Updike says, explaining why he regularly travels from his Georgetown, Mass., home for the occasions.

For another thing, Updike was class president. He feels an extra obligation to show up.

Besides, "It's fascinating to see time work its wonders on people you've known since they were 5," added the 48-year-old writer, who went on to top honors at Harvard and a brief career at *The New Yorker* magazine.

He is excited and touched by return visits to Berks, interested in

151

what's changed or hasn't, and may not keep a four-year-old promise to write no more about southeastern Pennsylvania. He immortalized Reading in *Rabbit, Run* and its sequel, *Rabbit Redux*.

"I still feel full of things to say and I'm never really totally dry. But maybe I'm not self-critical enough. I don't think being self-critical is something Pennsylvania writers have," Updike muses.

Updike, Reading's Wallace Stevens and Pottsville's John O'Hara are all different, but seem to share a capacity for being "serenely productive," Updike says. It's a talent he values dearly.

Each day after breakfast, Updike heads for his desk and three solid hours of writing, much of it recently literary criticism.

"The meaningful part of my day ends about lunch," he confesses.

But there are no blank spaces, either creatively or personally these days, particularly since he happily remarried nearly three years ago. The author of a consistently growing body of work, including four volumes of poetry, five collections of short stories and one play, Updike still finds writing a magical endeavor.

"I suppose I could rest on my oars at this point and not starve, but the habit is too ingrained," he says. "And I enjoy writing. It's still a magical act for me to have the things come out of nowhere. The happiest phrases and the happiest ideas often seem to come out of nowhere."

If this sounds idyllic, Updike does admit to struggling a bit harder every day to conquer the empty page. He confesses a certain suspense over his unfinished novel, a slight insecurity because he's not sure it's "terrific."

Well past his days as the critics' token WASP among New York's Jewish writers and then as an unwitting, he insists, 70s sexist, Updike resists a new typecast. He finds the critics kinder, if not a bit confused by his own new role as critic.

"Maybe the blood is so drained from the literary life of this country that there's not the energy to mount a real scornful attack on anybody," he says a trifle wryly.

Then, measuring each word slowly, he adds:

"I think I'm seen as kind of a respectable, graying, pale but sprightly inhabitant of limbo."

He doesn't laugh, until someone else does at the thought of a man in his prime as sprightly. But then a full warm laugh tumbles out, his eyes crease and sparkle, and he pulls up in the chair from a pensive slouch.

There is no pretense in the man, none in the living room with its worn furniture, piles of books, and old upright piano, nor in the house with all of its Updike family history.

"As a young man in this house," he recalls, "I would have done anything to get into print. I would have stood on my head, written in Sanskrit, or really tried to write any assignment handed to me. And I've never quite lost the sense of gratitude to be printed.

"I could never afford writer's block," adds the father of four children, ages 19 to 25.

Updike, who worked during his student summers at the *Reading Eagle*, believes a writer's ideas depend on enthusiasm, and disappear without it.

Journalistic fiction in the Capote and Mailer style is something Updike shelves in the "spurious category."

"Fiction by its very origin is so embroiled with the illusion of fact. And fiction perennially depends on some facts. It has some information contact.

"But if you begin with a lie, you're free to record the truth that somehow gets away from even the best reporting."

Nonetheless, he adds, "However fanciful our arabesques, we have to keep deriving energy from the way things are."

Fewer people, though, are turning to novels as a source of insight or wisdom about their own lives, and Updike sees few literary fires burning which would be capable of rekindling public interest in the serious novel.

"Books that do matter don't matter as intensely," he muses. "The kind of wisdom people possess now is derived from television. In a way, why do we insist that reading is good, and watching TV is dumb? I'm not sure it is that way."

He thinks writers must try harder to make reading worthwhile by offering more truth and insight. He is also aware of some obligation to make social comment.

He is not, or tries hard not to be, aware of his fame, choosing to live quietly with his second wife, Martha, in a small New England town far now from the "insulation and isolation" of New York.

"What fame means to a person who possesses it is mainly interference," says Updike. "But it's nice to know I've made my mark."

He is now adequately content.

"My personal life is in good order. I am basically happy. My children, for better or worse, are kind of grown.

"I have no excuse really," Updike continues, "not to concentrate on my art and make it better; although sometimes you do your very best work when you're not trying too hard.

"I have very little reason to complain," he adds. "It's almost frightening, since complaining is part of the human condition."

Updike: "I Think We're All Besieged by Books Crying to Be Read"

Karen Heller/1981

From the Rochester (NY) *Democrat and Chronicle*, 25 October 1981, 1C, 3C. Reprinted by permission of the *Democrat and Chronicle.*

Barely a fortnight passes without the appearance of John Updike's name on some new writing that is invariably precise and equally laudable for its elegant style and nourishing content.

Friday morning, sitting in a stark Strathallan Hotel dining room that he characterized as "for people who don't like orgies," Updike spoke of his writing and himself. His face, though clearly handsome and graced with a healthy, ruddy glow, is a map of wondrous divergencies: His ears aim backward, his aquiline nose dives downward between gray inset eyes while his head inquisitively juts a good three inches in front of a trim frame. To find that Updike speaks as commendably as he writes came as a pleasant discovery.

Updike, just shy of 50, has written 25 books that include novels, poetry, short stories, essays, children's tales and a play. His latest book is *Rabbit Is Rich*, the third Harry "Rabbit" Angstrom novel. In addition, Updike has written several introductions to other writer's works, delivered some excellently crafted lectures (including Friday's on Herman Melville, given at the Xerox Square auditorium as part of the Harold Hacker series sponsored by the Friends of the Rochester Public Library) and manages to monthly bang out perhaps the most thoughtful and compelling book criticism in this country.

But John Updike's first choice was to become a painter. He studied art in England after graduating from Harvard but since that time his painterly intentions have diminished.

"I don't know when I've last picked up a brush," he said in a deep, supple voice. "It's been at least a decade since I did and I miss it because there's nothing quite as exciting as drawing and painting . . . It teaches you an awful lot about precision. And about how hard it is to

155

see things really and how we by and large go through life without seeing a thing.

"The painting is *there* in a way a book is not there. Working on a
painting with pigments on a canvas, that dab can be no other, whereas
what does a set of words mean to a reader? You really don't know. It's
all kind of like throwing darts with a blindfold on."

Now Updike writes an average of three pages a day in Georgetown,
Mass., which he recently wrote of as "a town without qualities."
Without a grimace or smile, he refers to his books as "output" and
"production."

"It's been said I write too much," he said. "It doesn't feel to me as
if I do . . . I think we're all besieged by so many books crying to be
read that our impression of even a moderately productive author is that
he's cramming another book down our throats every time we turn
around.

"And I guess maybe I leave that impression. But a book a year, and
many of my books are rather short, is certainly not great compared to
the output of Dickens, say, or Trollope, or even somebody like D.H.
Lawrence or Evelyn Waugh.

"I think the American notion of writer as priest has also led us to
revere unproductivity as though something magical was happening in
those long gaps when a writer isn't producing a book, and I'm not sure
anything very magical has happened. I think Saul Bellow is a master
of pace in that by the time he does produce a book, we're all kind of
eager for it."

Updike's Rabbit novels have all taken place during the last year of
one decade and appeared in print during either the first or second year
of the next. His active preparation for this decennial event, he said, is
minimal.

"I did not, for example, reread all the way through either *Rabbit,
Run* or *Rabbit Redux* (he pronounces his word RAY-dux) for this, for
fear I would be depressed or somehow find the project not worth it,"
Updike said, twisting his wedding ring around his finger. "Instead, I
bank on my own memory and the faith that Harry Angstrom would be
there for me yet again as he has been before."

Angstrom, who resides in Brewer, Pa., does not stay with Updike in
the interim, "although I was conscious of him watching the Phillies

in those playoff games. I was aware that Harry somewhere was probably agonizing with the Phillies." And how did Angstrom feel last year
when his team won? "He was very pleased," Updike said, laughing.
"I'm sorry that I couldn't include that in the book."

The author believes his recurring protagonist is not "back home
with all the other people I knew in Shillington, (Pa., Updike's hometown). I'm fairly sure he'll be there when I need him. But in the
meantime I have a whole decade—or nine-tenths of a decade—ahead
of me when I should try to write about someone else." Updike is
asked whether Angstrom will outlive him. "I hope not," he laughed.
"I don't intend to go on and on like this indefinitely. I really think if I
can do a fourth (Rabbit novel) that should do it."

Dressed in a gray herringbone jacket, gray flannel pants and paisley
rust tie, Updike looked like a natty professor, an occupation he tried
only briefly during the summer of 1962 at Harvard and of which he is
not enormously enamored.

"Teaching takes a lot of energy. It uses somehow the very brain cells
that you should be writing with," he said. "The summer I did teach I
was struck by how good, in a way, the students' stuff was. I couldn't
see that my own stuff was much better. There was this awful effect of
being on a tightrope and looking down and seeing this abyss of other
writing beneath you. So I was frightened.

"My choice was to kind of make it as a professional writer even if
it was at a kind of humble level, you know, writing ketchup labels or
doing news stories.

"Instead of teaching, I do book reviews" that appear mostly in the
pages of *The New Yorker*. "It's a connection with the workaday world
and with some kind of stability . . . It mitigates my sense of isolation,
especially when I'm in the middle of a novel. You immerse yourself in
a novel for two or more years. You get to feel kind of lonely and a little
bit crazy. Is this really worth doing, and why am I wasting my life?"

The sense of isolation in writing a novel isn't one of selfishness but
rather "heroic, a martyrdom. That is, the world does not need this ur-
gently. There has been no S.O.S. sent out saying: 'Send us a novel.'
So you're doing it more or less out of kind of a sense of duty—duty
to your own talent."

Updike regards the book reviews and the lectures as "a post-college course. I think it helps a bit to be up on what other writers are doing, but only a bit, really. In the end you're very much stuck with your own vision and your sense of language."

His book reviews are largely confined to the works of foreign authors.

"I find that experimentalism lives in Europe at a higher level than it seems to here," he said, "that they still are trying to work out modernism and they are playful and confident of their playfulness, in a way not true of too many American authors."

Playfulness, Updike said, is a quality he'd like associated with his writing.

"I think if an author loses all sense of play in what he's doing," he said, "one loses that child who makes you scribble something. You're in danger of freezing up like an old engine."

Updike is currently working on his own 50th-birthday present, a new publication of his first book, *The Carpentered Hen*, a poetry collection that first appeared 23 years ago. He's also trying to get a book down to his New York publisher, Alfred A. Knopf, by the end of the year.

"It's kind of a novel. I can't talk about it because it will give it away if I say a word."

He also hopes to return to a more quiet existence back in Georgetown.

"I've been very mired in publicity and talk lately," he said, "and I would love to be restored to that state of idleness where one can actually have a poem occur to you." He said he has also, of late, been "slighting the short story."

Just before he left to lunch with friends Friday, Updike added another desire to his list.

"I'd like to go to Germany," he said. "I've never been to Germany. My ancestry is quite German on my mother's side." Updike paused, smiled and added as a footnote, "Before I go, I'd like to learn German."

Interview with John Updike

John Orr/1983

From *New Edinburgh Review* 64 (1984), 28–29. Reprinted by permission of *New Edinburgh Review*, Edinburgh University, Scotland. Conducted the week of 3 September 1983 at the Edinburgh Festival Book Fair.

The relationship of John Updike to his fictional hero Bech is clearly one of art imitating life and life in turn imitating art. At the Edinburgh Festival Book Fair [September 1983], Updike, the star attraction of the fortnight, had done both a Meet the Author session and a reading from his own work, and spent the time in between lurching word-drunk, like Bech, from one interview to the next. My own interview with him was toward the end of the second day just after his reading and second round of autographing books when by all mortal calculation he should have completely concussed. Despite the frenzied nature of such cultural discourse—being bombarded with detailed questions by people he had never seen before in his life and would never see again—Updike remained articulate and composed. Feeling he no longer had anything to prove, he was both modest and effortless, prepared to explore rather than evade aspects of his own work, prepared on occasions to confess error, or inadequacy.

In his first public session he had claimed that in his work he was searching for a "mystical sense of the real." I asked him if he meant by that a search for the miraculous in the detail of everyday life?

"I'm trying to capture, I think, the wonder of the real which is very easy to ignore of course since we're surrounded by the real day after day and it's easy to stop seeing and stop feeling. It's as if we go through life half asleep and wake up for brief moments to both the beauty and the terror of human existence. One couldn't live with the terror daily but the facing of it probably rounds out our sense of being human. I'm trying to convey the fact that the creation of the world is in some way terribly good. We love being alive."

Despite the affirmative note, it is probably true to say that his claim to literary greatness lies in the first of the Harry Angstrom trilogy, *Rabbit, Run*, which evokes less a sense of wonder than anguish and

159

desperation. I asked him if he thought anguish was compatible with wonder.

"I think there is an existential desperation which all men being mortal feel. In *Rabbit, Run*, Harry, having peaked so early, having tasted glory as a high-school athletics star, finds he is not good enough to become a pro and like so many others of his ilk, he becomes nothing. Perhaps in that circumstance you're more aware of your own nothingness. Rabbit feels trapped, trapped by marriage, by a society which asks him to get a job, trapped within his own skin. He has a terror of being himself and not somebody else. It is a specific body, a specific set of circumstances and there's something really claustrophobic about that."

In Updike's other famous and perhaps most controversial novel, *Couples*, which he wrote six years later, the situation of his characters has changed, from small town Pennsylvania to suburban Massachussets. The suburban couples of this novel of sexual manners clearly have an ontological society which Angstrom lacked. Did this not mean too the cushion of a sense of privilege within which to conduct their various rituals?

"Yes, it does. I think the shenanigans in *Couples* are financed by American prosperity and their advantaged position within it. They're not rich but they're not poor either. I think the novel is about the middle class suddenly having the latitude of behaviour the rich used to have. The rich behaved scandalously and now the middle classes can afford to behave scandalously too, to test the bars of their cages, to stray sexually, to be disdainful of their work in a way which was not true of their parents' generation. Their behaviour is a luxury."

Despite this admission, Updike has held in may ways to a positive view of the actual relationships which take place in the novel, seeing them as a fusion of sex and friendship in which one is impossible without the other. I asked if a cynical critic might not want to substitute for the terms "sex and friendship" those of "lust and propinquity"?

"I don't mind the terms lust and propinquity. As far as propinquity is concerned, a lot of our lives are governed by it, starting off with the family that we're born into. It's a kind of coping with the given, with what is handed to us than what is chosen. But what I try to say in the novel is more than that. It's about a moment of the American self-consciousness, about a loss of faith, particularly religious faith. The people in it are scoffers as most people are, but they have lost touch with the political life of the nation. The germ event in my life which prompted *Couples* was that on the night of Kennedy being shot, some friends had scheduled a party and after much agonising, decided to have it, as in the book. In other words we didn't know what gesture to make, so we made none. We had become detached from the national life. Our private lives had become the real concern. There was a monstrous inflation of the private life as against the merged life of the society which struck me and helped me think I should write the book."

I took the opportunity to voice my own misgiving about the novel, which is it elevates sex out of all proportion to its narrative importance. Was there a problem for any modern novelist in linking the continuity of everyday life with the continuity of sexual feeling, especially when the latter is explicit?

"I think there is. It's hard to present sex in fiction. Aesthetically the Molly Bloom soliloquy was a great breakthrough. The thing I like about it is the way the sex is muddled in with all the other details of her day, with various observations about Bloom and the people around her. That's the way I think sex should come. In *Lady Chatterly*, sex is somehow singled out, but it doesn't exist in isolation from the various functions of our social or financial selves. In this respect I would take Joyce rather than Lawrence. I admire his stance of looking at ordinary everyday life and people, his attempt to locate his art in what is instead of, as Lawrence does, in what should be. The 'what is' is the proper ground for the artist to stand on."

In *Couples*, politics is perhaps conspicuous by its omission. But Updike had earlier written about James Buchanan and the problem of presidential disgrace. His recent novel, *The Coup*, set in Africa, was also a study of political leadership and he himself saw it as an allegory of Nixon's term in the White House. I asked him why he himself had never tried to portray high Washington society and whether he thought there was room for a fictional realism in the portrayal of American politics?

"I don't feel the indignation about the Nixon/Kissinger administration which others have. There are things to be said on both sides. I think that in a way Nixon was his own worst victim. I also think there's danger of trying to fictionalize actual events which occur within the full glare of publicity. There are memoirs and revelations galore, so there's no real room for the novelist to function in. You can maybe write a novel about Charlemagne, but there's no point now in writing on/about Nixon since we know everything. *The Coup* was based on the country's rejection of Nixon. I tried to convey a sense of the country being stained from above. It is about the inertia and isolation of most political leadership as I see it."

If politics is surprisingly absent from much of his work, then he finds to his own surpise that religion is ubiquitous. I asked him specifically about the ending of *Couples*, where the local church is struck by lightning in a storm and is burnt to the ground. Was it divine judgment on Piet and Foxy, the central transgressors? Was it perhaps an act of disgust?

"Yes, I think that's right, a sense of saying 'this won't do'. And remember that Piet and Foxy flee. What is overlooked in the book and I tend to forget it myself is that Piet is not penalized for committing adultery with Foxy but for trying to legitimize the whole thing through marriage. It's the sin of that particular society. Piet becomes an outcast once he rejects Angela. It's a general problem which used to belong to the aristocracy but now afflicts the middle class, whether to keep the home together or seek the ideal mate and break away. I do think that in their own odd way, the people in *Couples* were trying to preserve their homes. There's some sanctioned dalliance outside marriage, but Piet broke the rules with this new woman who didn't know the rules because she was from the outside. Piet knew the rules and knew that he had broken them."

The central contrast and paradox in Updike's work probably relates to his sense of place. His evocation of Brewer, Pennsylvania, is so detailed yet so sparkling, so incandescent that it probably ranks second in American fiction of this century to Faulkner's legendary Jefferson, Mississippi. It is a small industrial town in northeast Pennsylvania which readers can easily populate without having been there. Apart from the Rabbit trilogy, however, most of his fiction, including his current novel-in-progress, is situated in New England. I asked him about the contrast specifically with reference to Brewer, and to Tarbox, the fictional habitat of the characters in *Couples*. Was Tarbox as vivid as Brewer?

"Probably not, because it's a slightly angry creation and the name is

not very affectionate. It's place where a bad utopia is going on whereas
Brewer is basically the world I was born into, and for that reason
seems to be nearer the human condition at large. It's a model for the
small American industrial city which has known better days. What is
amusing is that people are stuck with them anyway, so that they go on
living. Even a dreary city like Brewer has an intense human life in it.
In terms of the changes which have taken place there over the course
of the trilogy, I find a lot of them equally apply to changes which have
taken place in New England where I now live—the explosion outward,
the same rot of the inner city which doesn't really happen in Europe
on the same scale. It's the rot of an inner city inhabited exclusively by
blacks and Puerto Ricans and ringed on its outer fringes by malls for
white suburbanites, a curiously American phenomenon. I think the
flight from the cities is connected to a pastoral nostalgia which means
that every American wants a barbecue pit and a half acre of grass he
can call his own. I think the events which took place in Tarbox took
place to a greater or lesser degree everywhere else. I have a foolish
confidence that my locations will serve as an adequate symbol coast to
coast."

At the same time Updike found himself disturbed by that very uni-
formity, by the collapse of regional differences which made a modern
Faulkner or Hardy impossible. It seemed appropriate that we were
speaking in a hotel room opposite an international book festival, for
"the novel now has to work in a broader geographical frame." He did
not seem to think his own kind of achievement with Brewer could now
be repeated and cited the example of Donald Barthelme's brother,
Frederick, a native of Birmingham, Alabama, writing about it as he
sees it today.

"What you get is a totally plasticized accentless version of America
that is frighteningly cold. The relationships between men and women
don't exist. They slide by one another all the time. Here's a writer writing in the heart of Dixie about a post-passion America which could be
New Jersey or Southern California. It could be anywhere."

John Updike Says a Novelist's Job Is
. . . like Peeping

George Christian/1985

From the *Houston Chronicle*, 31 March 1985, 20, 23, 37.

John Updike cautiously pours himself tea, afraid the pot will dribble. "I adore Thurber," he recalls. "In fact, it's not too much to say that he was my hero." The pot dribbles. Updike smiles. There's no outwitting teapots.

Updike has been here to read from his work at the University of Houston. We're wedging in a chat before he has to go back to talk to some graduate students. An amiable, unexpectedly tall man whose nose arches from a face verging on the rubicund, he's fielding a question: What first drew him to fiction?

"My mother tried to write fiction for much of her adult life," he says. "In fact she's still alive and still trying to write fiction, so the idea of its being a plausible, or possible, activity hit me early. I used to read it and love it. I was a great mystery novel reader, a fair science fiction reader and a great reader of the then well-known American humorists, like Thurber and Benchley.

"About the nicest thing that happened to me as a kid was that when I was about 12 or 13 I used to write letters to famous people, bothering them. I asked Thurber for a drawing, which was quite a presumptuous thing, really. Why should poor Thurber, blind as he was?—but he did. He sent me one of the Thurber dogs. I took that with me everywhere I went, and I still have it in my study, so it was a great talisman, and I always remember his kindness."

Updike grew up in Shillington, Pa., a town of about 5,000, which gives its character to some of his early short stories. At the urging of his family he went to Harvard, hardly the usual route for Shillington boys, he says now, and later to Oxford to study drawing. He soon began to produce light verse and pictures which attracted the attention of *The New Yorker* magazine, Olympian home of Thurber and Benchley. After that he established a reputation for brilliant short stories and finally of novels. The best known of them are his *Rabbit* books, which depict the life and *angst* of Harry (Rabbit) Angstrom, a man on the run from himself. *Rabbit, Run* was the first of a trilogy which includes *Rabbit Redux* and *Rabbit Is Rich*, the latter a 1981 Pulitzer Prize winner. His most recent novel, *The Witches of Eastwick*, was published last fall. Simultaneously, Updike has continued to publish poetry, his latest collection, *Facing Nature*, has just been issued by Knopf.

"I really wanted to be a cartoonist," Updike remembers. "I did a lot of drawing as a kid. But I went to Harvard. It's very hard for me to reconstruct these days because this great leap up out of Shillington now seems kind of surreal."

It was not something the Updikes inevitably did. His mother, however, had noted that many noted American writers had gone to Harvard. She aimed her son in that direction.

"I suppose it was at Harvard that my vocation as a writer, such as it is, was firmed up. It was a very literary sort of place. I majored in English and took some creative writing courses, which were something of a rarity. Harvard did right by me, I must say. I went there a pretty ignorant fresh kid and they filled me in on the English classics."

By that time he had already been writing, though, writing as well as drawing.

"I began by writing a lot of light verse, light verse for the high-school literary magazine. It was a weekly called *The Chatterbox*. I think I began about 15. Verse seems easier to do when you're a teenager. A short story seems *enormous*. Ten or 15 pages of prose when you're 15 seems like an endless waste, but you could do a light verse poem. So I did imitations of Ogden Nash, Phyllis McGinley and a number of others. Light verse was then fairly common, not only in magazines but in newspapers. I wrote a lot of that. I tried a few short stories but I really didn't have a clue about fiction. I really needed those courses I took, in which a lot of fairly obvious things were said, but they weren't obvious to me.

"When I was a sophomore I thought I'd write a novel. It was called *Willow* and it was about what you might expect, a small town rather like Shillington, where I'd been raised. I got about two thirds of the way through it actually, before I gave it up—wisely. That was my first attempt at extended fiction. Somewhere it still exists. Harvard has a lot of my papers on deposit and I think *Willow* may be among those deposited. I wouldn't dare look at it for fear of being too intensely embarrassed."

Nevertheless, *Willow* forecast his later work, he says.

"It wasn't so different. A writer—I suppose any artist—will tackle a thing again and again until he sort of does it. So I came back to some of the themes of that book in writing short stories about a fictional town called Olinger. Those stories were published and have been collected, so I wouldn't say it was a wasted effort. It was just a premature effort."

Some time ago Updike said the Olinger stories were the nearest to his heart, the stories that most nearly represent him. He qualifies that now.

"It's probably less true now because I've written so much more. They appeared off and on in my first two collections. In some of them, I didn't even name the town, but it was obviously that same place. I didn't think of them as a series at that point. I was just trying to sell short stories and support myself and my family.

"But somebody wrote in to Knopf saying he thought it would be nice if my Olinger stories were collected. Alfred Knopf was still active. He liked this idea and said let's do it. So I put them together in chronological order—the order of the hero's age, not the order in which they were written, and made this little book of 11 or 12 short stories.

"In the introduction I did say I thought they were my best short stories. I might have to stand by that. They do have, I think, the most love in them, and I suppose that love is one ingredient of good writing. They're full of affection and the material was very important to me, which helps, I think, interest the reader somehow, the sense that the writer cares. They're very normal—it's about growing up. I do occasionally read one. I haven't written about Olinger in many years.

"They hold up for me, though you try to look ahead always as a writer and not back too fondly at whatever you've done. What's done is done. Your job is to stay alive and keep moving."

Growing up in Shillington was on the whole a good time for him.

"I was an only child and we were not rich but we were not exactly on skid row, either. My father was a high-school teacher, which didn't bring in much money but was respectable. We had some status in the town. It was a town of 5,000, so a high-school teacher's son was somebody. Many people knew me by name. We lived with my grandparents, my mother's parents, in their house. My grandfather was in his way a distinguished man, too. He was a lovely talker. He really had that old-fashioned way of talking as a kind of performance. He had been in his 40s when my mother was born, so he was 90 when he died and I was 23. That makes him almost 70 years older than I. So I had the benefit of living with a man of the past.

"I was born in '32 and we moved in '45, so those years were pretty· well frozen by, first, the Depression—nothing much happened except people struggled to survive. And then the war came along and froze things also. So I grew up in a town that was abnormally still. Nothing changed, except I grew slightly older every day. It was a very stable world.

"My impression of the war was a distant one. I was jumping on tin cans and collecting tin foil and all of that. From the standpoint of an adolescent boy it was kind of a good time, because there was no question that we were right and other guys were wrong and this was a great country and we were going to beat the Japs and the Germans. Everything was very simple. I emerged from that with a kind of simplistic fondness for this country that was tested in the '60s—I fear I'm a kind of simple-minded patriot in a way just because of those impressions.

"Anyway, it was a world in which things held still. The verities were pretty much respected. Bad and scandalous and unfortunate things happened in Shillington, of course. I remember the man next door to us committed suicide one morning. My parents woke up, having heard a gunshot, and he'd put a bullet through his head. But by and large it was an untragic world and a nice-sized world for a child. I felt in control of my environment."

Is he still in control? Updike chuckles. "Less so," he says.

"We moved to a farm where my mother had been born, strange to say. Her parents had sold it when she was in her teens and yet she remained nostalgic about the farm and thought we'd all do better there. It wasn't very far away—my father could still drive to work—but for me it was sort of a blow. I was suddenly surrounded by all this land and corn, and no friends, and I couldn't drive. I read, actually. It was probably a very good thing, looking back on it. Whatever creative or literary aspects I had were developed out of sheer boredom those two years before I got my driver's license."

Then he went to college and married and worked in New York and then moved to New England. He never went back.

"So I've had a rather static life. I've just stayed in New England and written."

Updike once observed that a writer's first 18 years are of critical importance, that somehow sensibility diminishes. He explains what he meant by that.

"One thing is true is that the impressions you get in your first 18 or 20 years are probably the most intense you get, and there's a danger for all of us writers, especially American writers, that after you've written out those first impressions nothing you write again is quite as intense or as intrinsically meaningful. You think of Hemingway's career where the Michigan stories and the first two novels have an effortless power that he never really quite got into again.

"Somehow the way the American psyche is set up, it's not easy to age gracefully as a writer in this country—unlike Europe, where you become an ever grander eminence and continue to pour out your memoirs."

He grins at the thought.

"You think of somebody like (André) Malraux, who got just more august and sort of better and better because he got smarter as he got older. Here we seem to get dumber for some reason."

Americans tend to write themselves out then? He nods. Perhaps.

"I think there has been that tendency. It may be less so now as we become more like Europe. But I think a noticeable pattern in the careers of American writers has been the first gush and then a slowing down or repeating yourself. Thomas Wolfe is another example of a writer who really had only one thing to say, which he said again and again, but it was best the first time. Basically raw stuff: 'This is what I suffered' in wherever. Asheville or Upper Michigan, 'This is my testimony.' It's like a giant revival meeting where all these writers are bringing all these stories of their youths."

I wonder if writers aren't still accumulating experience, still living a life. They don't just shut down, do they?

"It could be," he speculates, "that in some ways the life we lead as adults is basically offensive to us morally, and the American religiosity is such that we don't fully believe in adulthood and distrust adult experience. We'd rather write about being a little boy or a little girl."

I remember something Saul Bellow said: "What's a kid like me doing winning the Nobel Prize?" Updike nods.

"That's right. Bellow again is a writer who—to me his most poignant and moving and rich book is *Augie March*, which although it's
sort of shapeless, it's so full of the urgency of that Chicago material it
just knocks you right out of the page. His own concern, his own interest in these people—it's a fantastic book. Bellow really loved those
people, loved those trolley cars and stockyard smells, loved the hurly
burly and the confusion of it. The fellow loves people putting on an act
and people doing a deal. He likes that very much, but it gets a little
sour in some of the later books. *Humboldt's Gift* struck me as a somewhat sour book in which he didn't quite believe in all these antics."

I wonder how Updike deals with this American problem.

"One way," he says, "is to try to use your supposedly improved
smarts, your supposed wisdom—one should get a little wisdom as you
get older—to try to extend your range. I extended it more or less voluntarily when I moved to New England. I got away from Pennsylvania, so in a sense I shut the door on the Pennsylvania experience. That
was one way, and then I entered a new area with a new kind of material. And also I've written a few books in which I tried to animate
conceptions. *The Coup* is one, which is set in Africa and meant in a
way to be a kind of global parable. *The Witches of Eastwick*, to a lesser degree, is an attempt to write about women and nature and power,
all somewhat from the standpoint of opinion or belief, rather than 'this
is my material.'

"I'm not sure I'm succeeding in this attempt, but I am at least aware
of the problem. I look around for examples—when I review books I
tend to review Europeans because it seems to me they don't have this
particular problem and their writers do remain amusing and interested
through old age. Nabokov, now dead, was a man I greatly admired.
That kind of trickiness, though sometimes it was a little hollow, but at
least the trickiness and playfulness and willingness to combine supreme
mind and supreme cleverness I thought made his late books . . ."

He leaves the sentence unfinished.

"He was an example of a man who was also shut out of his youth.
His youth slammed shut. The revolution came when he was about 18.
So his home terrain was forever sealed for him a sort of magic globe—
you can't get back to it."

Nabokov, of course, began to write in a new language.

"I don't know how he did it except that language isn't as intimidating to Europeans as it is to us, I guess, and he had been raised to speak pretty good English and French, which was standard aristocratic practice. But to write that kind of spectacular English! To teach the native speakers tricks with their own language! To me *Lolita* is amazingly written. He never does rest. Every sentence does something extra, a little extra bit of poetry. He's an exemplar of a man who outwitted time to a degree. *Lolita* was written when he was in his 50s. That's pretty good. You're getting along when you're in your 50s, and to write a book that vital and that daring!

"Another thing that has happened to me, sort of by accident, is that having impulsively decided to write a sequel to *Rabbit, Run*, I've in a way extended my youth a bit. A lot of the *Rabbit* books is what I imagine Pennsylvania to be like from an adult point of view. But the impressions you get in your first 18 years, you do feel very sure about them, so that in a sense I know how things happen in Pennsylvania. It remains pretty much the world I saw in the '30s and '40s. It's a more clannish world than New England."

He's grateful for the 18 years he spent in Pennsylvania, Updike says.

"I think now a childhood spent in one country is a rarish thing and almost a kind of an asset. People move around a lot and they don't really develop any loyalties or any allegiance. We're living in an essentially regionless America, aren't we, where a piece of the Houston strip could be in Atlanta or Worcester, Mass. I hear very few Texas accents here."

Fiction is a form of spying, Updike once said. Would he explain?

"In a funny way, it's journalism of a kind. That is, we are reporting on the private lives of our fellow Americans, or our fellow whatevers. There's a scene in Proust where the Marcel figure, the narrator, looks in a window and sees an erotic episode going on. That kind of peeping into windows is, I think, part of the excitement that writers feel and maybe that we all to some extent feel when we read a novel. We're all voyeurs."

Readers, too?

"I think so. Here we are born into these bodies and circumstances and we're very curious to know how we match up against other people. One of the reasons we read novels is to see how other people live and to test our own solipsistic reality against theirs. Nothing quite does it like fiction, I maintain. I've read sociology, with the statistics and the very patient accounts of this or that family living in Mexico or wherever, and you don't get that spontaneous feeling that 'this is life' you get out of a good novel."

We get views of life in a novel which we can't actually get in reality, he suggests. Looking in windows is discouraged.

"We're born into a family of some kind, and a lot of what we know about how life is lived comes from that family. Maybe there's never again a family as intense as the first one. At any rate, in my writing I've always needed some feeling of bringing news. It may not seem like world-shaking news, but I'm trying to bring some report of how life is going on and how it's changing.

"In *Couples*, for example, I really was impressed by the erosion of not just the marriage vows but of loyalties of all kinds. I was raised in this sort of little make-believe world of war and depression. You grow up and discover that it's all very fragile. So the message of *Couples* was very real to me. Maybe I was a fairly innocent fellow and a less innocent man wouldn't have bothered. But I think being innocent is part of being a writer, probably, that you are struck by things.

"With *The Witches of Eastwick*, again, I was trying to bring word of somehow what it's like to be a free woman, the loneliness of divorcées and the financial pressures they almost all live under. And the consolation they find in each other."

He is in a way taking society's temperature? In a way, yes.

"Something like that, insofar as it more or less falls into my lap. I've just tried to live a normal life, had four children, so a lot of what I've reported on has just happened to me. I haven't gone out and searched for sociological morals. But I think that any of us, just by looking within, can take the temperature of the society. And you're fortunate if you happened to be born an American, because I think that America is kind of where it's been happening and is still happening. Because I think we're really on a kind of frontier here. Two-thirds of the world is trying to think of something better, but really the American style, I think, is a great improvement on past styles for human beings.

"So that whatever goes wrong here is important. That is, whatever is distasteful or sad or unsatisfying in American society, I still would prefer it to any other society that I've seen."

A Conversation with John Updike

Willi Winkler/1985

From *Süddeutsche Zeitung* 92 (20/21 April 1985), *Feuilleton* sec., 5. Translated by Marina Balina. Additional dialogue added from the author's original interview notes. Reprinted by permission of Willi Winkler.

He became famous with his "Rabbit" trilogy—*Rabbit, Run*, *Rabbit Redux*, and *Rabbit Is Rich*—where he describes, at ten year intervals, the life and sufferings of the former basketball star Harry Angstrom, nicknamed "Rabbit." He achieved notoriety with his novel *Couples*, where he brought to the forefront a chain reaction, by design, of broken marriages and spouse-swapping. Our reporter, Willi Winkler, spoke with the 53-year-old American writer in Munich on 18 April 1985.

Mr. Updike, when you were a schoolboy, it was your dream to be a famous cartoonist. What comic strip do you like best of all?

"Spiderman" is the only one which I follow every day in the newspaper. Unlike Superman, he doesn't fly, but he crawls up the walls as a spider—which is certainly something more realistic.

Henry Bech, your writer's alter-ego in the collection of your short stories that appeared recently, complains that Franz Kafka is his older brother who tyrannizes him. Does that also apply to you?

No. It rather applies to writers like Philip Roth, for whom Kafka is a kind of demi-god. In some way Kafka seemed to strike an essential chord. I read him first at the age of 18. I took his stories with me to a tropical island and read them, one by one, at night. There was no electricity on the island—in the darkness, only kerosene burners. The darkness, the hissing lights, the bugs that flew into them: it was a very Kafkaesque setting. Kafka suddenly opens up the desolation, the spiritual unrest which we all feel somehow and are unable to express. He is a very liberating author, and technically he does things that were previously considered impossible. No, for me he is a suffering older brother. And his life could be another important book.

Whom else among European writers do you appreciate besides Kafka?

Graham Greene, Iris Murdoch, Muriel Spark, Milan Kundera, and, naturally, Heinrich Böll and Günter Grass.

Do you know Martin Walser, with whom you are compared again and again in Germany?

No. But I've been directed to him so many times that I will read him.

In your critique of [Peter Handke's] A Moment of True Feeling, *you spoke of an unpleasant feeling that this story evoked in you.*

The fault is mine. I found this Keuschnig, who strolls the streets of Paris without purpose, too chaotic. One never knew what would happen in the next moment.

Once you wrote of Günter Grass that he "has gone so public he can't be bothered to write a novel." What about your political commitment?

I vote. But it is true that I am not much interested in politics. Unlike such European authors as Grass or Sartre, I always had a feeling I would waste my talents if I were to strive for positions of leadership. Traditionally, American writers didn't do that. The first great American writers kept their distance from the political events in the country. One exception was Emerson in the anti-slavery movement. Generally speaking, I try to be useful to my society by telling the truth in fiction without trying to be a politician. This, of course, doesn't mean that all [writers] should act this way. There are exceptions—like Norman Mailer, Gore Vidal, and William Styron, who orient themselves in the direction of becoming public figures—but I get the impression one runs the risk of speaking about something one doesn't know anything about. By European standards, I don't belong to the extreme left, but by American standards I think I do. Every election I have voted for a Democratic president.

For Jimmy Carter, too?

Of course. I could never understand why no one liked Carter.

If you consider yourself nonpolitical, one could be surprised how well politically-located your novels are. A party in Couples *happens the night Kennedy is assassinated in Dallas,* A Month of Sundays *oc-*

curs during the Watergate scandal of Richard Nixon, and it would be impossible to think about the third Rabbit novel without the oil crisis at the end of the seventies as a background.

Unlike most writers, I believe that there is a connection between political events and the life of a common working man. Basically, there seems to be a discrepancy in this country between those who are in power and the intellectuals. Businessmen run America, and business and art don't get on very well. If a new McCarthy should arise, would I stand up against him?—I would have my doubts if I could achieve much. Once I tried to write a historical novel about President James Buchanan, but I failed. There are very few books written about the presidency that one can consider serious literature.

Gore Vidal recently published a novel about Abraham Lincoln.

Gore Vidal is well suited for the task, because he has family ties to politicians. But he is also severely limited by his incredible rejection of the American lifestyle. Vidal writes as if he were coming from the moon. His characters are surprisingly stupid and angry. He also lacks the love one needs to write about something effectively.

Mr. Updike, you continue to write poetry. What do you think about yourself as a poet?

I don't know how one would rank me. Definitely, I'm not a major poet, but in poetry I can say something that cannot be expressed in prose. By working as a poet, I can keep my prose clean, make it free of feelings and words which are mine but don't fit my characters.

In one of your poems, you once sort of declared war against modern America: "An easy Humanism plagues the land;/I choose to take an otherworldly stand." What do you stand for?

I grew up Lutheran, but my parents were not especially religious. I decided then not to give it up, which maybe does make me a conservative in some sense. But because of that, I came to the decision to write about the imperfect world—a world that is fallen. That's why many people find my books so depressing. But for me it isn't depressing to say that the world is imperfect. Here the work begins: One confesses this imperfectness more or less happily and starts to think about what one is to do with the world in this condition.

You then consider yourself a Christian writer?

No. I don't want to be considered a Christian author. It would be more than it is in reality. I am simply a writer who goes to church. In moments of doubt, need, and in the boring moments of my life, I remind myself always that I pay homage with my writing. With writing, or generally with art, we show the world our admiration and express our thanks that we are here. I know that it sounds somewhat strange, but it's my intention to describe the world as the Psalmists did.

E.L. Doctorow said in Ragtime *that Sigmund Freud's ideas destroyed sex in America forever. How do you relate to Freud?*

I, myself, read Freud rather late in life, but I can say that he helped me. He also definitely helped America, because he—on top of the Calvinistic commandment to prove ourselves on earth through the accumulation of wealth—gave us the possibility to prove ourselves in our bedrooms. Since Freud, sexuality is also something positive, not something negative as it was suggested by the Puritans. Freud's concept of the death and destruction drive moves me, even if I can't agree with it.

Why, in your novel, The Witches of Eastwick, *do you bring the devil back to Earth?*

He was never away. *My* devil, Darryl Van Horne, is a weaker figure—no monster. I had an idea to create him as a kind of experimenter, where it would be possible for him, through some short-cut in the physical theory of thermodynamics, to forever solve the energy problems on earth. He's definitely not a Mephisto—but I'm also not an expert on devils.

Henry Bech said once that he became a character of Henry Bech. Are you afraid to become a character of John Updike?

The danger is definitely there, after a trip like this, that one comes back home and asks himself, What is actually happening to me? One has to try to stay as true to yourself as possible, and not to give yourself completely away.

Hawthorne, Melville, Whitman, and the American Experience

Jean-Pierre Salgas/1986

From *La Quinzaine Litteraire* 462 (15 May 1986), 11–12. Translated by Christopher Callahan. Reprinted by permission of *La Quinzaine Litteraire*.

John Updike: poet, novelist, essayist. Born in 1932 in Pennsylvania and raised in the Lutheran faith, educated at Harvard. From 1955–57, first a reporter and then a columnist for *The New Yorker*. His first collection of poems (*The Carpentered Hen*) appeared in 1958, his first novel (*The Poorhouse Fair*) in 1959. Since then, he has authored some 25 books, including the "Rabbit" series and *Couples*, which, in 1968, made him world renowned. He resides today in the Boston area. In France, his books have been published by Juillard, Le Seuil, and Gallimard. Few writers have discussed their tastes in reading as much as he has: *Picked-Up Pieces* and *Hugging the Shore* (Gallimard 1979 and 1986) are devoted to them. Also recommended are the two collections of short stories featuring a Jewish-American writer, *Bech: A Book* and *Bech Is Back* (Gallimard 1972 and 1984).

J.-P.S.: From Proust to [Robert] Pinget, by way of [Raymond] Queneau, Colette, Céline or [Roland] Barthes, your two collections of essays, *Picked-Up Pieces* and *Hugging the Shore*, are to a very large extent devoted to French authors.

J.U.: Yes, and I hope that French critics will not look at them too closely. I am writing for Americans like myself, who read these books in translation and who don't know a great deal about French literary history. I am not a critic like Edmund Wilson or Roland Barthes, I am a novelist who writes reviews. Quite simply, when I began to write [book reviews] for *The New Yorker* around 1960, I told myself that one of the things I could bring to the magazine was some attention to contemporary European writers. I still see myself as a kind of bridge between national cultures.

J.-P.S.: You yourself have been read that way in France: *Couples* was received as a novel about the pill.

J.U.: It was by my fellow countrymen as well. I wrote it because I was shocked by certain things. I really believe that you can read novels the way you would open a window onto another country. I would even say that nothing allows you to go more deeply into a place than a novel does. You can read everything you want about 19th-century Russia, but you are still left with only Tolstoy and Dostoevsky and Turgenev. That is what I am also trying to do: to say what is changing in the United States—through the imagination, to tell the truth about the U.S.

J.-P.S.: Beyond this concern with "national character," your essays surprise a French reader by their appeal at one and the same time to the works themselves and to biography, as well as by their extreme sensitivity to the physical features of the books—that is, their price, dust jacket, and so on.

J.U.: You ought to be able to hold a book in one hand. I am trying to resist a tendency among American publishers to make books larger and larger, more and more ugly, with knock-out covers that give away too much of the story ahead of time . . . all that is part of the text's context. Once again, I am not a critic; the things that interest me in my own books are those that interest me in other books. As far as biographical information goes, it's true that I like to include anything that I find relevant. I am not a reader of biographies; I couldn't read the life of someone whose books I didn't find interesting, like Lytton Strachey, for example. But I was just as enthralled by [George] Painter as by Proust. In the same way, having discovered *Buddenbrooks* for the first time last year—impressed by the contrast between the experience contained in the book, its gravity and wisdom, and the youth of Thomas Mann—I threw myself into Winston's account of Mann's early years.

J.-P.S.: I won't ask you about your great loves in literature; you talk about Proust, Henry Green, and Nabokov, in *Picked-Up Pieces* and *Hugging the Shore*. Conversely, you don't talk as much about your dislikes, with a few exceptions ([Francoise] Sagan, Cabrera Infante, [Jerzy] Kosinski). Are there writers whom you cannot read?

J.U.: Nabokov was very good at that game. He had a long list of people he couldn't stand, and he kept it up to date. I would say Faulkner. I've often tried to read Faulkner. He had a kind of genius, but I

find him greatly overvalued. His novels strike me as rather coarse and
oddly experimental. Otherwise, I have trouble reading blockbusters like
John Irving and Joseph Heller. They hit hard. I don't think a writer
should approach reality with his fists flying that way. Nor do I feel
close to the naturalist school of Norman Mailer or James Jones. Rather
than energy and violence at all costs, I prefer things to be neat and precise: "domestic" writing. I prefer Vermeer to Delacroix.

J.-P.S.: Are there any others among your great loves that you hesi-
tate to reread for fear of liking them less?

J.U.: In *Hugging the Shore*, there are three studies of Hawthorne,
Melville and Whitman which I undertook as part of my education. I
am trying to understand these authors in connection to the American
experience. Melville, for example, I still think is marvelous, but I'm
not sure that I want to reread him. We are sometimes reluctant to return to those authors who inflamed us when we were young and naïve.
But I open up Henry Green from time to time—an English author who
enjoys far too little recognition—in moments of doubt about my own
work. His phrasing reminds me what English allows us to do, to what
extent it is possible to be fresh, direct, casual. Proust also holds up, I
think, although I haven't ever managed to read *Jean Santeuil*. I've described what a revelation, what a shock he was to me at 23: A magic
spider spinning his web—I never imagined that language was capable
of all that! In my own way, I tried to imitate him. You know, the list
of authors who inspire one to imitation is not very long.

J.-P.S.: Which of your own books are you alluding to? *A Month of
Sundays* is a remake of Hawthorne's *Scarlet Letter*.

J.U.: I haven't, strictly speaking, written a "remake" of Proust, but
I feel that his tone is very present in my short stories from the late
fifties and early sixties—for example, in the last two stories from *Pigeon Feathers*—as well as in a novel like *Of the Farm*. It's very different with Hawthorne. He hasn't had anything like the influence on me
that Proust or other authors have. What's more, I only read him at
around age 30. If he really struck me, it is because he must be the
only classic American author who talks about sex! There aren't many
women in *Moby-Dick*, nor in Whitman, Emerson or Thoreau. Hester
Prynne is a very powerful female figure. From this stems my idea, in
A Month of Sundays, to write a parody or a variation, in the musical

sense of the term, on the triangle in *The Scarlet Letter*. You mustn't forget that this kind of thing happens frequently in the United States: clergymen are very vulnerable to the attentions of women.

J.-P.S.: Do you always begin a book under another book's influence?

J.U.: I have almost always begun a book with another book in mind. I think that that way, writers give each other the courage to carry on. Often, the sources would surprise you: *The Poorhouse Fair*, my first novel, was inspired by Henry Green's *Concluding*; the first "Rabbit" book, *Rabbit, Run*, by a novel of Joyce Cary's. For *The Centaur*, I had *Ulysses* in my head at all times. And Pinget gave me the courage to write *The Witches of Eastwick*. While, of course, there are American versions of the small-town novel—Thornton Wilder's *Our Town* or Sherwood Anderson's *Winesburg, Ohio*—it's nonetheless true that I owe to Pinget my interest in gossip, in malicious chit-chat, in the permutability of events as they are reflected and refracted in a community, in the voices of that community.

J.-P.S.: What book is hiding behind *Couples*?

J.U.: *Dangerous Liaisons*.

J.-P.S.: I could continue this line of questioning. What about *Bech*, or *The Coup*?

J.U.: Bech, the Jewish writer, the author of a single work (or almost), is inspired by [J.D.] Salinger or Henry Roth; his taste in farce comes from Saul Bellow. But the idea of putting together a kind of half novel out of short stories about a single character came to me from Nabokov's *Pnin*, which I love. Behind *The Coup* you can find, jumbled together, Nabokov, impressions of Ethiopia, readings on the Sahel, African novels (I'm mad about African literature—it's a different world, where magic really works), but particularly, to begin with, the works of Joyce Cary, who lived in Nigeria in the 1920s: *The American Witch* and *Mister Johnson*.

J.-P.S.: Let's look ahead a moment. What book is behind the novel you are currently working on?

J.U.: Again, *The Scarlet Letter*—*A Month of Sundays* was written from the minister's point of view. This new one, called *Roger's Version*, will be from the husband's viewpoint—*The Scarlet Letter* and certain chapters from *The Magic Mountain*, and even the dialogues of

Plato. It will be a rather difficult book which won't be a great commercial success: the bulk of it is presented in the form of debates. That's why I mention Thomas Mann and Plato.

J.-P.S.: "When I first read Proust, I also began to read Kierkegaard," you write in *Picked-Up Pieces*. You talk today about Plato. Are you interested in philosophy, or is your interest really theological?

J.U.: I won't say that philosophy *doesn't* interest me, but I don't follow the fine points of technical discussions. I read Kierkegaard for theological reasons. On the other hand, I am an avid reader of popular scientific essays, like Stephen Jay Gould's.

J.-P.S.: What books haven't you read that you would like to read?

J.U.: I should read more and write fewer book reviews. A writer certainly learns more from the great books than from the good books of his contemporaries. In the great books, there is an atmosphere which reminds us of our duty. So I would like to reread Shakespeare. I've been reading him since junior high, but I think that a writer in the English language ought to reread one play every three months, so as to recall what language is capable of. And then—I'm ashamed to admit these gaps—I should read *Jane Eyre* by Charlotte Brontë, *Middlemarch* by George Eliot, Flaubert's *Education Sentimentale*, and Balzac as well—I've only read few of his novels.

J.-P.S.: *Picked-Up Pieces* opens with a very funny text "On Meeting Writers": "The lust to meet authors," you say, "ranks low . . . on the roll of holy appetites; but it is an authentic pang." And you describe your first meeting with Joyce Cary. Have you finally met Vladimir Nabokov, whom you talk about next and who is quite obviously, among your contemporaries, the one you admire most?

J.U.: No, any more than I have met, with the exception of [Italo] Calvino, the other European writers I admire. I've exchanged a few letters with Pinget, that's all . . . otherwise, I haven't tried. In Nabokov's case, I was afraid to meet in person a man I admired so much on the printed page. You know, I like my writer friends very much, but I wouldn't go out of my way to make more. I'm convinced that the best part of them is in their texts.

Writers "Are Really Servants of Reality"
Alvin P. Sanoff/1986

From *U.S. News & World Report* 20 October 1986, 67–68. Reprinted by permission of *U.S. News & World Report*. Assembled from responses to the interviewer's unrecorded questions, and then revised by Updike.

Tension between science and religion is a major theme of my new book. People who pretend the tension isn't there just haven't paid any attention to the history of science since the Middle Ages. Religious authorities have tried to combat every basic scientific fact about the cosmos; they correctly perceived the facts as a severe threat to the view of the universe their religions were constucted upon.

Science has made human beings feel less significant: It has diminished our faith. How could it not? It tells us that we're specks of organic matter on an obscure planet in the middle suburbs of a galaxy that's one among millions. Just the scale of the universe that has been revealed to us is truly daunting. If you try for a moment to internalize these numbers, it's very hard to see yourself as a hero or heroine of a cosmic drama—which is, after all, what the great religions tell us we are.

In the conflict between science and religion, I'm very much my father's son. He was a teacher of mathematics and a man of great hardheadedness, in a way, who believed that facts can't be ignored. On the other hand, he was also a churchgoing man of a certain piety. I seem to have inherited both strains, and they somewhat awkwardly co-exist in me.

I do follow—maybe more than your average newspaper reader—the new developments in science. I think, for example, the entire Voyager sequence of photographs of planets is astounding. The close-up photographs of Jupiter, Saturn and now Uranus represent for me the most exciting intellectual adventure of the past 15 years. I'm interested in science aesthetically, really, and because it tells us who and where we are. We may not like what we're being told, but I don't think you can argue with it.

At the same time I find that just to be human I really seem to need a dose of church now and then. I need some sort of otherworldly point of reference. I go to an Episcopal church about once every three weeks. I was raised as a Lutheran, and in a way every service that is not Lutheran seems a little strange to me.

But all church services have this wonderful element: People with other things to do get up on a Sunday morning, put on good clothes and assemble out of nothing but faith—some vague yen toward something larger. Simply as a human gathering I find it moving, reassuring and even inspiring. A church is a little like a novel in that both are saying there's something very important about being human.

Insofar as I have Christian faith, it has helped me as a writer, keeping me from becoming unduly obsessed by commercial or critical success. Writing, after all, is an otherworldly thing to do—for rewards that may or may not be material. I try to write the best book I know how, rather than to write a best seller. This, in a way, relates to having faith that things will work out, that there is purpose to your life. My purpose has become very Gutenbergian-text related. It enables me to function and to, I hope, not become too distracted by the accessory aspects of authorship—such as doing interviews.

There is danger for a writer in doing too many interviews. Too much talk can make you fatheaded: You get the idea that everything you say is worth being recorded and that you are in some sense a wise man and an interesting person. The more an author thinks of himself in that way, the less attentive he's going to be to the business of trying to transcribe reality.

We really are servants, basically, of reality, aren't we? We're trying to get a little piece of it into print. And so—partly to avoid more attention than I can absorb—I have spent my life in small towns where I'm more or less accepted as another citizen and householder and not made much of as a writer, as I might be if I lived in New York.

An author today isn't the cultural superstar he once was. The middle class has, to a degree, phased out of reading and watches television instead. So there's no comparing the position of Saul Bellow to that of Sinclair Lewis or Ernest Hemingway in their heyday. The print culture is just more restrictive and academic—and the world of writers and readers somewhat smaller.

But I'm not complaining. Given these limits—and let's not kid ourselves that people have ever in great numbers rushed to books—I've been gratified by the number of readers my own books have reached. Maybe the lesser importance of the print world can be taken as an opportunity to do your own thing in a way that a superstar—the hot center of a culture—isn't allowed to: You are a bit in a side room. But within that side room maybe you can be more honest and creative. Creativity should be, in a way, play. Perhaps you can have a little more fun if you're not asked to tote the bales of the society the way others, including Lewis and Theodore Dreiser, felt they should.

There's something about the impressions gathered in the first 18 or 20 years of life that I think have shaped almost all writers. There's a kind of magic that is very hard to attach to later impressions that you involuntarily attach to your first ones. The world is more wonderful to you. The people look bigger. The smells are sharper. The sights are more vivid. Also, a child sees a relatively unguarded world. The things around him aren't defending themselves against him.

Pennsylvania, where I spent my first 18 years, is a place of vivid impressions even after more than 30 years away. When I sit down to write about the area of my youth, somehow I'm excited by returning— if only in my mind—to those rather pedestrian streets. I grew up in the Reading area. It was a grand place—thriving downtown, factories pouring out smoke and textiles and steel and pretzels and beer. It was a town that made things. It was a muscular, semi-tough kind of place. Now the downtown is a sort of empty, sad shell.

I was brought up in two houses within one county. And so I've had a more stable early life than most young Americans now, when there's a lot more moving around and a kind of placelessness that you feel in fiction written by young people. There's not that sharp sense of locality that you get in the Southern writers, who—above all others— are regionally attached.

My parents were very loving and encouraging, and if Freud is correct, those initial favorable impressions of the world stick with us a long time. So I have a kind of buoyant, optimistic nature. An optimistic person is perhaps better able to entertain pessimistic premises than somebody who is truly down. In other words, being somewhat up— from my name on—I'm able to look at the down side with the faith that maybe, in the end, up is stronger.

The people in my books are often driven by the wish to make connections, to explore their own potential, to be both safe and free at the same time. My characters are very fond of both safety and freedom, and yet the two things don't go together quite, so they're in a state of tension all the time. But I think of my novels as basically having happy endings. A book such as *Couples*, which was taken to be a distressing, ugly view of contemporary sexual behavior, was for me a kind of romantic book in which guy meets gal, guy gets gal—against a background of the nuclear family breaking up. I didn't create this breaking up; it was in the society around me. After all, I'm not responsible for the modern world. I'm just a portrayer of it.

I don't claim to be a proponent of the nuclear family. I think a lot of horrible things were and are done within it. In relationships, I vote for mutual respect that recognizes that there are areas of each other that we cannot possess and that each person should be given the dignity of certain kinds of freedom—and that includes spouses. But in my own life I've not found any better way to live than within a family. It gives me stability, companionship and the basis I need to do my work.

Some people think of me as a prolific writer. I'm sorry that I give that impression, because I distrust prolific writers. I think that if they'd write half as much, they might be twice as good. I think of myself as writing at a stately pace—a few pages a day. That's really less than a thousand words—a very modest quota compared with that which many writers have set for themselves. Evelyn Waugh was once asked how long a novel should take, and he said, "Six weeks." I take about a year. It's really two years between conception and publication of a novel. Since I'm a bit of a book reviewer and still try to write short stories, I generally have something to produce in between.

I do try to be a steady producer. You don't live forever, after all, and you're not going to know what you can do unless you sit down and try to do it. You don't learn much by sitting and thinking about writing; it's really in the act of writing that the design—the figure in the carpet—emerges and your own real feelings come out and are allowed to shape imaginative stories.

You begin with some notion of the overall milieu. In a way it's less important to have the characters in mind than a setting—some feeling of the place you're going to be writing about or the thematic concern. You should know where you're headed—if not exactly the last sentence, at least the last paragraph or so. Otherwise a book will seem to not quite end. In the middle you must hope for the unexpected. You can't plan it in advance, because you don't exactly know what parts of your subconscious or your memory bank are warm and which are cold until you begin to dip into them.

Once embarked on a novel, I keep at it until truly frustrated. Otherwise I run the danger of *not* writing, which is rather pleasant. If I let not writing become a habit, it might be the way I proceed all the time. Occasionally I have to stop and do some more reading or rethink what I'm aiming at. But the general trend is to keep it rolling for this reason:

A novel is going to be consumed by a reader in a few days. He will be aware of things fitting, of characters behaving in a consistent way. He will also be aware of a kind of music that the images make together. If you work too slowly or over too long a period, it's harder to weave this music in. Your book is going to be more chunky, more in pieces, and this will be noticeable to the reader, who consumes it at a rate 100 times faster than you wrote it at.

John Updike Still Finds Things to Say about Life, Sex, and Religion

Katherine Stephen/1986

From the *Los Angeles Times* 4 January 1987, Sec. VI, 1, 4. Reprinted by permission of Katherine Stephen and the *Los Angeles Times*.

BEVERLY FARMS, MASS.—John Updike's strikingly majestic New England home looks out onto the distant Atlantic from the top of a hill, elevating him above his neighbors on the outskirts of this rich and wooded village north of Boston.

The house—square, solid, imposing—is painted an intense, almost Melvillean white. "My God, it's awfully white," Updike said, casting an eye toward the paint work from his seat on a wicker sofa in the shade of a side porch. "On a sunny day, it's almost blinding."

At 54, Updike has earned an equally imposing stance on the literary landscape, earning virtually every American literary award, repeated best-sellerdom and the near-royal status of the American author-celebrity. In the vigorous, poetic prose of his many novels, he has made life in the American suburbs the universe of his concern, focusing with a particularly modern telescopic fascination on the frequently adulterous sex lives of his characters.

Updike is a great describer: His depictions of his *mis-en-scene* of life in mid-20th-century America—from dishwashers, to cars, to his sometimes rapturous descriptions of billboard-infested landscapes—may well be where future generations turn to discover what it was like to live in such a bountiful, confusing time and place.

But Updike is not just a superb novelist. He is widely regarded as the most astute non-academic critic in the United States. He has written poetry and he still produces short stories for *The New Yorker* that would, on their own, be enough to justify a literary reputation.

A tall, thin man, Updike leaned back on the wicker sofa and absent-mindedly nibbled a bit of pretzel that he'd taken out of his jacket pocket. He is low-key, free from obvious self-importance, willing to talk.

But if he appears casual, he is far from complacent about what he has accomplished. With almost 30 books in print, he still feels he has a lot to do, and that he has yet to write his masterpiece. "I like to think that's still ahead of me," he said.

Updike's most recent novel, *Roger's Version*, breaks new fictional ground for him and is perhaps a step nearer to that masterpiece. "I've been accused of writing novels without ideas, so I thought I'd write a book with a few ideas in it," he remarked with New England under-statement.

In *Roger's Version*, Updike has launched into a quest for answers to questions beyond the usual concerns of his suburbanites. In the course of the novel, he attempts nothing less than a discovery of a union of new scientific theory about the structure of the universe and the hopes of Christian theology: A tweed-jacketed professor of theology, Roger Lambert, chews his pipe over a mildly disappointed conviction that God is unknowable, while an obnoxiously clever perpetual student named Dale Kohler embarks simultaneously on an affair with Lambert's wife and a project to prove the existence of God via computer.

"I was sitting at my word processor one day, and I noticed this scramble of numbers that it throws up. The notion of there being a magical secret in that code of numbers occurred to me, being a super-stitious sort of person," Updike said.

The provableness of God is a subject Updike may have mused upon during the many Sunday mornings he has spent in church. Updike is a lifelong churchgoer. He was raised a Lutheran, became a Congrega-tionalist during his first marriage, and has recently joined the Episco-pal church.

"I don't see anything else around really addressing, for me, one's basic sense of dread and strangeness other than the Christian church," he said.

"I've written maybe all too much about religion here and there. But there have been times when I read a lot of theology. The year I spent in England [after graduation from Harvard] I was very nervous and fright-ened, standing more or less on the threshold of my adult life and ca-reer, if any. One of the ways I assuaged my anxiety was to read a lot of [G.K.] Chesterton and C.S. Lewis, some Kierkegaard, and when I moved to New England, I read a lot of Karl Barth. My intensive theol-ogy reading extends from about the age of 22 to, say, 30. I get great pleasure out of reading theology. Barth is always bracing and interesting. [Paul] Tillich, I've had a long tussle with. He is a fellow Lutheran, after all.

"I must have a certain amount of hostility, too, toward organized religion," he said. "I notice when I write about it that it comes out kind of acid. It is basically an amazing phenomenon among us. You could give a reason, I suppose, for the existence of gas stations. But it would be very hard to explain to a Martian what all these churches are doing. They're a little like books, in a way; a little like fiction. It would be very hard to explain to a Martian why novels exist."

If Updike readers are afraid that the concerns of religion are sweeping away the Updike they have known and loved so long, they need not worry. For as ever, in strenuous detail, in *Roger's Version* John Updike has been willing and eager to write about what may be his favorite subject: sex. "I don't know why I write about sex. It's sort of a weakness," he admitted. "You're stuck with what interests you as a writer and you have to keep writing about that instead of what *should* interest you or what interests other people."

Roger's Version is the second novel Updike has patterned after what he calls Nathaniel Hawthorne's "strange little fable," *The Scarlet Letter*. The first was a novel published in the mid-1970s called *A Month of Sundays*, narrated from the point of view of the adulterous minister. This time, Updike has chosen to tell the story from the viewpoint of the betrayed husband.

"There always seems to me to be something more to say about sex, and when I feel I have nothing more to say about it, I will probably try to stop writing about it.

"Since prose fiction from its origin appears to me to be about our private lives, I feel I would be a poor novelist indeed if I avoided trying to say what I can about sex."

Although his magnificent, gleaming white house, where he lives with his second wife, Martha, gives him the setting to play the almost aristocratic New England landowner, Updike says he is in many ways still more spiritually at home in the Pennsylvania of his origins.

Updike grew up the only child of a schoolteacher and a mother who encouraged her son's artistic interests. The future novelist was in part formed during a period of intensive reading in adolescence after the family moved.

"I was moved when I was 13, from the small town where I was very content, to a farm where I didn't have any friends and no siblings. So I read a great deal between the ages of 13 and 15.

"Adolescence is the time to really read. You're able to immerse yourself so easily into a made-up world. Almost any world seems preferable, when you're an adolescent, to the world you're in. But I think that my writer's duty to the unknown reader—my sense of the other side of the transaction—was formed in those early years. I try to create verbal engines that will in some way amuse and transport somebody as much as I was amused and transported.

"I read a funny bunch of not very high-class writers, although they seemed very high class to me. The Reading, Pennsylvania, Public Library had a shelf and a half of P.G. Wodehouse, about 60 books. I must have read most of them, with great delight. I was able to get into this artificial English world, maybe because it was artificial, with great ease and pleasure. I read about, among other things, golf for the first time in his many stories. I read a lot of Agatha Christie. So you can see a lot of my early reading was English. I'm almost an English novelist manqué."

He continues, more seriously, as Updike, the critic: "In a lot of English fiction—not to slam the English—you do feel a kind of contentment with a certain form, and a certain view of society that's been arrived at, and they continue to produce documents out of this. There are a lot of unexamined assumptions about society that makes it, in the end, a little smaller than it should be."

Updike does admire the outlook of British writers about their work, and partly attributes his own large output to this influence. "I've modeled myself, in some ways, on English writers who have a much more sensible and down-to-earth attitude about their trade than Americans do. There's something about being a writer in America in the post-war era that makes us think we have to be prophets or priests or politicians or something. There's a kind of grandeur in our ambitions which maybe does produce grand results now and then, but it also maims a lot of careers, I think. I prefer to think of sensible, hard-working guys like [Hilaire] Belloc and Chesterton and V.S. Pritchett, plying their trade every morning and that way accumulating a certain shelf of books."

With few exceptions, Updike's novels are divided into those books about the world of his past that has become a "largely imagined" Pennsylvania, and the world of his present, wealthy, suburban New England. "I understand the semi-poor the best, the social group I grew up in. I think their struggles are more authentic in a way."

In the minds of many critics, Updike's trilogy of novels—*Rabbit, Run*, *Rabbit Redux* and *Rabbit Is Rich*—set in rural Pennsylvania about the ex-basketball star, Harry (Rabbit) Angstrom, is his best work.

"I've always been rather attracted to rabbits in literature, from Peter Rabbit on. I was trying to write about that thing within us, which is rabbit-like: which is sort of irresponsible, and darts, and is timid."

Of his work, Updike said, "I'm not terribly self-critical. That may be one of my problems. I tend to do the best I can with the books and then let them go their own ways and develop a certain independence. Some seem happier than others or make me happier when I'm writing. None are totally easy.

"I'm fond of a book called *The Coup* and of one called *The Centaur*, books that I wrote along somewhat eccentric lines to please myself. But I don't want to stand in judgment on my own novels. Each one was the best I could do at the time."

Updike—still practicing the Puritan work ethic—takes the future seriously and has already planned what his next two novels will be.

He plans to retell *The Scarlet Letter* story once again, this time from the point of view of the woman, Hawthorne's Hester Prynne. He also intends to write a final novel in the Rabbit series. And he is looking forward to the release of a movie now being made in New England of his recent novel, *The Witches of Eastwick*.

When Updike finishes his two planned novels, he will be almost 60, and will then consider taking a year off. "I think it might do me some good," he says.

His career is an American success story, but an unusual one in that, so far, he has not been carried away by it. He has had fame; he's had money; he's had great praise; and increasingly it appears that literary history will judge him deserving of it all. Though critics might balk at calling him "the best" in America today, they would be hard-pressed to name anyone who is, with any consistency, better.

"I try to think about money as little as possible," he said, "because in the end there's a certain smell that a novel with money anxiety gives off, and I think it turns people off. People look to a novel to be in some way pure and to be honest, an intimate conversation with the author.

"The sheer number of books I've written by now—they each bring in their few little crumbs. So it's like a little procession of ants, bringing in their little royalties. But my crazy impulse is to write more because I still feel I have something more to say or do."

Updike indicated he has said enough for one afternoon. He got up and began to show the way down a path toward the road. He looked out onto the Atlantic, a safe distance away. "My wife and I didn't want to be too close to the ocean," he said. "We're both afraid of tidal waves."

An Interview with John Updike

T.M. McNally and Dean Stover/1987

From *Hayden's Ferry Review* 3 (Spring 1988), 102–115. Reprinted by permission of *Hayden's Ferry Review*, Arizona State University.

This interview, done by T.M. McNally and Dean Stover, took place at the Tempe Mission Palms hotel, in Tempe, Arizona, on the morning of March 24, 1987. We wish to thank Mr. Updike for his generous cooperation.

In their criticism of your work, critics range from praising the accuracy of your vision to criticizing its triviality. How do you see yourself as a writer and what you are doing?

Well, I didn't set out to be a social commentator. I write out of deeper, more childish motives than that, which begin with a wish to make a mark on paper—the perhaps irrational belief, which I began to get about the age of twenty, that I had something to say, that I was a witness of things which somehow should be told about and that hadn't yet been put into print.

I've led in some ways a sheltered life. I've not been wounded in Italy like Hemingway and I've never fought marlin at sea. I'm a product of the nearly forty years of Cold War. So naturally I've written about domestic, rather peaceable matters, while trying always to elicit the violence and tension that does exist beneath the surface of even the most peaceful-seeming life. That is, I think I see human life as basically difficult and paradoxical. Just being a thinking animal puts us into a paradoxical and somewhat painful situation: we are a death-foreseeing animal and an animal of mental appetite; we have a Faustian side, always wanting more or something else.

Anyway, I've never felt myself trivial. It's up to other people, I suppose, to decide how important or relevant what I deliver is. Each writer has to sing his own song, has to deliver what has struck him as worth telling.

What are the differences you see between being a poet, a short story writer, and a novelist?

I've explored the genres in that order. I was a poet first. Poetry very much belongs to childish making. I wanted to be a cartoonist, and from quite young on my love of humor and of things clicking and jumping and squeaking and talking led to an appreciation of so-called light verse. I began to write light verse at about the age of fourteen and have remained something of a poet ever since. I've tried also to write poetry that isn't light, or that says what seems to me to be true and interesting about the world. It's a satisfying thing to write a poem that you think works; it begins and ends rather quickly, often in one sitting. It has a neatness, an inbuilt order that we like. Somehow something deep in us likes looking for order, a completeness that composes well.

Short stories are something more, really; something that takes most of us several days if not several weeks to write. I didn't begin to write stories seriously until I was midway through my college career. If a story goes well, you feel it has a beginning, middle, and end, and in some ways, within its own terms, couldn't be better: I mean it couldn't click shut better.

I never saw myself as a novelist until my mid-twenties, when it seemed to me that this was the challenge in front of a so-called creative word person in the twentieth century: if you couldn't attempt a novel, you weren't really playing in the major leagues. This sounds a little false as I say it. I'm aware of Raymond Carver, Isak Dinesen, and a number of others who have done quite well without ever leaving the short story form; but it seemed to me something that I should try.

The novel is a little like living. You don't know what's going to happen from day to day. You have the general direction and a sort of general hopefulness that something nice will happen each day, and you sit down to it in that spirit. Novels have a slightly unsettling arbitrariness. I mean they could have gone some other way, very possibly, and be just as good or even better, but they do harden into the shape they take. You do your best by them and try to move on to something else.

What are the determining criteria for what becomes a poem and what becomes a work of fiction?

You don't always know, of course. Some things that begin as poems work out only as short stories, and some things which try to become novels maybe should have been poems. But in general it seems fairly clear that a little tingle or even a very small shiver, but a *distinct* shiver, should produce a poem if it's going to produce anything. And in the short stories—I don't write as many as I used to—the shiver is somewhat broader and often takes a twist or two of manipulation. There has to be some corner you turn in a short story. And in a novel you have a number of corners that have to be turned.

A novel begins with a wish to make a statement of a fairly large order about the society. It may not seem large when it's delivered, but it seems large to the writer. For example in *Rabbit, Run*, one of the impulses was the observation that the small city landscape I had come out of was littered with the unsuccessful later lives of heroic high-school athletes. At least there was something in the American society which led a lot of young men to peak at the age of eighteen, and left them really with nowhere to go but down; and this seemed an observation worth somehow embodying.

You also wrote a poem about an ex-high-school athlete.

Yes, I did. In fact I worked that idea all three ways. It also was in one of my early short stories, about an ex-basketball player, called "Ace in the Hole." So I've been lucky with my ex-basketball players. I really wasn't one, either, although I did, obviously, handle a ball and shoot a lot of baskets. In those days, in Pennsylvania at least, there were an awful lot of baskets up on telephone poles and above people's garage doors; and so we all were exposed to the glamour of basketball and the beauty of it.

I went to a lot of high-school basketball games, too, and still remember the smell and the sense of excitement and the mixture of the sexes and the cheerleaders out on the waxed floor with their sturdy, young legs and short skirts. It was a kind of romance, and it was something of what being an American meant to me: the ability to get turned on by basketball.

And *Couples*, a somewhat later book, had behind it a general sense that all of the old institutions which used to keep people in their houses and in their marriages had broken down, and that what had grown up instead was a kind of intensity of camaraderie, which led often to adultery and to the breakup of these homes. But I wasn't thinking this was altogether bad; I was saying that a kind of institution had evolved out of the decay of the other institutions.

Other than the obvious reason that most people think of you as a fiction writer, why do you think your poetry for the most part has been ignored?

Well, let's put aside the possibility that it might deserve ignoring. I think people who decide what is worthwhile poetry are by and large people who have devoted their major efforts to it. And somebody who writes poetry on the side is from the start looked on with suspicion. It's taken quite a while for example, for Melville's poetry to emerge from total insignificance to where it now has a standard place in the anthologies. And Hardy, too. Not that I'm Melville, or Hardy, but anybody who writes a lot of prose is viewed as a prose writer and his best self will be searched for there, and maybe found there. That might be a wrong supposition. In truth, the needs of my career, of supporting myself and putting my best self forward most fully, have led me to write more and more prose. And in a way I've abandoned the robes of poet. But I'm not ashamed of the poems, of course. In fact, some of them I like quite well. But they were certainly written at odd moments: often on vacation, an airplane trip. I'm not sure this is the way Yeats wrote poetry.

What is the relationship between imagination and personal experience in your poetry and your fiction?

My poetry is often quite impersonal, and may suffer because of it. I rarely put my most ardent and suffering self into it. Maybe my early light verse inhibits me, but the poetry tends to be observational. The short stories are probably the most me, the most autobiographical, because you can have even an uninteresting life and have short stretches of it that can be cut into short stories, with a little twist. Almost always there is an extra twist. I mean you slightly exaggerate, you sometimes combine experiences, you often combine experiences you had with ones you didn't have. But the short stories, on the whole, are the least fantastical. They're almost like scrapbooks to me now. I'm old enough to have forgotten modes in which I once existed—the whole experience of raising small children, for example, is quite far behind me, and I read with amazement that evidently I once knew all about it. And I must have, because I did have four children.

The short stories were a kind of running letter to mankind about my inner adventures, my domestic adventures; whereas the novels almost always are in some large part fantastic. There has to be something to make it interesting for me to spend the months or the years with them. There must be a kind of leap for me.

My first novel, my first published one, was about old people. I never write totally without some personal hook; I had lived with my grand-parents, so I knew a little bit about old people—how they smelled and talked, their cadences, and enough to feel the poignance that a whole world dies with them. It's not just that they die, but that they carry with them accents and memories and ways of construing reality that won't come again. A sort of extinction of the species goes on all the time in the generations. So I felt I had some authority to write a book about old people. In *Rabbit, Run*, without having been that guy who never left Berks County and the hometown environment, I still knew the landscape and I knew the way attitudes broke down, and what peo-ple said, or thought I did. The novel was an attempt to imagine what it was like, what it would be like to be him as a young adult—one of these basketball heroes that I used to idolize. A book like *The Coup* I wrote in part because I wanted to say something about Africa and about the world, but also I wanted to go to Africa. So, it was sort of my way of taking a trip.

I think unless we're going to become slaves to the autobiographical or only write one vast autobiographical book like Proust, or several vast somewhat autobiographical books like Joyce, the American novel must force its imagination outward, try to stretch it as much as possi-ble without losing that urgency of the person writing it, that personal urgency which makes a book alive.

How would you define American fiction?

There is certainly a distinctive American vein. Just for a matter of survival and trying to plot your own life, you have to do some thinking about American writing. I majored in English, and when I say English I mean the Metaphysical Poets, the Victorians, and I didn't really read much American writing in college. So I've had to slowly attempt to educate myself in the likes of Hawthorne and Melville, and in fact I came to Tempe with a novel by William Dean Howells in my suitcase because in a month I'm supposed to give a lecture on him.

He had a very instructive career: an American writer who was pre-eminent in his day, and who has distinctly faded now. The novels are quite readable and part of the fun of it is to (A) enjoy them, and (B) try to locate what makes them not terribly important now. But he was also trying to cope with this problem—how to be an American writer. And there was no doubt in his mind that one should deal with American materials and get away from the English models: get away from Sir Walter Scott, get away from Dickens, get away from Flaubert and face the American reality. Howells did try, and I think the Howells way still, one hundred years later, has to be our way. We must try to write about ourselves, and write about a continent and a social system which in some ways is still wild. There is something improvised about the American way of life and American art. When you look at what we view as our own classics, you're struck by how peripheral they are to ordinary experience. I mean, how many of us go on whaling ships? Hemingway also was a great avoider of the American landscape; he did not like to write about what went on inside the American home. The Great American Novel hardly takes place in America at all.

That certainly doesn't seem the case today in fiction, with its trend toward hyper-realism, especially in the short stories.

Yes. Post World War II American writers have tended to stay home at last. I think there was a way of looking at America as late as the twenties: either the writer like Hemingway left and wrote about charming European cafés and bullfights and everything in fact that was not American but appealed to him and entertained him; or the writer like Sinclair Lewis stayed at home and wrote critiques of the awful banality and suffocating hypocrisy and religiosity of American life. So when Lewis faced the music, he faced it from above; he faced it from a sort of superior position, saying this isn't me, this is what I'm avoiding or looking down on. My feeling is that if America and its manifestations aren't worthy of being written about now, they never will be. A writer like Bellow certainly can't be accused of avoiding American reality; that Chicago of his is so alive and so much Chicago it could only be Chicago. Indeed the American Jewish writers have been very willing to embrace their local reality.

My perception of the American writer's difficulties is that he lacks that sense of an embracing society which enables him to write easily about other people. The English, for all the rigors of their class system, seem to have wonderful imaginative access to each other, so that in Trollope or Henry Green or even the contemporary British fiction—

however pale or babbling it might seem—there is a wonderful ease about putting people on paper and making them talk the way they do. Whereas for Americans, we're locked into our life histories in an unhealthy but interesting way. I guess the flip side of this is that we write more honestly about the little we do write about. There is something about our sense of what a person is that compels us to be more searching. But if you're going to have an extended career as a writer, I think you do need to try to be empathetic and, in a way, playful.

In contemporary American fiction, what do you think are the differences between a work from the East and a work from the West?

I'm not sure I've read enough to really answer the question with any real intelligence, but my impressionistic answer would be that the basic violence that is part of the American reality is more accessible here in the West. And it's even true of California fiction; the West Coast you would think is a fairly settled coast now, but even there—I'm thinking of Nathanael West—lies a scary sense of there being a scorpion under any leaf and of violence breaking out abruptly, and of lives contending against Nature. Fiction of the East is a little more padded, has a little more greenery, a little more illusion of safety in numbers and safety in an established and long history. But the West is closer to the bone of American experience. Here in Arizona the quality of the landscape has to it this feeling of being very thinly covered and temporary, as if it all might be blown away; it's a subjective sensation. The East has, of course, the Atlantic, which isn't a very wide ocean, and the East has looked toward Europe often. I think you can kid yourself that you're a kind of branch of European literature more in the East than you can in the West.

Recently, a good many younger writers have been published: Jay McInerney, David Leavitt, Amy Hempel. What kind of effect, if any, do you think these younger writers will have in shaping fiction?

Well, I've read some and not all, and I just finished reading a long short story by a woman called Deborah Eisenberg who for my taste is one of the best of the youngish writers—but they tend to be a little less young than one thinks. At least they're in their thirties and not their twenties. I think it's a lot harder to get a career going now than it was. In my generation there were a number of us who published a lot, by the time we were thirty, for good or ill. I don't want to harp on the economics of it all, but I do think it's harder now to take writing seriously. When I went to college, Eliot was firmly on his throne; one had no need to defend writing as something worth doing. Now I think anyone who sets out to write must at some point wonder if it is really not sort of a dying little dead-end. The Gutenbergian age is in its twilight: why should I be doing this for an American audience which basically doesn't read anymore, just flicks on the tube or whatever else it does—goes out and has a beer?

Some of these new writers are very good. There's a strong sense of their coming out of very unsettled upbringings. The presence of stepparents or split families is almost more the rule than the exception now. There's also a kind of geographical wandering, people who have been a lot of places and haven't really put down roots anywhere, so that the America you see is an oddly generalized glittery America of parking lots and supermarkets that could be anywhere. This is the way they see it and this is where their lives have led them, so you can't quarrel with it. But it does make it harder for them to be warm. You think of the warmth that Faulkner's able to generate from a moldering old corner of the South, but in contemporary fiction there's a funny, shallow feeling of "So what?" And the "So what" extends even to "So what if my boyfriend and I broke up? So what if it turns out I'm gay and not straight? So what if I lose a job?" These things seem to happen almost as if on a TV screen. You don't feel they're so much happening *to* the people as happening outside of them.

So the traditional warmth and empathy and caring that leads us to enter fiction is not easy to generate. I read somebody like Carver— who of course is no young writer, he's about my age, but in a way he belongs much more to the younger writers now than I do—and his work, in spirit and prose texture and even in feeling, is sort of exquisite: his stories are like highly polished porcelain pieces. Every word is worked over. Under the seeming colloquial casualness there's this terrific craft. But you often wonder, "Why is he telling me this?"

As for Jay McInerney, I've read only *Bright Lights, Big City*, which seemed to me fine, as long as you were on this sort of stoned, disco-to-disco level—a life going in funny directions and no direction. When at the end he tried to pump a little warmth into it, it felt phony in a strange way. That is, the very wish to make you care about it made you care less.

Frederick Barthelme is a writer I read because he appears in *The New Yorker* and because he seems to me the master of a kind of glazed hardness: his fondness for describing the way the restaurant tables look; and the way the women are dressed; and the wonderful scary way the hero can never make a connection with these women, all of whom seem to be pretty much on the make. These women are still alive in the old-fashioned way, throwing themselves at this man, this narrator who's scarcely alive and can't often respond sexually, and certainly not emotionally.

But the young writers are each different. You can't generalize. Although many of them seem to share a fear of saying too much—of having too many adjectives and volunteering too much information and a fear of trying to steer you emotionally until there's something faintly repellent about the surface of the story. Obviously these young writers are interesting, and I applaud them for having been led into this venture of writing when so much would seem to mitigate against it.

Your work explores taboo, especially sexual taboo. What is the place of taboo in modern fiction?

Modern fiction, at least from Cervantes on, to some extent is trying to bring out the intimate life of the individual person, and part of that is his sexual life. And so I think it natural that fiction has again and again seemed to skate near taboos. There isn't much left in this day and age of triple-X films and triple-X books, and after respectable fiction like *Ulysses* and *Lolita* and *Lady Chatterly's Lover*. My own criteria is that we describe whatever we feel exists, but it must exist: it must be somehow mixed in also with the other parts of being human. In my rendering of sex, I try always to present it in the full context of the social embarrassment, the awkwardness, the unease, the rumbly stomach—the general human mess that these taboos are woven into. Freud said some very nice things about taboos, of course; he said that if the old ones break down, people have to construct new ones just to make sex interesting.

For every movement, there's a counter movement. There is, of course, a very strong Puritanical reaction in this country—Arizona's probably no stranger to it—that would put us back into Victorian clothes and Victorian mores; but also within fiction itself. Each fiction writer has to do something he feels hasn't been done before. And cer-

tainly I don't see much specific sex in the younger writers. My generation, and the one a generation before, was keen on breaking sexual taboos in print, but I don't think it is viewed as an artistic frontier now.

I don't know what's going on in writing courses, but what I feel in
the younger writers is their interest in seeing how much they can imply
and not say, on every level. The art of implication, the art of delicacy:
there's a frightful delicacy now that goes with minimalism, isn't there?
You often read a story and say, "What happened?" That seems to be
what interests the younger people who I read, instead of spelling it out
or shocking grandma or any of that stuff that used to interest me—
maybe *does* still interest me, since it's hard for an old dog to learn really new tricks.

Where do you think the strongest poetry and fiction is being written?
On the theory that enough butter gets in the middle of the sandwich
anyway, I've looked abroad for inspiration, away from America and
American writing. I've read people like Calvino and Grass and some
English writers whom I've really admired like Murdoch and Spark;
and the Latin Americans I've gotten into, not as heavily as many have
gotten into them, but I have read quite a lot of García Márquez—and
Mario Vargas Llosa and Machado de Assis. I think Latin Americans
are in some way where Americans were in the nineteenth century.
They really have a whole continent to say; suddenly they've found
their voice; they're excited about being themselves and their continent
and their history. And that's a great weapon in the armory of an artist,
to be excited by your subject.

I was chastised when I was in Paris last April, scolded for always
saying I wasn't aware of anything interesting coming out of France,
but it is true I'm not aware of much. I think criticism in France has
become almost the all-devouring art. Roland Barthes was, in his way,
a jolly life-enhancing figure, but deconstruction doesn't have much in
it to encourage a creative writer, because it says that everything you
say is not that at all anyway. As for Germany, I think it is a country—
a language, really—that has a lot to work out still, and there is good
stuff coming out of there. *Perfume*, for example, by Patrick Süskind.

The formal problems that were of interest to me when I was young
were exemplified by Robbe-Grillet and Donald Barthelme, who were
trying to reinvent what fiction could do, to make it look different. But

that has kind of run its course now. There were some wonderful formal experiments made, but I feel it's rather exhausted. You can still write a book with some trickiness in it, but you can no longer write a book just because it's going to be tricky. We're post-experimental in a way.

The American writers who still excite me most are people like Bellow and Roth and Cheever and Salinger and Malamud—writers who meant a lot to me when I was young. I suppose we're all in thrall to people who got their thumbs on us while the clay was still fairly moist. The older you get the harder it is to make a dent, so that although I can certainly admire the younger writers, I'm less apt to want to steal from them than I was from Bellow. I mean, you read a page of Bellow at his best and you think, "My God, nobody's ever written like this. Nobody's ever put those things on paper before." So, I guess I'm still reading fiction in hope of finding things there, news about life, news about what it's like to be alive in a certain place.

There seems to be a debate in your poetry as well as your fiction between the infinite nature of the spirit and the finite nature of the body. How has this debate changed over the years?

It's a large way to look at it, and we may be approaching an area here where psychoanalysis and not self-analysis is what's called for. I don't quite know why and I don't know why my poetry has taken the exact form it has. Religiously, I was raised as a Lutheran in a county where Lutheranism was taken for granted; just like anything that's taken for granted, it didn't seem very important. But it was worked into my system, so that when I left this world I found it was a part of me that I didn't want to let go of, couldn't let go of—I was scared without it, frankly. So in some way I've remained a religious person off and on, kind of a lackadaisical Christian, but a Christian nevertheless, and certainly it's figured in the writing.

You wonder in a way—why write about people if they're just bundles of neurons and cartilage and going to live and die like a set of chickens in the yard? I guess it does seem remarkable to me that we are inside these bodies and these appetites, and a lot of the fiction is about a certain strangeness here. My early novels were framed in terms of animals; that is, Rabbit being a kind of impulsive darting creature and the Centaur being a horse person. *The Centaur* is very much about this being half spirit and half body, or being caught in an incongruous physical frame. Not just incongruous, but of course painful: death is painful, toothaches are painful, love is painful; so much that our bodies ask of us is painful.

I don't know if I've changed an awful lot. Or enough. I should change. We all should change. One thing that's given me courage in writing has been this belief that the truth, what is actual, must be faced and is somehow holy. That is, what exists is holy and God knows what exists; He can't be shocked, and He can't be surprised. There is some act of virtue in trying to get things down exactly the way they are: how people talk, how they act, how they smell. So I have felt empowered in some way to be as much of a realist as I could be, to really describe life as I see it.

I'm not ignorant scientifically, but there is something supernaturalist in the way people have always written, from the Bible on. We are used to dualism in our fiction. We feel like spirits to ourselves as well as bodies. So, yes, it is hard for me to write, I suppose, without some sense of that dualism. It makes life interesting. We seem to be biune, we seem to be double in some odd way. We are witnesses to ourselves, too. We witness our intimate and helpless acts, except when we sleep.

I really never set out to be a Christian writer or theological writer. I'm just trying to announce with a sense of wonder the surprise that I'm here at all. It has always struck me as slightly odd that I'm me instead of you. There's a tendency to view most writers—especially when they come to Arizona State University or some such worthy place—as founts of wisdom who know something and who are writing away trying to deliver some instructions; but often they are creatures of wonder and surprise, and they're talking to themselves. I mean, you write as much out of ignorance as out of knowledge, as much out of surprise as out of any conclusion you've reached.

What do you think of the popular spiritual movement, as represented by Shirley MacLaine, which among other things believes in freedom from guilt?

Yeah, I think I believe in freedom from guilt too. I see myself described in reviews, and not always in friendly reviews, as a descendent of the anguished Puritan whatnot. As I say, I was raised a Lutheran and Lutheranism is of all the Protestant sects that I know of the least interested in guilt. It's interested in faith. I didn't think I grew up with

a sense of guilt. Most of the things we do in an animal way are probably forgivable, and we must forgive ourselves for growing pubic hair,
having smelly feet, needing haircuts, and the rest of it.

What do I feel about Shirley MacLaine? I think her creed fits our
general wish to be easy on ourselves. And there is this enabling thing
about any faith that the pragmatic American tradition encourages: anything that gets you through the night, as Frank Sinatra said, shouldn't
be ridiculed. What she says sounds to my prejudices pretty fantastical
and ridiculous and needlessly ornate and pointless. There's a kind of
horror: Asiatic cosmology taken seriously really is terrifying—terrifyingly endless, terrifyingly senseless. Nevertheless, you have Shirley
MacLaine herself, who is very charming on talk shows, very crisp, and
seems in many ways to me superior to the slightly needling, mocking
interviewer—Mike Wallace, or somebody else. I mean when she's up
against Mike Wallace, my sympathy is always with Shirley MacLaine
and reincarnation and whatever else enables her to be warm and relaxed and amused and a lovely woman. And her ideas are tied in with
her loveliness in some way that seems essential to her. I don't mind.

Perhaps America is especially prone to guilt because we don't have a
lot of institutions with which to get rid of it. There's nothing you can
do to get rid of it the way confession used to work or should work.
Participation in any large ritual or communal ceremony in some sense
relieves us of our individual burden of guilt.

I think there are other problems to being alive than guilt. Maybe our
age is less guilt-prone than it is anxiety-prone, and not just in the
sense that the atom bomb might go off. We are in some deep way
scared by how unthinkably small our place in the universe is, just how
fragile the planet is. We're almost creatures of gossamer, aren't we?
We're just barely here at all. Certainly all the teenage suicides these
days are an amazing thing to me who was always so afraid of death.
To rush forward and embrace it—I just can't imagine what's going on
in their minds.

In the poem "Humanities Course," from The Carpentered Hen, *you
write about " 'crucial figures' in the 'pageantry' of 'Western
thought.'" What do you see yourself doing within the pageantry of
Western thought?*

The poem was written with some resentment against Harvard. Harvard took me, a raw youth out of Pennsylvania, and did expose me to this pageant and made me to some modest degree an educated man, but I resented the process. I felt that it was frightening to be educated and in some way I lost something very essentially me. So the poem is meant to be satirical and I don't think I saw myself as enrolling in that pageantry, but now I wouldn't mind enlisting if I could think of a way. My aim is to witness the life of America in the second half of the century as best I can, and to keep my mind open more or less: to be open-eyed, and open-minded.

I'd like to try to do a kind of Emersonian self-exploration; that is, take my life not as the raw material of fiction, but as some kind of essential datum delivered to me, to write about being me in a way that would write about the problem of anyone being himself or herself. I'd like to say something about self-consciousness.

In a New Yorker *review of Emerson's work, you wrote about a coldness in Emerson that you didn't like. Is that what happens when you are looking at yourself? You develop a coldness in your view of things?*

I think Emerson, to his credit, was facing his own feelings. One passage I quoted in that review, to some people's irritation, was an interestingly frank set of remarks about his own response to grief, his son's death. He found that for all of the initial passion, after a while it didn't matter as much as it should. I think what he said of himself is true of most people.

William Dean Howells as a young man went and interviewed these New England literary giants when they were all still alive. He sat with Emerson for an afternoon and came away with an impression of coldness and distance. Of course, Emerson was on the verge of a long senility. I suppose he had Alzheimers, as we would say now, and he did have an extended dotty or absent-minded period. But I think there was always something detached about Emerson; and it might be true of the American character in general. I think if we look in ourselves with honesty we will find this Emersonian coldness that he spoke of.

Emerson was not only talking about his own coldness but about the something brutal in the American way of life. And foreigners feel this way when they come here; they see all the homeless and the bag ladies, and the communists never get tired of showing pictures of it on their television, because it is the other side of American freedom: you are free to succeed and you are also free to fail. I think we as Americans should recognize that bums are as logical an outcome of our wonderful freedom as millionaires.

We suspect we haven't asked the most "groping [and] truly interesting questions that one asks oneself," [1] *so we'd like to leave the last questions to you. What questions are you asking yourself?*

Well, the questions one asks oneself are best put, of course, in the form of fiction, of dramatizing aspects of your own self and taking an impulse and turning it into a person. That manipulation of the alternatives that we all have within us is the most creative and honest thing we do.

I'd like to take a breather eventually. Writing is so much a part of my day; I've structured life so I don't do much else, really. I mean, I'm not a teacher. So it'll be hard for me to let go of the writing habit, but I think the best use of my ability would be to let go of it a bit and try to regroup my alternative selves. I'd like to do a little reading, also. I wish I understood American history better.

I was one of those people who was brought up to believe, and saw no reason to doubt, that this was the greatest country in the world. I felt very lucky to be born an American, and I've carried with me all these fifty-five years that uninvestigated sense of being happy to be an American. But then I happened to be young when America was unquestionably the most powerful country in the world, and engaged in a very just war. Now we are becoming more and more one nation among many.

I'd like to look at our past in some intelligent way through reading. My reading has tended to be either directly for a book that I was writing or else a book I was going to review. This is not an intellectually ideal way to live. I'd like really to be more of a reader than I am and not just a reviewer. I'd like to work against my addiction to type, my addiction to appearing in print; I'd like to try to make myself into a slightly wiser person than maybe I am.

NOTE

1. John Updike, Introduction, in *Writers at Work: The Paris Review Interviews, Seventh Series*, ed. George Plimpton (New York: Viking, 1986), xiii.

"Fresh Air with Terry Gross": John Updike

Terry Gross/1988

As heard on "Fresh Air with Terry Gross," produced at WHYY in Philadelphia, Pennsylvania, U.S.A. and distributed by National Public Radio. Reprinted by permission of Terry Gross and WHYY.

John Updike is generally acknowledged as one of the most important living American writers. He's won just about all of the big literary awards including the Pulitzer Prize and the National Book Award. *Rabbit, Run*, *The Centaur*, *Bech: A Book* and *The Witches of Eastwick* are some of his best known novels. Here's how writer Scott Spencer described Updike in 1983. Spencer wrote, "Updike's genius is apparent in his use of passionately poetic language to describe a world utterly and unalterably everyday. Imagining the author Updike through his books, he seems to be a regular sort of well-mannered fellow, who just happens to be a literary genius." Updike grew up in a small town in Pennsylvania, not unlike the setting of his book, *Rabbit, Run*. After graduating from Harvard, he joined the staff of *The New Yorker* magazine in 1955. Although he left the staff two years later, he maintained a close association with the magazine which continues to publish his book reviews and short stories. I spoke with John Updike from the NPR bureau in New York. I asked him first about his new novel, *S.* which completes his trilogy of books inspired by Nathaniel Hawthorne's novel, *The Scarlet Letter*. I asked him why *The Scarlet Letter* has such a hold on him.

Well, it seemed to me it is a classic and one of the few books we can point to and say this *is* an American classic. Also, it's one of the few 19th-century novels that actually deals with men and women, and that seems to interest me—men and women. It all began like a number of my other extended projects: I more or less sidestepped into it by writing a book called *A Month of Sundays*, which was about a clergyman who had gone bad, and sly references to *The Scarlet Letter* slipped in, and the book became the first of the series. I didn't pick it up again until *Roger's Version*, when it seemed a good idea to give the hus-

band's version of this triangle, and having done the two men, it
seemed that the woman certainly needed a hearing. So, I've not only
written my third, but I think it's my last, since there are no more major characters in the novel.

In print, you once described The Scarlet Letter *as our classic novel
of religious conscience and religious suffering. At the same time, in
your own life, you've described Christianity as your curious hobby.
Can I ask you to explain what you meant by that?*

What did I mean? I don't know; I was raised as a Lutheran, and I've
never quite escaped the Christian church. I'm now an Episcopalian,
and at various points in my life I took a fairly intense interest in theology. My grandfather Updike was a minister, and my parents were—
and in my mother's case, still are—churchgoers, so I suppose I'm just
one more of the millions of more or less lukewarm, but not quite cold,
Protestants that fill this country.

*In the mid-'60s, you said that your subject was the American Prot-
estant, small-town middle class, and that middles really interested you.
Do you think that's changed much since then?*

Well, like many things that you've said and had quoted back at you,
you sort of wish to move on, and I wouldn't quite phrase it that way.
But as a matter of fact, yes, I do still live in a smallish town and I do
still seem to write about people who are somewhat in the middle. But I
don't feel it as a cause, quite the way I did. I write about more or less
everything I can think of—that is, I stretch my imagination as far as it
will go. I am kind of stuck in the middle, as far as my life goes, and
hence my imagination tends to zero in on things which are indeed in
the middle. I don't write about the very rich, whom I scarcely know, or
the very poor, whom I don't know very well either.

*Do you think your novels are getting less autobiographical as you
get older?*

I would say, yes, they are, slightly. I am older and so I've seen
more life and I should be somewhat wiser, and should have a certain
repertoire of stored images from other lives that I can draw on and I'm
trying to use them. Certainly, in *S.*, only the innermost essence of my
heroine could be called me. The rest is all made up, and indeed her
age is nowhere near mine. In writing about her, I had to sort of rethink

what her past would have been. In my own defense—not that you're
attacking me—I would say that all of my novels have been somewhat
*un*autobiographical. In every case, there was something that kind of
stretched me. As well as the facts and things I had seen and cities I
had visited, there was always something which was not true of me. I
was never a basketball star, like Harry Angstrom, and I was never a
black dictator like Ellelloû in *The Coup*. So always, I think, for a novel there has to be something out of the autobiographical to excite the
author, and one hopes to excite, then, the reader.

*Most of your novels have been about people from the middle class
but I think there's something in your life that you've never done that's
always a part of the middle class, and that is reporting to work, reporting to a job. You worked at* The New Yorker *for a couple of years,
back in the mid-'50s, but you've been a writer all your life and have
been able to make a living from it, which meant that you never had to
go to work at a job in an office, or a plant, or something like that.*

No, exactly so, and I think that it is an area of American experience
which most people have, and which I have, by my own early and
lucky success, somewhat skipped. I'm sorry, in a way, that I did not,
like Joseph Conrad, ship out and be a marine captain for many years.
Because it gave him, when he did sit down to write, a lot to write
about. He never was in danger of running out of material. I did have a
number of jobs as a teen-ager, and I did watch my father go off to
work everyday, and I've lived among commuters for much of my life,
so I don't feel entirely locked out. But you're right, I began to write
quite early and to get published early, and to some extent this has
made me an oddball and a bit to one side of the mainstream of American experience.

*Have you ever had the desire to try a very unusual experience that
would take you far away from your life so that you could use it in your
writing? Between your own writing and all the reading that you do for
the books you review, you really have to be home a lot, reading and
writing.*

I'm home a fair amount, and do enjoy trips and have taken a number
of them with the idea of expanding my horizons and perhaps leading
me to some new room of reality. Africa was the main trip I took. I've
been there a couple times and I've written about it, both in a few short

stories and also in a novel called *The Coup*. So that was one place that did seem exotic and interesting to me. I wanted to get there and I *did* get there, and I did write about it. Every writer has to find some balance, surely, between being at home and doing the work and getting out and living and seeing the world. I've maybe stuck to my desk more than most, but plan in the future to get away a bit. I think we have to, just to let ourselves know that there's more to the world than our desk and our window.

You've extolled accuracy in writing, accuracy in describing the details of objects and settings and of people in their lives. Why is that kind of detail so important?

I find that the main charge, let's call it, that I get out of writing is when I feel I've gotten something down accurately. The main bliss, whether I read Henry Green or Nabokov or Proust or Tolstoy, is the sense that they've described precisely a certain moment of experience, whether it's a dress, a chair, or how a person's face looks. The literary art is a parasitic one, in that its energy comes from the energy of the real, and so "accuracy" is one term for the close approximation to the real that we all sort of live for. There's other kinds of accuracy, of course. There is the larger attempt, in the shape of your novels, to give something of the texture and the ambiguity of life itself, which makes, perhaps, for novels that don't end as conclusively and as satisfyingly as 19th-century novels did. But I think it's our fate as 20th-century people to live with ambiguity, and so I've tried to make my books in some sense reflect the ambiguity as it exists.

Do you think that great novels have more to do with "perfect pitch" than they do with great stories or great themes?

I think the storytelling instinct has to be part of the writer's equipment. In the end, the novels that we treasure as classics are those which tell a pretty solid story. *The Scarlet Letter*, *Moby-Dick*, and *Huckleberry Finn*, to name three American classics, all have a strong story line that you can retain in your mind. So I would say that this is one piece, and maybe the main piece, of the puzzle. Having the story in your mind, then I think it's the sentence-to-sentence pleasures—the little surprises of a surprising style, of an acute style, and also the way things happen one after the other—that make a book interesting to read page to page. So you try to do both things. You try to have the

page-to-page interestingness so that any page of a novel could be
ripped out and read as kind of a poem, plus the fact that when the
book is closed, some kind of whole image will be in your mind and
stay with you—in some way your mind will have been changed by
the book.

*You review a lot of books, and you once wrote that when you review
a book you should review the book and not the writer's reputation.
With the reputation that you have as a great American writer, do you
find that it's frequently your reputation and not your latest book that
gets reviewed?*

I feel that less lately than formerly. I did feel as though a number of
critics had appointed themselves, when they sat down with a new book
of mine, to rectify what they felt was my inflated reputation, so that
the book in hand was not really given a chance, but was made a kind
of weapon in the general attempt to bring me down to size. I've tried
to avoid doing that to other writers, and I must say—and maybe I
should knock on wood—that the last couple books of mine have been
reviewed in, I think, a basically fair and attentive way. All a writer can
ask, really, is that the reviewer read the book and say what he thinks
about it, instead of trying to readjust the American literary scene by
means of this book review.

Does the critic in you ever threaten to stifle the novelist in you?

Yes, all the time he threatens to do that. I kind of sidled into reviewing. I never really set out to be a critic, and my mother didn't raise me
to be a critic, but in the '60s it seemed a convenient and nice thing to
do. I had a number of authors whom I was enthusiastic about and I
wanted to share my enthusiasm with the reader, and so it's gone on for
thirty years. I've reviewed a lot of books and would like to review less
in the future than I have in the past. There was a time when *The New
Yorker*'s book department had a fairly small number of members, and
we all had to pull our share. Under the new management, others are
being brought in, and my own responsibilities are somewhat less. But
yeah, it's not good to think very critically when you're trying to write,
because any sentence could be stifled by the critic in you, if you allow
him to get the upper hand. By and large—and keeping in mind that I
am a little wary of the critic in me—once you start to try to put images and words of dialogue together, in some way the imaginary world

takes over and mercifully shuts out all these harassing critical thoughts that you might otherwise entertain.

You wrote a satire of the literary life called Bech: A Book, *and the literary figure you write about is a Jewish novelist. I wonder if you felt that when you were coming of age that many of your peers who were coming of age as writers were Jewish?*

They were, and they are collectively and one by one the chief glory of postwar American literature. It has been Jewish and urban. I'm Protestant and kind of a country boy, so I did feel that occasionally I was chastised for writing out of such an unfashionable corner of the American experience. But I persevered because it was the only corner I had. Who knows what went into the creation of Henry Bech? For one thing, a writer, especially as he ages and if he has some success, has experiences which only a writer could have. So it was helpful to me to invent a fictional writer, and I tried to make him as unlike myself as I could. Instead of a father of four, he's an unwed bachelor. And he is Jewish and urban, which is, in a way, something I would like to be.

Jewish and urban?

Yes, I think it would be nice and kind of lively and a lot of fun, as I imagine it, really. Although Bech's life isn't all fun, it's been fun for me to try to imagine myself into the skin and the mind of Henry Bech.

Do you feel that you missed out on something because you don't have a kind of obvious ethnic heritage? WASPs in this country are not assumed to have the kind of ethnic sense of past that, say, Jews do.

You don't have a subject quite in the way that the Jewish writers of a certain transitional generation did, it's true. I was raised in a town that did not have much ethnic self-awareness because, basically, it was all Protestant, all white, all Gentile. On the other hand, it was in Pennsylvania; we had a sharp sense of ourselves as Pennsylvanians, and there was a feeling there was something here, that we *did* have an identity. It's not exactly like water, it's more like milk. That is, there is a color even if it's white and even if the milk is a little stale, now, in the glass. You know, I think any life has in it enough material, enough points of departure, to fuel a writer's career, and that we shouldn't worry about what we're not, but try to focus on what we are and what we do know.

You grew up in a small town in Pennsylvania where I'm sure there wasn't a big writers' community.

To say the least.

Did writers seem somewhat magical to you, growing up away from writers and the publishing world?

Yes, that whole world seemed magical. There was, however, my mother, who was trying to be a writer, so that the basic tools of writing—that is, the typewriter, the paper, and the manila envelopes—were all in the house, and I used to watch her type and I used to watch her send the things off and hope for the best. Eventually she did get published, although perhaps never as much as her gifts deserve. So there was my mother, and there was some literary activity in the near-by city of Reading. We're talking about an eastern area, basically, which was only a train ride from New York City. So although it seemed quite magical and distant, it was not as distant and magical as it might have seemed to a boy, say, from Alaska or Nevada.

Were you anxious to leave home?

I thought it was time, when the time came. I had been home very much. Unlike many children, I didn't go to summer camp. I didn't go for the summer to France. I was home more or less for my first 18 years and enjoyed it quite a lot and learned a lot, being home. But yes, when the time came for me to go to college, I thought I should do this. It was a nice home, and my parents were very loving and encouraging. But there comes a time when you must test yourself against the world, and I went away to college and more or less stayed away for the rest of my life.

Your father was a math teacher in your high school, and I believe you even had classes with him. Most of us, as children, didn't get to judge our fathers at the work they did, because the work they did was far away from where we were. What did we know about their professions, or their factories, or whatever? But all students evaluate their teachers, so you knew your father on a kind of different level than most of us knew ours.

It was a strange exposure. My father taught junior high math, and I was his student for not one but three years—all those junior high years. Indeed, he was my homeroom teacher for one of those years.

What can I say, except that he made it kind of painless? I was not
pressured to behave better than the other children, and he somehow
continued to express paternal feelings toward me when I was not in
class, and luckily I was a good student and liked math, so there wasn't
really any basic conflict. But, yes, it is a strange thing to see your father at work, as it were, and what I got out of it was two things really:
A sense of pride, seeing him perform—because I saw him in high-
school assemblies, and he was the funniest of the teachers and would
say things which would make the whole auditorium roar with laughter.
And I thought, crouching down in my seat, that that's my dad and was
kind of amazed. On the other hand, I did see, especially as he got older, the real struggle that teaching is—keeping discipline and saying the
same things for the 15th year in a row—and so a sense of his agony,
that is, the agony of the working teacher, was born in me also.

*You must have been known, at least partially, in school as your fa-
ther's son, since everyone knew who he was and who you were. Was it
a relief when you left home not being known as your father's son?*
I think on teacher's children—and there were a number in my
class—and on minister's children in a small town there is a certain
pressure or expectation that you will be good. Since I basically was
kind of timid and good, it wasn't an inordinate pressure on me, but I
both enjoyed the role, kind of—it gave me a tiny bit of celebrity in
this small town—and in a way was happy to get out of Shillington
into an area where nobody knew me, or my father, or my grandfather.
Yes, it was a kind of a relief.

*It seems to me that you are one of the writers who really dislikes the
"literary life" and being in literary circles. You've made a point of
leaving New York—you only lived there for a couple of years. What do
you find so distasteful about it?*
Well, it's not so distasteful. I have a number of writer friends—I'd
like to think that they are my friends—and I very much enjoy their
company, because, like any other profession, we enjoy the camaraderie
or the collegiality of people who do what we do and know what it's
like, and so on. Philip Roth and Kurt Vonnegut and so on—I'm very
happy to see them, but I think a life devoted to seeing them or people
like them or editors and agents would not be very helpful for a writer.
I, at least, wanted some sense of isolation and some sense of space to

do my own thing. And New York did not offer that kind of space. It offers many other delights, but mostly distractions, as far as I was concerned. Also, I had a family to raise and thought that one of the good things a writer can do for himself is to live as cheaply as he can. So for a variety of reasons, I moved out of New York and into a small town where I could live without much pressure, I thought, on my slender talent.

For years, I'd really hoped that I'd someday have the opportunity to do an interview with you, but I was very scared of it as well because you really dislike interviewing. You dislike being interviewed and you dislike the form. You've called interviews "a form to be loathed." I think of all the people I've met, you have the strongest anti-interview feelings.

And yet, I've given my share of interviews, as you may notice. I seem to be giving more and more too, which just goes to show that these high principles. . . But I think what I was objecting to mostly when I made the remark about them being "a half-form, like maggots, and a form to be loathed" is that once you've put yourself on record in an interview, and you're sort of thinking fast and saying the first thing that pops into your mind, basically—anything to fill up the air-time or the reporter's time—it's a little disconcerting, when you're younger than I, to realize that these remarks, which you toss off, once they're in print have an equal weight with all the words that you've labored to polish and make come out exactly right. So in some sense I do resist and resent the tendency of our age to milk people through interviews to get them to betray the "real" whoever—John Updike, let's say—when John Updike has been trying to show the real John Updike in his writing all these years. However, like traffic jams and flying in jet planes, it's part of our penance for living in the 20th century.

You've said that an artist of any sort in our society and most others is a privileged person, allowed to stand apart from some of the daily grind, and is supposed to be closer to the gods and to have access to the divine sources of tribal well being. This is quite a responsibility, and I'm not sure if you think that that's an appropriate way of seeing an artist or if you think that that's an absurd way to see artists.

There's been quite a lot said by the classic modernists—Wallace Stevens, James Joyce, Proust, and others—about the sacred importance of the writer and about their sense that God, being either dead or asleep—that the writer has inherited what once was the priests' function. And this high concept of their importance certainly enabled the modernists to write marvelous stuff. That is, to do anything well you have to believe in it, and such a creed enabled them to believe enough to devote their lives to writing well. I don't know as I quite subscribe to this elevated notion of the writer's role, but I think people *do* look to us to tell the truth in a way that nobody else quite will, not politicians or ministers or sociologists. A writer's job is to, by way of fiction, somehow describe the way we live. To me this seems an important task very worth doing, and I think also to the reading public, even though they might not articulate it, it seems something worth doing also. By describing, as best you can, the fantasies of your own life, you are showing other people what their lives are like, and in a way you are giving people life, you are clarifying their lives for them. So this is not an insignificant task, is it?

No, that's a great way of looking at it, too. One last thing: Do people still say, "Run, Rabbit, run" when they see you?
A little less than they used to, and it was mostly in Pennsylvania that people used to say "Run, Rabbit, run" at me. I guess, though, he is my most famous character, and I meet people now and then who ask about the fourth book, if any, and say how much it's meant to them, that Rabbit has been their life, they are Rabbit, they tell me—they don't look like Rabbit, but that's what they say—so I've kind of become a little more mellow about me and Harry Angstrom. I don't mind people saying that, or whatever. It's funny. As a child, you sort of hope for fame of a kind, and when you get it you find that it has its thorny side as well as its roses. But thorns and roses go together; you must take the sour with the sweet.

Interview with John Updike

Christopher Lydon/1989

From "The Ten O'Clock News," WGBH-TV (Boston), broadcast
21 December 1989. Reprinted by permission of Christopher Lydon
and the WGBH Educational Foundation.

*Our guest is the great American man of letters John Updike, whose
new book is called* Just Looking. *And it's not about letters, it's about
art—especially painting. What I really love about this book is that I
feel connected not to the eminent John Updike, but to the Everyman
John Updike. It's a book by little Johnny Updike, in a certain way, at
home with his crayons and drawing as a boy.*

It is sort of about that. I did draw a lot as a kid. In fact, my first
hope was to be a cartoonist or an artist of some sort, and it died slowly. Going to Harvard, was, I suppose, the crucial mistake, because it
turned out not to be a very good school for training practical artists,
but it is pretty good for writers. So I emerged more of a writer than an
artist—although I did draw until about the age of 22–23. I even went
to art school. So I had some training, but, yes, I'm very much an amateur, and my enthusiasm, maybe, is very amateurish.

*It's interesting that you mention the art school. Every one of your
books, it seems to me, mentions on the dust jacket that you spent a
year at the Ruskin School in Oxford. And I wonder, why? Obviously,
that's something important to you.*

It takes a lot of words to say. My wife, too, wonders why I keep
saying it. I don't know. It's my education. My education was the Shillington public schools, Harvard College, and the Ruskin School. I
guess I'm amused that I went there, and sort of pleased. I'm proud of
the fact that I went for one year—I'm not a graduate.

Do you brag about it?
I don't, really. Only on the dust jackets.

Do you still draw?
Rarely. It's Christmas season, so I've been trying to draw a few
cards. My drawing really hasn't advanced over what it looked like

217

when I was 22. In fact, it's getting somewhat worse, because my eye-
sight is worse and my hand shakes a little. But yes, I occasionally try
to draw.

Do you doodle?
Yeah, I do doodle, Doodle I do.

I remember a signed drawing in The New Yorker *of a man's view of
his own feet under a hot sun on a beach, with a very modest JU in the
corner.*
I was allowed to do the artwork for two autobiographical pieces. I
also did the drawing for the Shillington piece. The name of the one you
remember was "At War With My Skin." It was about skin and sun-
bathing. There were three drawings *The New Yorker* printed of mine,
actually. I also illustrated "A Letter from Anguilla" many years ago.
But I've never had the wit to submit any successful cartoon ideas. In
fact, that's why I became a writer—you don't need as many ideas as if
you're a cartoonist.

*What is it about you and artists, though? Obviously you admire
them. Some of them have led you by the hand, artistically. But do you
envy them too . . . or not?*
I do sort of envy them. The pictorial arts seem to me to be the
heroic modern arts, somehow, and also they're the most lucrative, it
turns out. What writer makes the money that Jasper Johns' paintings
bring now, and what writer was quite as dashing and as endlessly productive as Picasso? So, yes, it's the heroic art, and I, myself, in my
attempts to be an artist in words, have looked to museums—especially
modern museums—as some sort of example of what art might do
now. The little *frisson* or big *frisson* I get in the museum is something
I hope to translate into my own writing.

*One of the interesting things about this book is that it begins, as I
say, with little Johnny Updike and his drawings and his cartoons and
comic books, and yet you very adroitly make the leap into modernism
and modern art. You pass through that looking-glass rather easily and
gracefully—enviably, for a lot of people.*
This book was made up of pieces I had done, plus three I wanted to
write to round it out. The first one, about my visit to the Museum of

Modern Art, is one I wanted to write, and that does describe the transition or the shock that a provincial but interested, comic-book-loving,
cartoon-loving boy from Pennsylvania experienced when he went to
the Museum of Modern Art at I think about the age of 13. Many of
the things seemed kind of funny, the same way that comic drawings
did, so it wasn't such a big transition. I was enchanted that these
amusing things could be on the walls in all solemnity, and apparently
were art. And I've always loved the museum for providing that gate-
way into the mysteries of modernism.

*What would you say to people who have never made it over that
threshold into modernism? How would you give them a hand?*
   Well, I would tell them to relax in front of the *objet*, instead of
fighting it. We used to talk about modern poetry—"Now, what does it
mean?"—but meaning really dawns upon one, or sneaks up behind
one, and I think you should try to, as non-verbally as possible, enjoy
the color and the shape and the fun and the energy of modern art. I
don't enjoy it all, myself. I sort of winked out about 1970, but certainly between 1880, let's say, to 1970 it's almost all delightful—to
me, at least, and it should be to most people.

*Should we be surprised that you haven't written about painters, as
far as I know? You haven't imagined the minds of painters.*
   The voice who narrates *The Centaur*, the boy, says that he's an abstract expressionist living in New York with a black mistress. So he
was a painter, and the work is some kind of a painting he's doing with
his voice. And there's been a short story or two—one called "Still
Life"—but you're right, I've not written about painters very often. I'm
not a painter, but occasionally it has pleased me to try to imagine what
it's like. Certainly the creative thrill is accessible to all of us: painters,
writers, commentators. Most people, in fact, have some memory or experience of the kind of bliss that a painter must feel fairly often.

*Is there one painter you've mentioned in your book that you'd most
want to meet, interview, imitate?*
   Well, the painter whom I admire, I suppose, most of all is Vermeer,
who might not have much to say. I think the good painters probably
did say what they had to say in the painting, so I'm not sure I would

like to meet Vermeer, except to thank him for painting so terribly, terribly well. Of living painters, there's a painter called Richard Estes—he's a photo-realist of a kind, and I devote a little essay in this book to him—and I would like to meet him, to see what he's like, because I love his stuff.

Forty Years of Middle America
with John Updike
Melvyn Bragg/1990

From the *South Bank Show*. London Weekend Television, June 1990. Reprinted by permission of Melvyn Bragg and LWT.

John Updike's subject is small-town life in Middle America, and in this quartet he charts the progress of Harry Angstrom, nicknamed "Rabbit," an ex-basketball star who lives in the fictional town of Brewer, Pennsylvania, closely modeled after his own childhood town of Reading, Pennsylvania. *Rabbit, Run*, published in 1961 [in the U.K.] was the first of the series, and since then, in *Rabbit Redux* and *Rabbit Is Rich*, he's returned to look at the changing fortunes of Rabbit in his country at about 10-year intervals. The latest, and possibly last in the quartet, *Rabbit at Rest*, is published tomorrow. Updike has written many novels, as well as poetry, short stories, and essays, but we've chosen to take this opportunity to focus on the Rabbit quartet—which amounts to a chronicle of American life over the last four decades, and a round portrait of their central character. We took John Updike, who lives in New England now, back to Pennsylvania to talk about his 20th century mid-American man.

Q: Do you think of Rabbit as a good man?

A: I think of him as kind of a hopeful man, who, at his best, was in love with life. Certainly he's not a moral ideal—he doesn't deny himself much, he yields to impulse, and there's something even a little mean about him—but I think of him as a man, a mixed blessing, really. I think life is a mixed blessing, and that people are mixed blessings. But he's good enough for me to like him. I've liked him for more than a thousand pages, and I like him because he's alive. When I put him on the paper, he talks and walks, acts like a character.

When I first began to write, Reading and Shillington and Berks County were simply life to me. It was all I knew. I had hardly left the county until I was eighteen, so that my first stories and novels were very unself-consciously about this area. Berks County is one of the main centers of what they call "Dutch Country," meaning "*Deutsch Country*," so there's a kind of flavor here. Along with a lot of other imported Americanisms, there's a German base. I think that people have that Germanic conscientiousness. They try to keep their places clean and, generally, if they're given a job, they do it. Even I, I'm told, am a rather hard-working author. I think it's a county of hard-working people.

Reading is a beautiful city. It hasn't grown a lot, really, in the last fifty or more years. The courthouse is still the tallest building in town. As you know, Rabbit's kind of conservative, if you'll notice, and that, I think, is typical of Reading. He's remained attached to the area, also—which is true of an awful lot of the children in this area. They don't find it easy to leave for long. I managed the trick, but even I had my parents to come back to. Also typical is the primacy of athletics in his life and a certain sensuousness. He's rather concrete, you know. He feels things and likes to touch things and doesn't have an awful lot of Platonic imagination, the way a New Englander might. He's down-to-earth, as they say, and I think in all of those respects he's a typical Reading-area product.

We're at 117 Philadelphia Avenue, which is the house I was brought back to as a baby, having been born at the West Reading Hospital. I never know quite where to say I was born, but there I literally was, and I came here at the age of one week and lived until I was thirteen. The neighborhood—the feeling and the kind of houses—is certainly all in my fiction. I do get very excited here. I find I begin to talk very rapidly and jump around a lot, just being in the blocks, the streets. It all looks rather ordinary, in a way, although it's a nice spring day.

Q: And you've endowed Rabbit with that sort of powerful memory of place. You're giving him your memory, in that sense.

A: A child sees things that an adult never does, and a child gets impressions stronger than an adult usually does, so in some ways it's fairly easy to write about the world you knew up until you were twenty.

Q: What attracted you about the character of Harry to start with?

A: You write about characters often because you wish to be them, and as a high school boy I admired and really adored the good basketball players. I loved the idea of pretending I was a six-foot-three, blue-eyed hero of the basketball court. I wanted *Rabbit, Run* to be about an American predicament, the predicament of the ex-high-school athlete.

Basketball is very much a thing here, as it is in Indiana, and indeed throughout much of so-called Middle America. I don't know where Middle America begins, but probably this is part of it. And in *Rabbit, Run*, I was trying to write about a predicament that was true of Americans in general, and to that extent, Brewer was anyplace.

Q: Can you tell us what Rabbit's character is, who he is when we meet him at the beginning of *Rabbit, Run*?

A: He's a working-class stiff who suffers this little rejuvenation of playing a little "scat" basketball around the net, so he has a momentary vision of how far his life has fallen and he's ready for a violent move—which he then makes.

Q: In *Rabbit, Run*, the twenty-six-year-old Harry Angstrom is working as a Magi-Peeler salesman and living in a poor part of town. He's frustrated by the realization that his glory days are over, and increasingly he begins to take it out on his young wife, Janice.

A: There was more sex in it and more explicit sex than was usual in America at that time. My theory was not so much that I was trying to make a point about censorship, but I did feel that this particular hero lives so exclusively in the realm of the present and the sensational that, once sport was gone, sex was about the realest thing left to him—and so I should try to make it real for the reader as well.

Q: Did it feel to you, as a writer, controversial and daring, sitting down and writing about sex in that way, then? Did you have to take a deep breath to do it?

A: There was a tradition among my peers for frank and open talk, and I'd always been a rather shy, priggish, unexperienced adolescent. So maybe my revenge as a young adult was to put down all the dirty words that I'd always been a little shy about using. I think I might have known that I was putting my respectability at some risk. On the other hand, I was fresh from college and emboldened by the example of *Ulysses*, and I knew that this was the right thing to do—to write about sex on the same level, as explicitly and carefully and lovingly as one wrote about anything else—so in a sense I had doctrine behind me, as well as these almost unexaminable, subconscious or semi-conscious wishes to "let go." Philip Roth about this time wrote a book called *Letting Go*, and I think letting go was sort of in the air, then. *On the Road*, by Jack Kerouac, had just come out and made a great stir. As an even younger American writer, I was, of course, jealous of any stir that was being made, and I read the book with some antagonism because it seemed to me to be so very unreal, so very evasive—about these more or less privileged people zipping back and forth across the country with no visible means of support. And I was trying to make the good Protestant point that we're all involved with our fellow man, and we're all members of families, and so the basic image of [*Rabbit, Run*] is of a man running or leaving or going on the road and disrupting his own family.

Q: What did make Rabbit run?

A: Fear, certainly. "Angstrom"—he is a man of angst, and he is afraid. When you're doing something you tend to be less afraid; there's this "fight or flight" impulse, or reaction, or adrenalin rush, that we all have. One thing to do with your human angst is to run with it. The running associates, for him, with running back and forth on the basketball court, and there is a sense of emotion as joy. That was what I was trying to close the book on, that sort of open-ended "Ah, runs." It feels good to run—some rejoining of his animal self. Animals run without thinking, and he's for the moment free of all these bothersome moral worries that human beings have to carry.

Q: *Rabbit Redux* is the second book in the sequence. Harry has become caught up in the turbulence of sixties' America. His marriage has collapsed, and he's working as a linotype setter in Brewer.

A: The books are all about his education, and he's a somewhat slow learner, you may think. Vietnam was a considerable shock for middle-of-the-road Americans who had known nothing but victories in wars, who had no reason to doubt that America was always right and would always win. And suddenly we couldn't seem to win, and it wasn't very clear that we were right, either. It was very hard to feel enthusiastic for the war; on the other hand, the opposition to it seemed kind of alarming to me. There was a violence in both the rhetoric and the deeds of the anti-war forces. A kind of American self-hatred emerged in a way that I still can't quite approve of. I felt conflicted, as they say, and rather more conservative than most of my literary friends, which was really my problem. The Shillington boy in me was at war with the Harvard graduate and the eastern liberal, I suppose. On the other hand, a crisis or a series of crises like that does not evaporate a country. We still have our wheat fields, our coastal cities, our people, and so on, and so it seems to me that the America of the seventies was really a better place for having gone through the sixties.

Q: A major part of *Rabbit Redux* is taken over by a character called "Skeeter," a black . . .

A: Militant.

Q: Or I was thinking of the word "evangelical," as well, because he keeps saying "I might be Jesus Christ," and "I will come again in glory." I think those were almost his last words, aren't they?

A: It was an audacious thing for me to attempt. For a white small-town boy to try to write about a militant black *is* audacious. My experience with American blacks was quite limited, but in the sixties there was no avoiding black anger. Eldridge Cleaver and a number of others had all made the angry black a newspaper figure and a figure on campuses, so there was a lot of visible black anger. The Civil Rights movement was one of the more constructive turbulent flows in all that, and that little house of Harry's becomes, in a way, America suddenly playing host to, first Jill, the white, spacey, upper-middle-class drop-out type, and then she brings in a black radical. And these things did happen. There was a peculiar attraction developing between the privileged classes and the black underclass.

Harry is always looking for a kind of religious center, and this encounter has a religious meaning for him. Throughout the entire history of America, the blacks have not been just slaves and an underclass, but they've also had something to offer which whites have coveted. They've made America what it is, to a great degree. The blacks, however disadvantaged their own lot is, are very much a part of the American psyche, so that Rabbit is facing up to this, facing up to the fact that we're all black, in a way.

Q: By the time of *Rabbit Is Rich*, Harry's fortunes have changed. He and his wife, Janice, have reconciled. She's inherited a thriving business: the local Toyota franchise, which Harry is running. He's settled into middle-aged affluence, enjoying the fruits of new wealth: golf and country club security.

A: *Rabbit Is Rich* is a happy book. I was happy, I was feeling rich. My own exuberance spilled over, somehow. He's happy his wife has turned out to be a winner. She who seemed to be such a loser when she was in her twenties now is a kind of heiress, and he's a man of some standing in the community and making good money, as they say around here.

It was written in the late days of the Carter administration, when the overall sense was that America was running out of gas, and there was a sort of deflation of expectations and of actual prosperity, and so it's a flimsy America in which he has risen. I was trying to investigate or trying to look at the malaise Jimmy Carter referred to in his famous "malaise" speech that might have cost him the re-election, because he looked, himself, like a victim of malaise. He was trying to put his finger on what he thought, as a good Christian, was somehow wrong, and I suppose *Rabbit Is Rich* is mucking about the same area.

Q: By the time of *Rabbit at Rest*, he conspires in his own eventual death very heartily, doesn't he?

A: And in that, maybe he's making a kind of semi-conscious protest. He also is an addict—a junk-food addict, a salt addict—like his son is a dope addict. But they're all addicts, and I think there's the idea floating around in there that America makes us addictive, that there's so much more food here than we can possibly eat that you feel you should be eating your share all the time—or at least *I* feel it. The consumeristic tone of television is constantly making you feel you should go out and eat something, so in a way he's going down like a good American by trying to be a consumer to the end. And his pleasure centers have become pretty much located in his mouth. I noticed that the most fond descriptions of what he does in the book are of what he eats, the way different foods crumble in his mouth.

Q: Harry recovers from his heart attack, but *Rabbit at Rest* charts his declining fortunes. His son embezzles the profits from the family business, Springer Motors, which prompts a visit from the Toyota area manager.

A: The Japanese now have the money. They are the world's rich nation, and this was a role that America had ever since I was a boy. So it's a bit of a shock, but I think this trend certainly exists. What's happening in 1989, which doesn't quite get into the book in any forceful way, is that the postwar world is surely ending. Harry does reach a point where he asks himself, "When the Cold War is over, what's the point of being American?"

Q: What's Rabbit's view of the America of the eighties?

A: He seems a bit overwhelmed and lost in it, doesn't he? When I cast my mind back, maybe I feel overwhelmed and lost in it. There turned out not to be an awful lot to say about the Reagan years, except that they were a little dreamlike, that things seemed to work out but felt basically unsound. He thinks about the debt—the way Reagan kept spending money that wasn't his, and the way we're sort of owned by the Japanese, or part of us is—and it corresponds to the debt being run up in his own family. It's almost as if he feels he's kind of worn out by America.

He is Uncle Sam in the book. I was invited to be in a parade in a town I lived in, as one of its celebrated citizens. Anyway, I walked [in the parade], and the sense of the aloneness of being in a parade when you're sort of the only float, it was just amazing. It took so much courage to take those steps on that wide empty street—the itch to run and hide, and the kind of toppling feeling you get when you're in a parade like that—so I just grafted that onto poor Harry, and made him into Uncle Sam. And yet, the people are nice. It was America, really, and everyone was so cordial and looked so cheerful and healthy that you *did* come away with the feeling that, when all is said and done, this is a terrific country. It makes terribly nice, hopeful people.

Q: And that comes through, as well. Is there a feeling in you, in the book, that there is still an essential aspiration towards goodness that is the fortress, the last redoubt, but also the first cause of America?

A: I think we were founded as a utopia, and that's always in our minds—that we're falling short of being a utopia. It's one of the things that makes American self-criticism so savage and relentless, and I guess it controls the tone of American fiction, to a degree. That is, we're extra hard on ourselves. But it gives a kind of point and a bite to American fiction, also—this feeling that we should be better, that there should be paradise of a kind, and why isn't it? Why is it full of junk? Why is it full of cruelty?

Q: Near the end, Rabbit goes on another run, which proves to be his final run. He runs from the city of Brewer down to Florida. But this time he's reaching a destination where he will not achieve anything more than dying—which might be a great achievement, in a way. What's the balance, though?

A: There is a pattern in life whereby you do tend to complete motions that you begin. The things you really care about you wind up often *doing*. Sex is an area where it first seems very mysterious and

august, but most people who care about it get to *do* it. And so he has
become expert at this drive to Florida. I don't know, maybe it was too
neat a way to cap off the four [books] to have him really drive south,
and really describe it.

Q: If you were to give Rabbit an epitaph, what would that be?

A: Here lies an American man—something like that, something
kind of vague. The last book tries to pick up the epigraph of the first
one, which was a quotation from Pascal. I talk about the movements
of grace, the hardness of heart, external circumstances. I think our life
is a mixture of these things, and in the fourth book I perhaps especially show the hardened heart becomes no longer a metaphor, but an
actual physical thing. External circumstances are always there, and the
movements of grace have become somewhat dimmed, but not entirely.
I actually enjoyed writing those last pages in Florida. It all kind of
lifted off the ground for me.

Q: What else are you saying goodbye to, besides Rabbit, with this
last book?

A: This farm [in Plowville], for one thing. It was 1945; we moved
on Halloween day, I remember. It had been my mother's birthplace.
She thought that Shillington was sort of a small town, and small-town
people had small minds. And this space here and the freedom of country space was important to her. My dear, departed mother would have
loved it if I'd been able to see my way to come in here and carry on.
There's a certain something a little oppressive about the places you
grew up in. You love to have been there, you love to visit, but to live
here day in and day out would be too strange. I think a writer is a little strange for this part of the world, so as a favor to the place I must
sell it.

One of the reasons I wanted to make the Rabbit book the last was
that I felt that my Pennsylvania connection was on its last years, that I
wouldn't be coming back and refreshing my memory enough. So yes,
I've been saying goodbye to a lot of things—saying goodbye to Rabbit, saying goodbye to my mother, saying goodbye to this farm. It's all
a little sad.

A Conversation with John Updike

Dick Cavett/1992

Originally broadcast on "The Dick Cavett Show," 9 November 1992, on CNBC. Reprinted by permission of Dick Cavett and CNBC.

Q: Only a very tiny list of writers comes to mind when you think of the finest American novelists, and John Updike is certainly upon that very short list. His series of what might be called the Rabbit novels— from *Rabbit, Run* through *Rabbit at Rest*—are alone a splendid account of American life following the Second World War. And he will grimace when I refer to him as a literary giant, I have a feeling. His 15th novel is called *Memories of the Ford Administration*, and it's just been published. And John Updike, I thank you for being here. By the way, did anybody say to you, perhaps, *Memories of the Ford Administration*—could you come up with a slightly sexier title? You know, we *do* have to sell this thing.

A: I'm surprised nobody resisted the title, since it doesn't sound like a novel, is the main trouble with it. On the other hand, it was my working title, and after a while the title becomes almost inextricable. It would take a lot of thunder and lightning from the head office to make me change a title. But I'll tell you a title I did change, if you care. I wrote a book about theology, and my title for it was *Majesty*. That they did balk at, because there were several books about the Queen of England called *Majesty* or *Her Majesty*, so I changed that to *Roger's Version*. But in this case, it seemed to slide through. I think the idea of there having been a Ford administration is amusing enough that they'd like to keep that smile in the title.

Q: You said backstage that this is a hard book to talk about. That intrigues me. Why is it hard for an author to talk about a book that he's written?

A: Most books have a beginning, middle, and end—and one level, more or less. This is distinctly a two-level operation, because the hero, having been asked to contribute his memories of the Ford administration for a symposium for an organization of historians in Vermont, not

229

only tells more than they ever wanted to know about his own personal
life during the Ford years, but he also dumps on them large segments
of a book about President James Buchanan that he was trying to write
in the interim. So you get his life in the mid-'70s alternating with
Buchanan's entire career, and it's a hard idea to describe, and harder
to justify to anyone why did I do this monstrous thing. I've been car-
rying Buchanan around with me for years, and I had to get rid of him.
And this was my only way.

Q: The average boy doesn't grow up obsessed with former President
Buchanan. Are there things other than the fact that he may have been
our only virgin president—a fact trivia experts will cherish?

A: The fact that, beyond dispute, he was the only Pennsylvania
president—and I'm from Pennsylvania—and I often wondered why he
was so little mentioned in the schools, or why there were such few
Buchanan Avenues, or any of the other tributes you would think would
exist to your large state's only president. I began to do some research
on him after I wrote *Couples* and discovered that he was, in fact, an
interesting man, with an interesting long career, and a terribly interesting time when he was president.

Q: Did you really say, when you came off a show of mine some
years ago, "Cavett only seems to want to talk about sex," and if you
had, would you have said it jokingly?

A: I don't remember saying it, but had I said such a wicked thing,
I'm sure that it would have been very much in jest. You're known for
your high-mindedness—above all that, is how people talk of you.

Q: Is there what you could call a healthy obsession with sex?

A: Freud says, only an obsession with sex is healthy. Isn't that the
truth that we all are weaned on?

Q: He's a dead white male.

A: He is, like so many of us are going to be. But, no, I don't think
you can have too much sex in a book, since it is very much a part of
people's actions, even when they're not doing something sexy. It
would be hard for a Martian, I suppose, arriving in New York City, to
figure out immediately that sex was on everybody's mind, but if he
lived here long enough, certainly it would become clear to him. As to
my sex scenes, in this book they felt much lighter. In *Couples*, I was
sort of a crusader, in a way, trying to make the reader read explicit
sex: this is what sex is, blessed reader, take it or leave it—sort of an

"in your face" approach, whereas by this book we're beyond all that, right? It's 25 years later, and they're meant to be kind of joyful, playful . . . funny, even. Didn't you once smile, in those sex scenes?

Q: Yes, I did. Also, the nostalgic smile, when you recall that that was the last time when sex could be indulged in with the most serious danger being something maybe one shot could cure you of.

A: There were very few fears. There was no fatal fear, and pregnancy was no big deal either, because the pill hadn't gotten its bad knock, and we didn't know what we were doing to women's bodies. So yeah, it was a kind of a paradise, of a sort.

Q: Fifteen novels. Let me ask you this: do you have them all nicely placed on a shelf, happily together, and does it give you a good feeling to look at them?

A: I do. I'm afraid I'm one of those anal-retentive authors. John Cheever, whom we both knew, often had no copies of his books in his house, and I thought that was very swanky. But I'm not up to that kind of swank, and all of my 38 or so books with Knopf are in a row, without their jackets, and it's in this set that I note the typos and gaucheries, so in a sense I have a master set, ready for the new editions and to be further refined. And it gives me some pleasure to look at them. It certainly did when there were maybe six or eight of them. Now waves of disgust come over me when I see all the books I've written, but I can't make myself stop. I'm like that serial killer out in Chicago years ago who scrawled in the bathroom, "Will somebody please stop me." But each book when it's new gives me a lot of pleasure—just the smell of it, the shine of it.

Q: Book collectors would be horrified to know that the dust jackets aren't on.

A: Only this one set. Elsewhere, in the same small room, there is a full set of them in their jackets and in their several editions and in their translations. It really is a room to enter. You've got to be pretty fond of me. Maybe only I can enter it.

Q: Where is it you became annoyed first by people calling you "John"? I think I read where you said there's a tendency to call people by their first names that irks you.

A: It doesn't irk me very much, but I'm concerned enough about it to have put it in a self-interview by Henry Bech, which the fictional Henry Bech did with me in *Vogue* a month or two ago. My mind must have been fresh from some encounter with a phone operator. They are instant intimacy. If you make a collect call, they say, "Thank you for using AT&T, John." Maybe it's the name John I'm resisting, since it's slang for so many marginal things. I don't know, but there's been a real loss of "mister" in our society. I get more and more letters addressed just to John Updike.

Q: Among the many things we have in common, aside from having a first name that's slang for everything, is that we are both only children of schoolteachers. Do you think that's influenced your life in any profound way that I ought to know about, that I might not have perceived?

A: It's probably a very good way to be trained in the arts. It makes you somewhat bookish. Being an only child does give you more time on your hands, and what better to do with that time than to read a book? At least it was that way in Pennsylvania, where there wasn't television. As to the schoolteacher thing, my father was not the happiest teacher who ever was. He complained about going off to face the— he didn't say "monsters," but that was the sense of it, and to teach in classrooms of 40 children in the public schools in a small Pennsylvania town wasn't the easiest kind of teaching, but he also kind of loved it. My mother, I should say, was a failed teacher who fled the classroom after her one day of practice teaching, so I was really the only child of a teacher and a would-be teacher who often referred to this failure in her life. But teaching was very much in the air, and in my case it produced a strong wish not to teach, to do anything *but* teach.

Q: I remember a statement you made once, where you said that teaching might not only be difficult, but corrupting. Why corrupting?

A: I think it would corrupt your head, with all respect to the teachers watching us—especially after the first couple of years of lectures and presentations, when you've done everything several times, and must keep catering to these young minds. What I find sickly in college teachers is their speaking of the young as though they are really calling the shots—the young don't want to read Charles Dickens anymore, the young find *War and Peace* very boring—so I think in that sense it is corrupting; your mind slowly drops to the level of your students, as it should, to establish a camaraderie. Corrupting also in the kind of attention you get. You have a captive audience who are more or less adulatory, at least at first, whereas a writer's audience is invisible and somewhat hostile, and it's helpful to feel that you're working against a sort of silence, instead of getting cheap laughs by being a teacher.

Q: What would you say to a kid who says, "I tried reading this *War and Peace*, and I can't get interested"?

A: I'd say, "Maybe you should plan for a life of ignorance and menial work." What would I say? I would say, "It's really terrific once Napoleon invades Russia. You won't be able to put it down then." I would say, "That's your problem, not mine or Tolstoy's." That's what I'd say.

Q: One of the things that I am so attuned to in your writing and strikes some chord in me is what I suppose makes people talk about you as a "lyric" writer. You seem to celebrate the passing of things in a way that I find I'm totally in tune with. The immediacy of things can be bright, but there's always a sense that these things are evanescent and passing away—and a kind of nostalgia for them. Or am I full of crap?

A: Not a bit of it, sir, and don't let them tell you you are. In this book, especially, I think, there was that sense of getting toward the end of this particular ride, and there's very much a sense of loss and the magical way that the present becomes the past—even as we live it— and, I suppose, the overall point of the book, if it has an overall point, is the way that neither history (the determined study of past events) nor memory (in the form of nostalgia) can really bring back the past. We forget. My hero finds that he's really forgotten the Ford administration, just as he can never really exactly exhume the reality of James Buchanan and his time. So this sense you feel of mourning, we could call it, is certainly part of the book's texture.

Q: Would you play a silly game with me for a second? Pretend you have to teach this summer for money. I'm going to read you three first lines of short stories, and you get the chance to tutor one of these students: 1) "It was one of those gray days when you seemed to be looking at life through the bottom of a Tupperware bowl." 2) "If you told me I'd wake up and see a UFO in my yard, I'd have laughed in your face." 3) "'Mingo?' I repeated, and for the first moment I didn't know what my aunt meant." Can you think which of these shows the most promise?

A: They're all very promising and exciting. I wish I could read those stories. They're good, don't you like them?

Q: " 'Rattlesnakes, my foot,' said Ayden Pryor, slamming down the plate of griddlecakes so hard he thought it would break." And I just have one more for you. "Larry Husser came for me wearing a good suit." I don't know if we've invented a game show here, or if we're simply embarrassing ourselves nationally, but does any of those ring a bell?

A: The last one sounds a little like one I once wrote: "Neil Hovey came for me wearing a good suit."

Q: As a little joke, I thought I would change the name.

A: Yeah, and mine is the most limp of the five, actually, but even that has a little something.

Q: What have we learned here?

A: That the first sentence of a short story should always make you curious to read the next, because it should have a little bit of a puzzle or a poke. The reader's interest must be earned. It isn't just there for the asking, which is more and more true as TV and other entertainments compete with the printed page. Some of these, I suspect, were real pros—not students at all.

Q: Well, I blushingly confess to having written all of them except the ones that you and Eudora Welty wrote. Does that startle you?

A: You wrote them all? And you're wasting your gift on this TV show when you could be home writing stories?

Q: I wrote them all on the Mac before coming over here. Is there a way of saying the impossible interview-sounding question: what's the deepest satisfaction a person can get from writing? Can you say, if you had to, not only what satisfies you the most, but what is the thing that you would most miss if you were told by a commissar, "You can no longer write"?

A: There are a number of satisfactions, some of them trivial, and some of them deep and major. What comes to mind is the sense of life quickening under your hands, of one sentence linking into another and a character developing a kind of plausibility and a kind of solidity. And the story or novel or poem, as a whole, taking on a kind of life— that's very exciting, and you need silence and patience to bring it off, and sometimes you may only *believe* it's happening. But in general, this is what you're there for. The joy of creation.

Q: The sense of onrushing life happening—does that make you a fast writer?

A: I'm not slow, but I wouldn't think of myself as fast, either. I think of myself as about the middle. I try to do about three pages a day, which is about a thousand words, a fair quota. It enables you to pile up manuscript, but it's by no means what Trollope did, or what a number of contemporary writers can do. I find that you begin to lapse into cliché or to cease to really try to see the imaginary events if you write more than three or four pages a day.

Q: I liked the way you told me to get out of television, in a disguised sort of way, a moment ago. You have said somewhere that you felt that television poisons the mind. How does it do that? We hear that kind of thing all the time. Need it? Does all television poison the mind?

A: Not all. But a lot of it does. In a way, it's too easy. It comes to us maybe 90 percent of the way, and we have to go 10 percent to it. With the printed page, we almost have to go about 60 percent. We have to (a) do the actual reading, which is a highly unnatural act—witness the many people who have trouble learning it—so there's that, and then (b) you're supplying, out of your own memories, images to go with the words put down, so there's a lot of creative work in reading. Whereas in receiving the images that so fascinatingly and excitingly pour forth from television requires less mental effort. It's a little like the banality of the everyday given a kind of shine by the fact that it's being televised—that somehow this conversation, among others, is being ennobled and broadcast and multiplied a millionfold, and yet it is that same old banality. And I think if you watch it six or seven hours a day, as they tell us American children do, you have a lot of brain cells that you're not really challenging.

Q: Mailer said he envied you your withdrawal, that you write in a kind of secluded area. He tends to live in the city and be in the social whirl. Would that be hard for you, would that cut into your writing in some way, or, in fact, is there a danger in being out-of-touch with the world if you're around too many elms and maples?

A: Of course you lose a little something by moving out of New York City, which is what I did at the age of 25. You lose city smarts, the kind of smarts that Mailer certainly has and continues to sharpen. On the other hand, I, in particular, with my temperament and background—which is not like Mailer's city background—found it too distracting, exciting, interfering. Maybe interference is the major note to strike here. I felt that I had to hatch my books in a nest of relative quiet, and also I felt that the kind of life that I would witness in a small town would be more representative of American life than what I would see in Manhattan, had I stayed.

Q: One last question: People have mentioned that Rabbit is dead, and a friend of mine who reads more carefully than I do pointed out that Rabbit doesn't *clearly* die in the last sentence.

A: But he's getting close. I'm no doctor, but I would say he's in big trouble, physically. He's dy*ing*. I do miss him, in a way, and readers write and tell me they will miss him. But we're all mortal, including fictional characters.

A Timeout to Talk about Words

Paul Galloway/1992

From the *Chicago Tribune*, 29 November 1992. Copyrighted 1992, Chicago Tribune Company, all rights reserved, used with permission.

John Updike, perhaps the nation's best novelist, and Phil Jackson, coach of the NBA's best team, got together on a recent Saturday morning at the Chicago Bulls practice center in suburban Deerfield.

It was a chance to get acquainted. The next day Updike was to deliver the keynote address at the Illinois Humanities Council's annual festival, and Jackson was to introduce him.

The festival invited Jackson after learning of his love for books. And Updike and Jackson seemed an especially good match because of Rabbit Angstrom and basketball.

Harry "Rabbit" Angstrom, a former high-school basketball star, is the flawed hero of Updike's celebrated four-novel series, which started with *Rabbit, Run* (1960) and continued with *Rabbit Redux* (1971), *Rabbit Is Rich* (1981) and *Rabbit at Rest* (1990).

In chronicling Rabbit's up-and-down life from his 20s to his death at 57 from a heart attack, Updike provides an absorbing portrait of an evolving modern America.

After the author, 60, and the coach, 47, took seats at a long conference table at the new facility, Jackson asked Updike to autograph his copy of *Rabbit at Rest* as *Tribune* reporter Paul Galloway listened in.

Jackson: I went to the bookstore yesterday to buy some books for the team. I give each player a book for the road trip we take each season at this time of the year. When I was there I picked up your book, which is the only "Rabbit" I haven't read. But I didn't really want to read this one.

Updike: Why not?

Jackson: Because it seemed to me that Rabbit was going to die. I didn't want to put him at rest yet. I've just started reading it, and I'm amazed.

Updike: In what way?

237

Jackson: Rabbit's chest pains are causing me problems right now.

Updike: They did me too. When I was writing this book, I had a lot of aches and pains. I'm surprised the book didn't kill me, in fact. I did a little research into cardiac difficulty, and I started to get all the symptoms that I'd been reading about. So maybe you should wait until after the season to tackle this book.

Jackson: I've been diagnosed as having atrial fibrillation [an abnormality that causes an irregular heartbeat], and my wife has been all over my case about not taking more stress tests. When I was a player with the New York Knicks, I was diagnosed as having arrhythmia [an irregular heart rhythm], so this has been going on for 20 years.

Right now I'm reading *A Month of Sundays*. I'm enjoying all the theology in it, which is intriguing to me. And I'm also a minister's son—both my parents are ministers—which makes the book a lot of fun for me. [*A Month of Sundays* was Updike's 7th novel, written in the form of a journal by Thomas Marshfield, a Protestant minister undergoing counseling for his sexual affairs with female parishioners.]

Updike: I wrote this in the mid '70s, and you may find it not very authentic, but one of the hazards that apparently affects the profession is sex scandals.

Jackson: I could tell you some stories about that.

Updike: I'm happy you're enjoying the theology. I was raised as a Lutheran, and Lutherans don't give up their faith easily. I read a lot of theology in my 20s, when I was sickened by angst and anxiety—Kierkegaard and Karl Barth and others.

Jackson: Religion was one of my composite majors in college.

Updike: I've known ministers. Nobody exactly like [Marshfield]. He, too, as a matter of fact, is a former jock, isn't he?

Jackson: Yes.

Updike: I recall he talks about being a shortstop, not a basketball player like Rabbit.

Jackson: Right.

Updike: Yes, an infielder. The book came fairly easily because so much theology was in my head. I couldn't write it now, because there's not as much as there was then.

It's also my quickest novel. I wrote it in two months. I had frittered away a lot of time on research about James Buchanan, intending to write about him. [Updike's research on Buchanan surfaces again in his just-published novel, *Memories of the Ford Administration*.]

In the rhythm of my work, I thought it was time for me to produce a novel, and so I put Buchanan aside and tried to think of a way to do it quickly. Suppose I have a guy writing a journal? He writes every day, and I'll write every day and that way I'll accumulate a book very rapidly.

Jackson: The book of yours that was most meaningful to me was *Of the Farm*. [Published in 1965, Updike's fourth novel has been described by Updike as about "an aging mother and an adult son negotiating the acceptance of what seems to each other the sins of the other" during the son's visit to his parents' farm.]

It's interesting how I found your book. I alluded earlier to the time when I had heart trouble as a player. It was at training camp.

I had driven 36 hours straight [to get from home in Montana to camp in New York], and the next day we had our physical examinations, and the following day we started training camp.

I'm on the court practicing, and one of the assistants runs in and says we just got a call from the medical staff and they said to take you off the court and put you in the hospital.

I had only a few minutes to get something to read and I ran into a drugstore, and *Of the Farm* was the only thing that was any good in those book racks you find in a drugstore. It jumped out at me.

It was a very meaningful book, I guess because you're in intensive care and everybody around you is on monitors and you're on a monitor, and it's about your mother getting old and dying, and about the land. I really enjoyed that book. It was a good time in my life to have something like that to read.

Updike: I'm flattered you took it with you on this critical journey. That book was written quite a while ago, when I was in my early 30s. Unlike the woman in the book, who seemed on her last legs, my own mother lived a long time. She died three years ago, at 85.

It's a book people mention to me and I feel kind of embarrassed about it, like I was somehow too naked when I wrote it. I never read it again after the last proof. I never pictured anybody reading it in intensive care. Certainly you can't picture where some of your books will be read. It would freeze you right up.

But if you come from farming country, it does sort of stay with you, doesn't it? There's a feeling about land.

Jackson: Yes, the land and the attachment to it. We have some land in Montana. I bought it with a playoff check when I was with the Knicks. It's only six acres, and my parents have a couple of acres next door, but it means a lot to me.

Updike: Six acres is about the right amount of land for one man to take care of.

Jackson: Where do you make your home?

Updike: I live north of Boston, near the sea. I'm from Pennsylvania, and I've lived in small New England towns most of my life. You've always been in Montana?

Jackson: I went to college in North Dakota. Bill Fitch was my college coach. The former Celtic coach?

Updike: Yes, I remember the Fitch years.

Jackson: He was hard and fair, a good college coach. He had a quick wit. After college, I went to play in New York. I was there 15 years.

Updike: I knew you played with the Knicks. I didn't know it was that long.

Jackson: I spent 13 years with the Knicks, and I played two years for New Jersey.

Updike: Were you able to read much when you were an active player?

Jackson: Well, you know we spend so much time on the road. You can only read so much on airplanes. I'll read Elmore Leonard. I read mysteries when I'm on an airplane. You need something light there, something you don't have to digest. But you're in a hotel room a lot on the road when you can read. If you were on the road today, you'd have a shoot-around this morning and then you'd go back to the room and wait till 5:30 and then get on a bus and go to the arena to play. So that's four hours in the room.

If the team is staying in a hotel in town, I like to walk. But a lot of times now, these arenas are in the suburban beltways—Washington, Cleveland, Detroit. You're in the countryside in places like this, and you have no place to walk, so you're basically room-bound in the middle of a winter, so reading is very natural and easy to do.

The place I loved most for reading was in Puerto Rico. I spent four summers down there coaching and learning this craft, and it was a place you'd be lost without books. I lived out in the countryside, and I could read four books a week very easily.

The games were at 8:30 at night because of the heat, and I'd get up very early and work out and run before it got to that 90-90 phase—90 degrees and 90 percent humidity—like it did every day. Then maybe I'd go for a swim and then I'd get in a hammock and read until it was time to take a siesta.

Updike: One of the things you worry about as a writer is when do people read?

When I was a kid there were those endless afternoons where it was easy and pleasant to read and to escape your own house and get away from your parents just by getting into a book.

As an adult, it's not so easy. Most jobs take you all day, then you're too bushed to really do anything but turn on the television, eat your dinner, and go to bed.

It's nice to talk to a real reader.

Jackson: We're very tied to television and video now. I thought my kids would pick up the reading habit because I'm a reader, but they're very tied to video.

Updike: None of my kids, I must say, is a reader the way I think I was. Looking back, I may be glamorizing my adolescence, but TV wasn't that interesting. You couldn't turn it on at any hour of the day or night and find something to look at.

Jackson: I was from a very fundamentalist home, and my father did not think television was a good medium. He thought it was a worthless, mindless thing.

Updike: He was right.

Jackson: He was right. So he didn't own a TV set until he finally realized it was worth it if he could see his son playing for the New York Knicks.

So as a kid I was forced to go to the library because there weren't a whole lot of secular things in the house and no TV. That was what made me a reader.

Updike: I was an only child, which helps. There wasn't a sibling to restrain me. I had a lot of time on my hands, it seems.

But that period when I read intensively was really not very long. It was about the age of maybe 12 to 18, and then I went to college, where they told you what to read, and then I became a writer, and a writer reads but in more of a professional way.

It's rare for me to pick up a book just for the fun of it, and read it and just get lost in it, the way a reader should. The ideal way is you should be relaxed and give yourself to the book. I'm kind of fighting the book I read now because I've either got to review it or I'm trying to learn something from it or I'm a friend of the author.

Jackson: Are you still reviewing a lot of books?

Updike: Less than I used to, by my own design. I was doing one a month for *The New Yorker*, which was fine when I was in my 40s, but now I'd like to try to write books and not read books, so maybe I'll do six reviews a year for *The New Yorker*.

Jackson: Do you like the change at *The New Yorker*?

Updike: I think [new editor Tina Brown] has not an easy task, to try to breathe some life into the old horse.

A lot of us like it the way it was, of course. And every little change you kind of resist. Or I do. The whole coolness of it, the way the names came very discreetly at the end of the article, whether the writer was a Nobel Prize winner or a nobody. Everything was very cool.

And now she's making it more hot. The makeup is very jumpy and jazzy. But I must say it does seem to be more entertaining. At least it's an easier magazine to get into. All these little short things. And it's very political.

So on the whole I think she's doing a pretty good job, considering this isn't the 1950s, and you can't really continue to sell a '50s-style magazine, which it was. So we'll see.

Jackson: I thought *The New Yorker* got very political during this presidential campaign.

Updike: Very. The magazine was very openly partisan, openly pro-Clinton or anti-Bush or whatever.

Jackson: I think most of the press was noticeably pro-Clinton. Being a Democrat since I could vote and prior to that coming from a conservative family, I'm very objective about the press. Or I like to think I am. And I think the press was noticeably pro-Clinton.

Updike: I think so too. I'm like you, a Democrat. I didn't even have to change, because my parents were Democrats—Roosevelt Democrats—so without much reflection I've remained a Democrat.

But I think even if I weren't a Democrat, I might have thought this time, let's give the Republicans a rest now from being President. It really was time for a change, like Clinton kept saying and saying.

It's interesting to me that now that he's President, he looks different. He suddenly looks like a President. He no longer looks like an overweight kid out of Arkansas, but even looks a little like Franklin Roosevelt in his photographs.

Jackson: Elijah's mantle has fallen and Elisha has picked it up. It's a pretty heavy burden.

Updike: It is and yet, as he said the other day, he's asked for it, and I think he's a very bright guy and full of energy. If he can't be a good President I don't know who can. Maybe nobody can in this day and age.

Jackson: I notice that you were born in Shillington, Pa. Where's Shillington?

Updike: It's near a city called Reading.

Jackson: So did you go to the Poconos or the Jersey shore in the summers?

Updike: The more affluent people went to both places. We took a few trips to the Jersey shore, but we were too poor most of the time to take vacations. I used to go to Shillington playground. I thought that was very exciting. I played a lot of basketball there.

Jackson: When I introduce you tomorrow, I'll mention your awards. Which ones are you particularly proud of? The Pulitzer Prize, I'm sure, is one.

Updike: Certainly that's the one people know about. The Pulitzer has charisma. It's sort of the Michael Jordan of literary awards. But I was very pleased to get the National Arts Medal the other year from President Bush. I got it in company with composers and painters. Dizzy Gillespie was one of the honorees.

Unlike a basketball championship, however, a writer doesn't really earn a prize. You just hope for a bit of good fortune.

Jackson: It seems to me you're a literary champion.

Updike: But a writer doesn't perform before a very big audience. And he certainly doesn't hear his audience, as you do.

Sex, Religion, and Politics:
Interview/John Updike

Edney Silvestre/1993

From *O Globo*, Brazil (31 January 1993), Livros sec., 7. Introduction translated by W. Michael Weis. Reprinted by permission
of Edney Silvestre and *O Globo*.

NEW YORK—According to Camille Paglia, as stated in an *O Globo* interview, there aren't any great intellectuals in the United States today, which makes the position of John Updike difficult. Novelist, poet, playwright, essayist, contributor to the most sophisticated American magazines (such as *The New Yorker*), winner of the Pulitzer, the National Book Award, the American Book Award, and the National Book Critics Circle Award—how else could he be classified? Updike is one of the best writers in the country, according to his admirers; an author without the social relevance of his contemporary Norman Mailer, in the view of his critics; and accused of being representative of right-wing thought by such fellow writers as Gore Vidal.

Having recently turned 60, with a new novel out in American book-stores (*Memories of the Ford Administration*) and a book of poems (*Collected Poems: 1953–1993*) announced for spring, Updike lives far from the polemics that surround his name, in bucolic Beverly Farms, Massachusetts, from which he rarely leaves. To promote *Memories*, his fifteenth novel, he made only a few television talk shows (including one with the sophisticated Charlie Rose) when it's normal for authors to make a marathon circuit of studio appearances.

With a nimble style, in which intense sexuality and metaphysical anxieties combine with positions frequently touched upon in his own autobiographical writings, John Updike has found his niche in the American literary world: prestigious, remote, Olympian, insuperable chronicler of the suburban American middle class and its neuroses.

In this exclusive interview [conducted by mail in English in the second week of January] with *O Globo*, the author of *Rabbit, Run, Couples*, and *A Month of Sundays* did not shy away from making some surprising revelations about sex and religion, refuted some critics, threw more wood on the fire of the feud that exists between him and Gore Vidal, considered nonsense any comparison between Camille Paglia and Susan Sontag, and showed himself concerned with the prospects for success of the Clinton administration, as well as arguing with crystalline simplicity the role of the writer in politics and society.

Q: Mr. Updike, why did you choose an administration as anodyne as Gerald Ford's as the setting and title of your latest novel? Would you say that there is a close connection between the plot and that it all happens during the Ford administration?

A: I am always interested in the overlooked, and of the presidents since Roosevelt, Ford is the most overlookable. I think many Americans have forgotten that there was a Ford administration. The connection with the plot exists principally in the way in which the sexual revolution came to its high tide under Ford. My hero, the historian Alf Clayton, when asked to contribute to a symposium on the Ford administration, responds instead with a torrent of confession about his personal life in that period.

Q: *Memories of the Ford Administration* sets a rupture with your former work, confirms its continuity or could be seen as a sign of evolution—please classify your book and tell us about the symbols and intentions it contains, establishing whatever possible parallels there may be with your other novels, other plots and other characters.

A: Like *A Month of Sundays*, it takes place in the mid-1970s and has a sexually hyperactive hero. Like *Buchanan Dying*, it tells about the fifteenth American president, James Buchanan. Like *Roger's Version*, it takes place within an academic community. It takes place in both Pennsylvania and New England, and thus includes the principle locales of my fiction. Like *The Centaur*, it has alternating chapters of contrasting textures and epochs. And it takes the form, like a number of my novels from *Of the Farm* to *S.*, of a first-person confession, in the Puritan tradition.

Q: Two recurrent themes in your work are eroticism (since *Couples*) and religiosity (since *A Month of Sundays*). Sometimes the two intertwine. However, there is not much about either theme in your autobiography, *Self-Consciousness*. Could you tell us, as extensively as possible, about the importance of these two themes in your work? How and when were these preoccupations born and how much have they changed through the decades?

A: There seemed to me quite enough about both in *Self-Consciousness*—the third and sixth chapters, specifically. Perhaps, also, I felt I had written enough about them elsewhere. Surely sex and religion are such basic human concerns—the first a tribute to our bodies and animal selves, the second a tribute to our mental and (some would say) spiritual selves—that I cannot imagine myself without them, even as a small child. Both are inextricable from human vitality, and tracing their forms is one of the tasks that fiction performs uniquely well.

Q: Camille Paglia, whom some consider the most controversial contemporary American essayist, said in an interview to *O Globo* that there are no intellectuals in the U.S. According to Professor Paglia, "an intellectual is a free-spirit, even somewhat eccentric, and apart from the establishment." Do you agree with that definition? Who are the great contemporary thinkers in America? Are you familiar with Professor Paglia's work? What do you think of it? Do you think it is fair that she is considered "the new Susan Sontag" (in her own words)? Why?

A: I have read her two books—skimming, perhaps, parts of *Sexual Personae*—and I wrote a review of her *Sex, Art, and American Culture* which appeared in *The New Yorker* and was translated into a Brazilian newspaper. I like her quite well, especially her qualities of courage and daring and intellectual ambition. She and Susan Sontag are very different, in style and era, and I think it fairly futile to link them. Paglia perhaps aspires to the celebrity and panache of Sontag, just as she also aspires to the fame and notoriety of Madonna. Paglia is a strange mixture of stern scholar and starry-eyed groupie, but she is a creature of the academic world, and if/when she says that there are no intellectuals apart from "the establishment," she would have to include herself. I think she means that the level and abundance of thought expressed in widely-read newspapers and journals has gone down since, say, the 1920s, and most intellectual activity comes from persons employed in universities and colleges. That is true, but where else will intellectual activity, at least in the humanities, find sponsorship in an increasingly non-Gutenbergian, post-literate world?

Q: Some of your colleagues—if I can put it that way—like Gore Vidal see you as a man of right-wing ideas, something probably born from the fact that you did not oppose the Vietnam War, unlike most at the time. Is this correct, or is it a misconception of what you stand for? Do you believe that a writer has a social and political role in the present time? What would that role be?

A: I don't think of myself as right-wing. I consistently vote for the Democrats, the more left-wing major party, and support abortion rights, non-censorship, equal rights for women, homosexuals, etc. It is true, I give the American people and their leaders credit for more good sense and good intentions than Mr. Vidal does, but then I would see him as an elitist who feels at home in an attitude of aristocratic disdain. I disdain nothing, not even the struggles of presidents and politicians. My father was a public-school teacher, and I do not share many of my colleagues' reflexive contempt for middle-class life and attitudes. I do not stand for anything. I write fiction, poetry, and literary criticism that seek to describe the world as it is, with its surprises and its paradoxes. Telling the truth is the main, and perhaps the only, social service a writer can perform.

Q: The election of Bill Clinton has been widely celebrated as the victory of a new generation. What do you think of that? Can Bill Clinton really mean a new era in American politics? Is America ready for deep changes? Do you believe there will be some?

A: As Clinton gets ever nearer the Presidency, it appears that any hope of radical change or instant improvement is unrealistic. The problems and their inertia are too great. However, even a change of emphasis and announced goal is useful and welcome. After twelve years of conservative presidents who financed tax breaks for the wealthy with enormous deficits, and spent much of their political passion in trying to make abortion again illegal, the United States needs a broader and more humane approach from its government, and if Bill Clinton cannot provide this, I do not know who can.

Thoughts of Faith Infuse Updike's Novels

Jan Nunley/1993

From *Episcopal Life*, May 1993, 1, 4. Additional dialogue added from the interview audiotape that was the source of the interview conducted on 3 February 1993. Reprinted by permission of Jan Nunley and *Episcopal Life*.

As with so many places in New England, you have to know where you're going to find this village. It's an appendage of the town of Beverly, a small, well-manicured seaside village a few stops out on the commuter rail from Boston. Its streets wind past Colonials and Capes with red doors; several private schools call it home; and in its midst is a 90-year-old replica of an English country church, St. John's. Here, on a Sunday morning, you may find novelist John Updike sitting in a pew on the baptistery side; when the service ends he strides out and up the hill to his home.

The 61-year-old Updike and his wife, Martha, who have seven children between them, moved here a decade ago. The writer joined St. John's about the same time. Raised a Lutheran, he was advised by a local Lutheran minister that in New England the Episcopal Church was closer to the "relaxed, establishment Lutheranism" of his Berks County, Pa., home.

He'd detoured through Congregational church while living in nearby Ipswich, but recalled the minister's advice upon settling in Beverly Farms.

"Episcopalianism is fairly close to Luthernanism," Updike observes, though with more emphasis on rite than creed: "a bit more of a 'works' kind of place, I think. I notice that the theology is kind of 'do-it-yourself.' But I'm comfortable with that, and even happy with it. There is a kind of broadness to the Episcopalian outlook, a tolerance that you have to like, that makes it a very gracious church."

Updike is grateful for that. Churches, and the clergy in them, have not always been gracious places and people in the works of this writer, whose career spans nearly 40 years and with just as many books. The struggle—and frequent failure—to be faithful, sexually and otherwise, while wearing the collar consumes characters like the Rev. Thomas

248

Marshfield in *A Month of Sundays* (1975) and Prof. Roger Lambert in *Roger's Version* (1986). It's a theme that pops up often in his fiction: the links between religion and sex, both "modes of self-assertion, of saying, 'I am.'

"What has interested me as a writer," explains Updike, "has been the betrayals: the clergyman who doesn't practice what he preaches. I think the most important ecclesiastical fiction I ever wrote was the story 'Pigeon Feathers,' which reflects my own shock when it seemed to me that the well-intentioned, sweet, bright, liberal Lutheran minister who was confirming me didn't really attach any factual reality to these concepts.

"I was distressed, because I saw that without these supernatural assurances we might as well all be dogs and cats and cockroaches. And so that boy's struggle as reflected in the fiction, I suppose, continues to tilt my portraits of the clergy. The Rabbit books have a couple of clergymen in them, and I guess I want the impossible for them. But then, I guess religion is the request for, if not the impossible, for the unlikely."

The series of novels recording the travails of Rabbit Angstrom included *Rabbit, Run* (1960), *Rabbit Redux* (1971), *Rabbit Is Rich* (1981), and *Rabbit at Rest* (1990).

But clergy aren't the only Updike characters who wrestle with religion.

"The books right up to and including *Couples* (1968) were rather specifically Christian," Updike points out. "I'm not trying to force a message upon the reader, but I am trying to give human behavior theological scrutiny."

Frequently those earlier works cite Karl Barth and Paul Tillich, the "crisis theologians" of the '50s and '60s, whom Updike says were "theologians I could trust. Not every theologian spoke to me—in fact some of them affected me sort of like the minister does the boy in 'Pigeon Feathers': the very hollowness of their voices frightened me."

He is still a Barth aficionado—"I haven't altered those views; I haven't really refreshed them either"—but his theology is less overt in more recent works.

"I don't want to write tracts, to be more narrow in my fiction than the world itself is; I try not to subject the world to a kind of cartoon theology which gives predictable answers."

His own faith, for all his Lutheran roots, has more than a little of
Anglican ambiguity in it.

"I wouldn't say that I'm one of those who's certain that God is
there at all. I find it hard to imagine anybody who is that certain, in
fact. But it's always seemed to me that he should be there, and that
our best self is called forth by acting as though he is."

Updike sees faith as a response to anxiety about the possibility of
death—"the natural product of having a mind that can foresee a future, which a dog, say, doesn't have. That is the human condition
which leads us to theologians we can trust, leads us to church on a
Sunday morning, leads us to pray in the space behind our eyelids."

Whatever leads him to St. John's, he's called a "faithful parishioner" by head usher Caleb Loring III. "He's very much a part of
the congregation," Loring says. "And he makes you feel that way as
well." The rector, the Rev. James Purdy, says Updike seems to find
"genuine joy in participating as a person in a pew, rather than as a
person who is pressed forward. It's a joy to preach to him as a parishioner too. John is a quiet and generous critic; he has a certain sparkle
and twinkle in his eye so that you can tell when you're on. And when
you're off, he masks it well."

There isn't much trouble with "sightseers" coming to the parish to
gawk at Updike: "We have other spectacles in this congregation," he
teases. "And I don't think he's among them."

Indeed, the parish has a full list of activities for its 2,000 or so
members, including English classes and resettlement for Cambodians in
Beverly, a food pantry, clothes collection and outreach to the homeless.

A frequent lector, the author sometimes writes the introductions to
the lessons he reads as well. Each year he donates cartons of books to
the parish fair, where autographed copies of his works are auctioned
off.

He's also known for smaller generosities. Parishioner and friend
Judy Cabot says that over the years, Updike has brought audio tapes
he's made of his works to her mother-in-law, who's been blind from
girlhood.

"There's a real gentleness about John," she says, "a sweetness and
a thoughtfulness. He seems to take pleasure in just coming into the village, to the post office, and then he comes into the kind of easy
rhythm of the Sunday morning service."

It fits, somehow, with how Updike sees himself. "I'd say I was a hopeful person. Hope is only one of the three virtues that St. Paul enjoins upon us, and without lacking faith and charity I think I am truly hopeful. I think people are by and large well-intentioned and benign, if you let them be. They are beautiful, if you see them in the right light, and there is something inspiring about ordinary life as it is lived."

That's very Episcopalian, John.

"Oh, is it? Yes. Well, you see, maybe I am in the right church after all."

Q: What was your first encounter with the idea of the holy?

A: The memory that keeps coming to mind is attending my Aunt Hannah's funeral, when I was, I think, nine. It was an old-fashioned Lutheran burial in the country, and they propped her up in the casket and her profile showed against the hangings behind the altar. I don't know if that's holy, but it made a very vivid impression on me. Another early religious impression had to do with the ants that lived between the bricks of our little patio underneath the grape arbor. Their little teeming lives, running back and forth, seemed to transpose me into the position of the deity—these little scurrying ants, whom I occasionally stepped on, were, I supposed, a God's-eye view of humanity.

Q: How did that make you feel about God as "the Other"?

A: God as the enormous Other, yes—and when many years later I came to read Karl Barth, the concept of the totally Other, the totally inscrutable Other, seemed congenial. But God had a friendlier face. [Shillington] was a small town, all white and mostly Protestant, divided very much between the Lutherans and the Reformeds, and there was a geniality to the religion. My father was a Sunday-school teacher, and a number of his colleagues were also Sunday-school teachers, so the Sunday school and the church had a kind of familial, communal dimension that was not intimidating, but the opposite.

Q: How did those ideas change as you grew older and began to write?

A: Well, I'm not sure they did change. I think the function of a church . . . it's kind of a gratuitous thing, after all. People show up voluntarily. It's one of the few really voluntary things that people do—they could all still be at home in their bathrobes.

Q: Did that affect your ideas as a writer?

A: The sense of the sacred or the religious, let's call it, certainly does play into one's art. Art is also a gratuitous realm, where certain absolute standards seem to obtain. Just as the ideal Christian in his behavior does good acts that go unnoticed, so an artist tries to put a little something extra into the work of art for which he receives no money, and may not receive any credit. When you write, you do feel you're functioning by laws that aren't entirely human. They're somewhat absolute and otherworldly. The notion of the other world certainly figures in each time you write a novel, or an even briefer flight. You are trying to create another world. I don't feel like my characters are ants and I'm looming above them. Rather, I'm among them as a kind of invisible brother. Not only am I not larger than they, but in a way I'm smaller, because I'm trying to get inside them and figure out what they're feeling and what they'll say next.

Q: That's very incarnational.

A: I suppose so. I wouldn't have used that adjective, but it's certainly empathetic. One tries to empathize. Christ advised us to empathize, and even a non-Christian writer is perforce obliged to try to empathize and try to feel what it's like to be in some shoes other than your own.

Q: In your memoirs, you talk about your struggle with stuttering and with psoriasis. You frame those as part of what shaped you as a writer, gave you the ability to step outside the "universally human." Do you feel that outsider observational vantage point of being different, of being "other," is an essential element for a writer?

A: The artist and the writer is, to an extent, an outsider and probably is attracted to it because he feels like an outsider already. Most writers begin with accounts of their first home, their family, and the town, often from quite a hostile point of view—love/hate, let's say. In a way, this stepping outside, in an attempt to judge enough to create a duplicate of it, makes you an outsider. That is, you are outside your material to the degree at least that you are writing about it, and indeed that is a big step, a big-*feeling* step when you begin to write fiction—the fact that you are on one side of the glass window and human events are on the other side. Yes, I think it's healthy for a writer to feel like an outsider. If you feel like an insider you get committed to a partisan view, you begin to defend interests, so you wind up not really empathizing with all mankind.

Q: How has that affected you spiritually—how you've grown in your relationship with God and human beings around you?

A: I don't know. I've been very grateful that I've been allowed to be a writer or something artistic. I wasn't too fussy as a child. I wanted to draw, basically, but I remain grateful that I've been lucky enough that in some ways my life has been charmed or my endeavor has been blessed, and to that extent I've tried to remain grateful and to give praise. Any act of description is, to some extent, an act of praise, so that even when the event is unpleasant or horrifying or spiritually stunning, the very attempt to describe it is, in some way, part of that Old Testament injunction to give praise. The Old Testament God repeatedly says he wants praise, and I translate that to mean that the world wants describing, the world wants to be observed and "hymned." So there's a kind of hymning undercurrent that I feel in my work.

Q: That reminds me of the idea that the act of observing, in a sense, creates reality.

A: So scientists tell us, and so indeed Berkeley and Locke and others have told us, and I suppose it's true: that reality is a mixture of stimuli from the outside and a recording, a sensitive ego that sees it. I've never, though, had the feeling that I am the only reality. I've always devoutly believed that the external is real, and what's frightening and dismaying about being alive is that the outside would appear to be fairly indifferent to your presence. A thunderbolt in the wrong place, a slippery road on the wrong night—all that can wipe you out in a twinkling.

Q: Particularly as a novelist, you've engaged in a form of expression that, at least in my mind, is closest to that of the biblical writers: the telling of stories rather than preaching sermons or creating an academic discourse. So your theology comes out in the story, rather than explicitly being stated, even when you're quoting. That tends to make for a wider range of interpretation from critics and the reading public. Do you find that they often miss what you intended?

A: A critic never quite describes the work that you thought you were putting forth. My most Kierkegaardian or Barthian, or whatever, fiction was, I think, that which was written in my twenties and thirties, and a book like *Rabbit, Run* is a fairly deliberate attempt to examine the human predicament from a theological standpoint. I'm not trying to force a message upon the reader, but I am trying to give human behavior theological scrutiny as it's seen from above, and the emotions the characters have. Rabbit is not a formal Christian, really. He's been exposed to it, but he proceeds by a few more basic notions: an instinctiveness that somehow his life must be important, even though there's no eternal confirmation of this—only the belief that the reality within must matter and must be served. A figure like Caldwell in *The Centaur* is a Christian, he keeps announcing, and is trying to lead a good life. So these books, right up to and including *Couples*, were rather specifically Christian. I think the later books were a little less so, although a book like *Roger's Version* certainly is, in a way, an essay about kinds of belief.

Q: Why do you think that movement happened, away from being specifically Christian, as your career has progressed?

A: Who knows? Maybe I'm becoming a less ardent Christian, or perhaps the struggle whereby I established my theological ideas climaxed in my early twenties in a set of conclusions along the lines of crisis theology, and I haven't altered those views; I haven't really refreshed them either. Also, I don't want to write tracts or to be more narrow in my fiction than the world is. God presumably sees Christian and non-Christian alike and is familiar with our modes of despair and absence, and so on. So I try to include those and not subject the world to a kind of cartoon theology which gives predictable answers.

Q: How does it feel to know that people will probably learn more about Barth, Tillich, and Kierkegaard from your writing than from reading them, or, frankly, from the pulpit?

A: I'm afraid if they depend entirely on my writing they won't learn enough, although I have actually reviewed Barth and, in a lesser way, Tillich. They were the poles, as I saw it, of possible theologies in the '50s and '60s, when I was concerned. I can't believe they will not remain important. I'm not a divinity student and never have been, so I've no idea what's in fashion now in the schools. I do notice that, when in a bookstore, you go to the theology section to see if they have any Barth in print, it's like Zen and various kinds of neo-Hindu tracts, and very little that I would call theology by anybody. . . . Earlier, for me to find, in this welter, books by Barth and Kierkegaard, it meant a lot to me. I can't believe, in short, what you say is true. It's always better to go to the source. I only really took out of Barth what I wanted and what I needed. There's a lot left-over that I didn't use.

Q: In the end, you hope that you may lead people in that direction?

A: Yes, that would be nice—those who feel the need. There are various degrees of, various kinds of anxiety in the world, and many people don't seem to be anxious at all. I suspect that anxiety, fear, is the natural product of having a mind that can foresee a future, that can picture death, which a dog, say, doesn't have.

Q: Is being a Christian something that you feel that you do as an individual, or is it something you find as part of a congregation?

A: I think the sense of community is real enough, and a real enough comfort. The Christian religion is hardly something that you can do alone. It's quite a concoction, after all, and no single person could have invented it. I think it's helpful to be a member of a church. There is the danger, of course, that church observance becomes merely formal, and that the struggle part of it—the winning-through—you've left up to the rest of the group. As in any group endeavor, it's always a temptation to shift responsibility and ride along, so I suppose that could be said about not only the Episcopal Church, but any church. It can encourage a kind of spiritual laziness.

Q: Are you a fairly active churchman?

A: No, I've tried not to be. I've dodged—not that I've really been asked to do an awful lot, for which I'm grateful. I occasionally read the Bible verses of the day, and I'm active enough in the annual church fair, but I would say that that's about the extent of my activities. It was in the Congregational church, oddly enough, that I got involved in the committees, and that was fun and useful and instructive, and it heightened, really, one's respect for your fellow parishioners, since you saw them trying to debate real issues—money issues, and so on. But I kind of had enough of that, and have been grateful not to have been asked to take it up again. It's hard, if you are a Christian, to say "no" to your pastor, but I have stayed out of the business end of St. John's.

Q: I found that what attracted me to the Episcopal Church was a "high tolerance for ambiguity," and I sense those themes in your writing.

A: I noticed that the theology is kind of do-it-yourself, as you said—a high tolerance for ambiguity. It comes out in the sermons, even in the kind of hymns we sing. But I'm comfortable with that and even happy with it. I think life and faith are both ambiguous. Ambiguous

isn't quite the word—it's faintly unkind—but there is a kind of broadness to the Episcopalian outlook, a tolerance, that you have to like.
The tolerance of each others' lives, spiritual lives, is what makes it a
very gracious church to be a member of.

Q: You've dealt extensively with the intersections of sexuality and
religion. So many of your fictional clergy are men—so far as I'm
aware, no women yet—who struggle with their sexual lives in the context of wearing the collar. Why is that?

A: It's a problem I've noticed in clergymen, both the ones you read
about and even the ones you know. You have a lot of time on your
hands; a clergyman's weekdays are his own, more or less, to organize
as he wishes. You have the freedom of peoples' homes; you go back
and forth. It's an ideal set-up, if you're going to sexually wander. It's
certainly an ideal profession as far as technically being able to do it,
and it does happen. The first time that a young person sees it happening, you're thunderstruck by the incongruity of this sermonizer also
being an adulterer. Later, it doesn't seem such a paradox, in a
way. . . In sexual encounter, you get the kind of confirmation of your
own existence and tremendous intrinsic worth that you don't get elsewhere, except maybe in your mother's arms when you're an infant. So
it's not surprising that churches are sexy places. The Puritan, the ideal-
ist in me or the shockable pre-adolescent is enough struck by it to have
written a couple of novels about it: *A Month of Sundays* and also
Roger's Version. It's no paradox: religion and sex are traditionally
linked in the United States, at least; the camp meetings our ancestors
went to were also mating parties. It's kind of lovely, in a way.

Q: But the church struggles so much with coming to terms with
that, at least in its public discourse: sexuality, women in ministry, *et
cetera*.

A: You describe what seems to be the case, and it exists less out
there in Protestantism, in Episcopalianism, than in many of our more
Puritanical sister sects. Methodism and Presbyterianism had a long
stew recently about appropriate sexual attitudes and the place of homosexuals in the church, and all that. It is a problem, but it's not my
problem, and it's not a problem that interests me as a writer terribly
much. . . As to now, with the issue of consummating homosexual
marriages or not, I have no idea what's right; it depends on how far
you're going to ignore the Bible, which does have some things to say

on these topics that aren't really in line with modern liberal thought. I recognize it as a problem for church administrators and for right-thinking church-goers. The issue of the female clergy is, of course, behind us in the American Episcopal Church, and once you see them in action you realize how very well suited the gender is for the pastoral function, and you wonder what the fuss has been about. And so it is with some contemporary problems. You may look back 20 years and wonder why you bothered. But the Bible does take some conservative positions on sexual behavior, and the church is caught between modern mores and biblical mores, and I don't think it's a false bind. It's an actual bind. Although, the Bible is a sexier document than our Victorian grandparents admitted, isn't it? There is sex in the Bible, not just the "Song of Solomon," but really constant acknowledgment of the power of sex—David's behavior, and so on.

Q: When you created Tom Marshfield and Roger Lambert, I sensed that despite your years of worldly wisdom and sophistication, there's still something in there that wants people to do what they say they're going to do.

A: Yeah. . . I do hold them to a higher standard, as I hold myself. I mean, I expect a lot of them, and this is unreal of me, but it does seem to be a part of me. My father's father was a clergyman, a Presbyterian—if you read *Self-Consciousness* I mentioned this—but a failed one. He didn't lose his faith, but he did lose his parishes and finally had to go into the real estate business. And my father was haunted, I think, by his own father's failure to uphold the faith somehow. It was a strange little shadow in the religiosity of our family.

Q: Failure to uphold the faith, or failure to uphold a congregation?

A: Well, they could have seemed the same thing—you know, if he had the faith, why didn't it work? Again, the expectation of a miracle, or maybe the expectation of earthly prosperity, to confirm our state of grace.

Q: There's John Calvin.

A: Yeah, the Calvinist notion that if you're good, where are the results? And my grandfather didn't come up with the right results, somehow.

Q: Is there still a strain of that in you, of that Calvinist uncertainty?

A: Probably, probably. It's not very fashionable, is it? But it's hard to get rid of in myself. On the one hand, it's made America, it's what made the U.S.—that Calvinist drive. We became the wonder of the world through our Calvinism, and we musn't be too hard on it now. It still is, I think, part of our approach and our high expectations. Clinton's inaugural address even reflected somewhat the sense that we can do anything if we work a little harder.

Q: According to the *Chronicle of Philanthropy*, Clinton was the only one of the candidates who tithed his income. Perhaps it's a measure of how far away we've gotten from our Calvinism, that sense of giving back to God in gratitude for what we've received. At some point we say, "Thanks for the keys to the car, Dad. I'm out'a here!"

A: I don't want to sound pompous or pious, but I really have been strengthened and emboldened by the notion of gratitude and the idea that it is a service to both the universe and to fellow man to try to write entertainingly and accurately about the world. We've spoken about empathy and about giving praise, and there's something in what the fiction writer attempts, of searching out . . . it's almost a scientific attempt to find those spots where a God shines through, as it were.

Q: Which is ideally what ministry is all about, as well.

A: I suppose so. But I must say that I never for one moment thought of becoming a minister. I admire people who are. To me it seems a very thankless recycling of the same human stuff that, like a heap of sludge, keeps coming back on you. Whatever I said about the ministers' not having enough faith must be qualified with my admiration for their willingness to deal with human distress first-hand, not to sit in a room and write about it, but to actually go out and try to help it, to soothe it, to direct it, maybe.

Q: But in a sense, you're doing that as a novelist. It's a different kind of mediating function, but there's a sense in which it's a priesthood of its own.

A: There's a tendency of American writers to see themselves as priests, actually. Wallace Stevens said it, but I think many have felt it, that we are, in a way, trying to offer spiritual leadership, moral leadership. Even though my books strike many people as immoral or morally useless, to me they are really moral investigations of how we live, and harsh, perhaps, because the standards are otherworldly. I judge, in a way. I see my characters' confusion and rapacity and callousness against some kind of background of ideal behavior that I suppose is part of my Christian inheritance.

Q: That's what makes people squirm when they read them.

A: Somewhere Flaubert was described as reading the French people a series of lessons in human vanity, and in a way fiction could be said to be that. If nothing else, you're trying to read lessons in human vanity to your readers.

Q: Ecclesiasticus?

A: Yeah. . . I have never been an unbeliever, I guess you could say. Somehow it struck me quite early that the church, whatever its faults, was speaking to the real issues, and that without the church I didn't feel anybody would speak to the real issues—that is, the issues of being human, being alive. I've remained loyal to the church. Spires you see in a small town or a city do bring hope, and hope brings energy. It's certainly brought me energy.

A Conversation with John Updike

James Plath/1993

From the *1993 Hemingway Days Festival Annual*, Key West, Fla.,
12–16. Reprinted by permission of James Plath.

Like Ernest Hemingway, who wrote every morning and tal-
lied the word count on the walls of his study, John Updike is
disciplined about his writing. He works for three hours each
day, six days a week, limiting himself to polishing only three
pages or some 1000 words per day. But how those words add
up. Including his most recent book, *Collected Poems: 1953–
1993*, Updike has produced over 80 books in a distinguished
career which began in 1958 with the publication of a slender
volume of poems titled *The Carpentered Hen and Other
Tame Creatures*. Between those two poetry titles are enough
important and successful novels to have earned Updike the
status of major American novelist.

A 1963 tribute to his father, *The Centaur*, chronicled the
mythic struggle of a beleaguered teacher, and won the National Book Award for Fiction. Myths had long been the aqui-
fers which fed the wellsprings of American fiction, but to
deal successfully with myth on the surface was then (and
still) a daring fictional achievement. Likewise, Updike's
''Rabbit'' tetralogy of small-town American life stands alone
in the canon of contemporary American fiction. Rabbit Angstrom, the ex-basketball star who married too young and settled for selling kitchen gadgets, began ''running'' in 1960.
Roughly every decade since, readers have followed Updike's
renewed chronicles of middle-class life in Middle America,
through the turbulent sixties (*Rabbit Redux*, 1971), the ''me
decade' which followed (*Rabbit Is Rich*, 1981) and the inevi-
table Florida retirement home that awaits (*Rabbit at Rest*,
1990). The last two books in the series were awarded the
Pulitzer Prize.

With *Couples* (1968), a novel of spouse-swapping, Updike brought down-and-dirty sex out of plain brown wrap-
pers and into mainstream American literature. And with *A
Month of Sundays* (1975), *Roger's Version* (1986), and *S.*
(1988), he explored adultery-as-American-myth by contem-
porizing Nathaniel Hawthorne's *Scarlet Letter* and re-telling
the story from the point of view of the adulterous woman

(Hester/Sarah), the philandering minister (Dimmesdale/ Marshfield), and the cuckolded husband (Chillingworth/ Lambert).

Hemingway once referred to the New York literary scene as a bottle of tapeworms feeding on each other, and while Updike early in his storied career was a "Talk of the Town" reporter for *The New Yorker*, he also wanted no part of the Big Apple. While still a young writer with a family to support, he gambled on his talents and left *The New Yorker* and New York City to live and work in downtown Ipswich, Massachusetts, not far from Hawthorne's Salem. The rest is literary history.

Although Updike dislikes interviews, he has given more than 200 of them—few of which deal with *The Witches of Eastwick* (1984), a novel many are beginning to regard as one of his strongest books. Hence the focus of this interview, which was conducted by phone on June 6, 1993, in anticipation of Mr. Updike's arrival in Key West to accept The 1993 Conch Republic Prize for Literature—awarded to an author whose life's work reflects the daring and creative spirit of the Keys.

Q: Given your oft-stated aim of transcribing middleness, *The Witches of Eastwick* seems not only representative, but perhaps, as Harold Bloom writes, your most remarkable book as well. In it, all of your themes and images seem to coalesce in a rich and resonant swirl: sex, religion, art, death, male vs. female, science vs. nature, yin and yang, shadow and light, in a fictional world that feels suburban, yet touched by magical realism. How do you see the novel in relation to the Rabbit series or the *Scarlet Letter* trilogy?

A: Well, unlike Harold Bloom or yourself, I'm not really able to rank the novels in terms of excellence. I did think of it as one of my small-town novels and, in some ways, more concentratedly about a small town than *Couples* was. It was written after *A Month of Sundays* but before *Roger's Version*, and I felt good while I was writing it. I felt as though I was inhabiting a real enough place, and that the "magical realism," let's call it—the touch of having the divorcees acquire the power of witchcraft—gave it a kind of spriteliness for me. I was pleased Bloom liked the book, but at the price of all the others, it was kind of a heavy price to pay, I thought, for Bloom's approbation. But

I'm happy to take praise where I can get it. The book felt complete and kind of *replete*, when I was done with it.

Q: You once wrote me that you thought of the book as your Pop Art novel. Could you elaborate?

A: Darryl Van Horne, the devil figure, is a Pop Art collector, and it was my chance to pay homage to Pop Art, which came along at a time when I was still trying to keep up with contemporary art movements. I think I'm fonder of people like [Claes] Oldenburg and Jasper Johns and [Andy] Warhol than of the high abstract expressionists who came before them, and it gave me pleasure to assemble, for my devilish hero, a pretty good Pop Art collection. That was all I meant. I don't mean that my novel is a Pop Art novel, because Pop Art doesn't translate terribly well to the written word. Some of Barthelme's books, I suppose, are as close as you can get to the Pop Art feeling.

Q: Why were you more drawn to Pop Art than to Abstract Expressionism?

A: I suppose because I was an aspiring cartoonist once, and I could "relate," as they say, to the Pop Art imagery. It made sense to me and amused me. In a way, the great abstractionists demanded that you develop a vocabulary of appreciation from scratch, almost. I wasn't quite up to it, whereas Pop Art seemed to come halfway to meet me.

Q: All the Pop Art statues in Van Horne's mansion are gathering dust, though it's in this room where "the women were free, on holiday from the stale-smelling life that snored at their sides." Not only the husbands return to dust in this novel, but the artworks as well.

A: The novel takes place at a time, I think, post-Pop Art, so in a sense dust has gathered on the movement, which was fairly short-lived. And there was something furthermore dusty about the mansion and the accoutrements within it. That is, Van Horne is keeping up pretenses. He's one of the characters with which we've become very familiar: the apparent rich man who, in fact, is not rich. Maybe that dustiness, of which I've forgotten the exact context, may have been a little way of saying that not all is as it seems, and that things are shabbier than they seem here in the Van Horne mansion.

Q: It's interesting to hear you refer to Van Horne as the novel's hero, because as I read it for the first time, it seemed very Edenic in nature. You have three divorced women—"witches"—whose lives seem stable, their relationship with each other happy enough, when suddenly there comes this man, this devil-figure into their garden-variety lives who becomes a disruptive force. Sisterhood evaporates.

A: Well, he stirs them up in ways that the other men in the book don't. This is a book in which I, having been accused of writing only about men, made an effort to keep the male figures in the background—except for Van Horne, who has that quality that women seem to like, of stirring them up and permitting them to *be*, permitting them to self-explore. He indulges them, he's a playmate, he's kind of an educator, in a way, as well as a liberator. So yeah, he's certainly the hero of the book. Who else? Clyde Gabriel, the editor of the *Word*, is the other character who might aspire toward hero status—and he does in the little episode that he stars in—but basically no. The book is meant to be about a coven, and the hero of a coven is surely the person who puts on the devil costume.

Q: Yet, there's a section in the book which reads, "Like all men, Van Horne demanded the women call him king," and he clearly manipulates and dominates the women. He has a sexual power over them—the same kind of power the women had previously enjoyed over the hapless men in town, once they turned their husbands to dust, herbs, and placemats.

A: He is a kind of king. My head was full, then, with reading about witchcraft—the numerous trials and the alleged concessions and so on—and that thing of being called "king" and paying obeisance to the devil is, of course, a central feature of devil worship and meeting in covens. So some of the behavior in the book relates to the old covens and the vocabulary of kingship and subservience, and so on. But Van Horne, in exchange for this (I think) playful demand, offers something. What he offers them, really, is the chance to be with each other. He gives them a theater in which they can explore their mutual fondness and, I guess you could even say, their latent lesbianism. So he's a facilitator.

Q: A believer in the Big Bang theory, Van Horne tells the congregation that he's looking for "the big interface" between electrical and solar energy, which strikes me as terribly Freudian. Even his name suggests not just satanic horns, but a phallic symbol or a rhinocerous horn, a common aphrodisiac. Is this Freudian underpinning something you were doing on purpose?

A: Well, it's hard to write about sexual relations without having some Freudian undertone or overtone. I don't know as I felt especially Freudian in that sermon-speech. He is devilishly trying to control nature, to find a short-cut through it, like the alchemists of the late Middle Ages, and this I think of more as blasphemy than anything Freudian. But maybe you're right. I don't want to deny any reader whatever he can find in the book, if it will make it intelligible to him.

Q: *The Witches of Eastwick* strikes me as being much more complicated than what Bloom described as a book with the antagonist located among "three natural women." To me, it also suggests the ways in which "paradise" or human happiness can be lost, because stability and power always shift in any relationship. Such shifts occur in the novel with the arrival of each new character: first Van Horne, then Jenny, and finally Chris.

A: I never saw Eastwick as a paradise, exactly—certainly not for these divorcées. The book was somewhat about the predicament of divorced women. Now that divorce has become common, what do women do with their freedom from male or patriarchal authority, and how do women handle power? It was a convention of feminist thought, at least in the sixties and seventies, that men were murderous in their use of power, and that women, were they allowed power, would of course *not* be—even though Indira Gandhi and Golda Meir and other female leaders throughout history had not proven to be conspicuously more clever at avoiding war than men had. So I was trying to explore, on the realistic level, the whole question of power in women. Would it become less murderous in female hands? And, of course, my thought was, it wouldn't. Witness their own murder of their fellow witch, the ingénue witch, Jenny.

Q: Which is motivated by their jealousy of a younger woman.

A: Yes, of course. She's stolen their hero, their lover and facilitator. Sure, they're very miffed about that.

Q: In the novel, women's power does seem sexually rooted, and there's a line about "the equilateral triangle being the mother of structure." Readers familiar with your work, I suppose, can't help but associate "triangle power" with the female pudenda and sexual power. In the original version, though, that line read "isosceles triangle."

A: Yeah, I think somebody pointed out that I didn't mean "isos-

celes," that I really meant "equilateral"—a triangle with equal sides—
and that's why I changed it.

Q: Well, the book is certainly triangular in structure. Triangles keep
shifting and forming and re-forming until, at the end, a rather surprising triangle emerges with Jenny, her brother Chris, and Van Horne living together.

A: That's right, because he's really a homosexual. His real interest
is in the beautiful brother of Jenny.

Q: That *is* what you intended, then. In the novel, though the lesbianism seems fully explored, the homosexuality is only implied by off-
handed remarks the witches make, and kept offstage at the end, with
talk of his running away with Chris to New York.

A: Right. When they're talking in the first conversation of the
book—they don't use the word "gay" then, but there's some apprehension that [Van Horne] *would* be, that he sounded like what we now
call a gay . . . and, of course, he reveals himself as one. The comedy
of the book, if there is any comedy in it, is these women fighting so
hard over a man who is essentially homosexual and isn't really interested in them in that basic way. It happens. I've seen it happen,
actually—one of nature's jokes, I guess.

Q: Is Sukie's last name—an obvious reference to Denis de Rougemont, the author of *Love in the Western World*, whose sequel you
reviewed—meant to imply that de Rougemont's ideas are embodied in
her more than the other characters, or is it just a reminder of the complexities of male/female interaction?

A: Yeah, why does one give characters certain names? Faulkner
once said you have to wait for a character to name himself or herself,
and I forget exactly what was going on in the waiting period for Sukie.
Of course, there is a self-referential tip of my own hat to my much-
earlier declared interest in de Rougemont and his ideas about *Love in
the Western World*, but other than that I think it just kind of fitted her.
And after all, it's not her name, but her former husband's name. I
don't know. When you have a lot of characters, you try to find names
that are distinctive enough so the reader can remember them from one
to the other. If you name them all Brown and Miller and Turner, you
get a greyness. And that name seemed spritely and sharp. I'd have to
reread the book to be sure about this, but I don't think she especially

embodies this whole notion of what de Rougemont decided is *the* central myth—that is, the unattainable love, and really the charm of having love be unattainable, but as the distant, unreal woman, as opposed to the closer, real one.

Q: She's the one whose features are constantly referred to as being "simian."

A: In a *nice* way, though. She's perhaps the most lovable of the three—at least in my mind—and she's the one whom you see actually involved in an affair that means something to her. It certainly means something to Clyde, so maybe in a way she's the one who's more real. I was pleased in the movie that she was played by the most engaging actress, too. Michelle Pfeiffer, I think, took the Sukie role, although she made it different. Funnily enough, in the movie—which I had nothing to do with—she becomes a very fertile woman. She can't stop getting pregnant. It was the one inventive or added touch that I kind of liked in the movie. It showed that the scriptwriter wasn't entirely numb to the inner life of the book.

Q: Although Cher as Alexandra was not exactly type-casting.

A: Not quite—not how I pictured her at all. I thought of Alexandra as the earthiest and biggest, the most Junoesque of the women. She was sort of the head witch, the most witchy, the most powerful. And also, the sorrow of being a witch was keenest in her.

Q: You observed in the book that "precision is where passion begins," and while that statement almost sounds Hemingwayesque to me, this is a book that so precisely focuses on your major themes that a great and resonant passion does emerge. It's full of energy, and I suspect that it will stand every bit as tall over time as the Rabbit series and *Scarlet Letter* trilogy, as well as *The Coup*, which also doesn't seem to get as much critical attention as it probably deserves.

A: Well, what is attention? Now there are so many other claims on our attention, I guess an author is lucky to get *any* attention. And many quite good ones don't get any in the landslide of books, all of them aimed at what seems to be a narrowing sector of the average bourgeois's energy dispersal. *The Witches of Eastwick*, as I remember, was reviewed well enough in the leading journals—by women, oddly enough. Margaret Atwood gave it a nice review, as did Diane Johnson. They're both writers that I admire, and I was happy to have their good opinion. I was told, then, that feminists hated the book, and maybe they've a right to, since it *is* a male attempt to look at the female revolution or aspects of feminism, or women alone, women in a group, women as power centers. All that was certainly an investigation I didn't think a hostile one, but it could be construed as such. So maybe that shadow has somewhat depressed the book's reputation. But I'm glad you and Bloom, at least, like it. It sits firmly in my mind. It's a fairly solid novel, with quite a cast of characters, and it does do something with the sexual *seethe* that underlies many a small town.

Index